THE SPANISH COCKPIT

THE SPANISH COCKPIT

An Eye-Witness Account of the
Political and Social Conflicts
of the Spanish Civil War

BY FRANZ BORKENAU

Foreword by Gerald Brenan

Ann Arbor Paperbacks
The University of Michigan Press

First edition as an Ann Arbor Paperback 1963
Foreword copyright © by The University of Michigan 1963
First published by Faber and Faber Ltd.,
copyright by Franz Borkenau 1937
All rights reserved
Reprinted by special arrangement
Published in the United States of America by
The University of Michigan Press and simultaneously
in Toronto, Canada, by Ambassador Books Limited
Manufactured in the United States of America

'Los paisanos armados eran ciertamente muchos; pero habia muy pocos fusiles, y de estos la mitad resultaban inútiles por falta de cartuchos; y ¿con qué se hacían los cartuchos si no había pólvora? A esto habíamos llegado cuatro meses después de la victoria de Bailén. Todo al revés. Ayer barriendo a los Franceses, y hoy dejándonos barrer; ayer poderosos y temibles, y hoy impotentes y desbandados. Contrastes y antítesis própios de la tierra, como el paño pardo, los garbanzos, el buen vino y el buen humór. ¡Oh, España, cómo se te reconocer en cualquier parte de tu historia adonde se fije la vista! Y no hay disímulo que te encubra, ni mascara que te oculte, ni afeite que te disfigure, porque adondequiera que aparezcas, allí se te reconoce desde cien leguas, con tu media cara de fiesta y la otra media de miseria, con la una mano empuñando laureles y con la otra rascándote tu lepra.'

('Certainly, many of the burghers had arms; but there were very few rifles, and of those half were useless because cartridges were lacking; and how to produce cartridges without powder? To such straits had we got four months after the victory of Bailén. Now it was just the reverse. Yesterday we closed in upon the French; now they were closing in upon us; yesterday we were powerful and awe-inspiring; now we were impotent and in disintegration. Contrasts and antitheses belonging to the soil as white bread, beans, good wine, and good humour. O Spain, how thou art the same into whatsoever part of thy history one may look! And there is no dissimulation to cover thee, no mask to hide thy face, no ointment to adorn thee, because, wherever thou appearest, thou art recognized from a hundred miles away; one half of thy face in the mood of a fiesta, and the other with misery grinning through it; one hand bearing laurels, and the other scratching thy leprous sores.')

GALDÓS, *Episódios Nacionales*.

FOREWORD

by Gerald Brenan

When *The Spanish Cockpit* came out exactly a year after the outbreak of the Civil War it made an immediate impression on everyone who had not been blinded by the propaganda of one side or the other. The account it gave of the political situation was something that few people had been prepared for. We learned that the Communists were not playing their historic role of leading the proletariat, but on the contrary were allying themselves with the shopkeepers and rich farmers and doing their utmost to damp down the revolutionary impulses of the peasants and factory workers. We were told that the chief reason for this was that the real revolutionary forces in Spain were the Anarcho-Syndicalists and for the first time got an intelligible account of this huge, loose organization which seemed mysterious and incomprehensible because it had no counterpart in any other country. The author's comments on what he saw were brilliantly acute and penetrating and his desire to get to the truth so evident that no one could doubt that he had given a trustworthy account of the evolving situation.

Behind every important book there is a long history of study and preparation and Franz Borkenau's was no exception to this. His father had held a position as judge and professor in the Austrian Empire, and Franz was brought up as a Catholic, although he was of Jewish descent. He joined the German Communist Party, and here his intelligence got him a post in the Comintern, where he worked for several years till he became disillusioned both with communism and with Marxism, characteristically giving as his chief objection to them their lack of realism and their pedantry. He then decided to become a sociologist and after a course of study went out to Panama where he remained, I think, for six months. He had only just returned to Europe when the Spanish Civil War broke out and he saw his opportunity.

The Spanish Cockpit is a classic of its kind because Borkenau is the only person to have written on the Civil War who had both a mind of the first order and a thorough political education. He knew what questions to ask, he visited the front and the back regions, and he was an excellent observer. No book on this war is more perspicacious or more truthful. Yet Borkenau, whom I got to know and like, was not, as he thought himself, a democratic liberal, but a sort of Nietzschean romantic, who only arrived at the truth after a struggle with himself. This unfitted him for understanding the English character—he regarded it as weak and colorless—but helped him to understand and deeply admire the Spanish. For this reason *The Spanish Cockpit* is not only a model of what the study of a revolution should be, but one of the best books ever published on Spain. Franz Borkenau died in 1957.

PREFACE

This book is written with a double end in view. In the first place, it wants to give an idea of the political developments in the camp of the Republican Government in Spain. Of these developments, both among the masses and among the ruling strata, relatively little has been said in the already voluminous literature about the Spanish civil war, and not much more in the daily Press. Attention has been directed almost exclusively to the military operations. Yet the Spanish civil war is not a war in the ordinary sense of the word. Both armies are extremely weak numerically; their technical outfit is limited and their command lacks military experience. The decision of victory will largely depend on political developments behind the lines, and on the international situation. The international situation will not be dealt with in this book. But the history of the Spanish Left, in its various shades, its specific characteristics, its antagonisms, achievements, and failures, is its main subject matter.

If the present international situation is outside its scope, that is not to say that in this study Spanish affairs are viewed from a purely peninsular standpoint. Its second aim is to describe the specific characteristics of the Spanish conflict, as contrasted with conflicts in other countries. All Spanish parties, even those like the Anarchists which have hardly a counterpart abroad, claim to be Spanish specimens of international movements. In most cases the claim, in my opinion, is entirely unjustified, and in those instances (such as the Communists and Trotskyists) where it is justified, it means that the movement has failed to take deep roots in the

PREFACE

Spanish soil. I began my studies under the common delusion
that the Spanish revolution was simply an incident in the
fight between Left and Right, Socialism and Fascism in the
European sense of the word; I have been convinced by observation on the spot that this is not so, and have since tried to
discover, under the external appearances which present the
common form of political struggle throughout Europe, these
actual driving forces which really differ widely from the
conventional European patterns that are being generally
used to describe them.

I do not expect that any of the parties involved in the
struggle, either in the Right or in the Left camp, will be
pleased with my description. It is critical of all of them, not in
the sense that it passes judgements about whether they are
right or wrong—who could provide the objective and absolute measure for such judgements?—but in the sense that all of
them, in my opinion, suffer from a deep antagonism between
their official aims and their real trend of evolution, and in the
other sense that none of them, I believe, has a chance to win.
In the military sense, to be sure, there will finally be a con-
queror and a conquered. In the political sense, I am afraid,
there will finally only be vanquished and no victor in the
field. And nobody likes to hear that he will probably fail to
attain his object. There is, however, a greater actor than the
political factions on the stage, the Spanish people itself,
which is not identifiable with any of the factions which to-day
tear it to pieces. This greatest actor in the struggle will perhaps emerge not beaten, unshattered. Only the Spanish
people, as distinct from its factions, parties, newspapers, and,
last but not least, foreign allies and enemies, is inarticulate.

But the sociologist, the student of politics, and the historian
ought not to mind too much the displeasure of all factions.
The simple fact is that a party that has succeeded in taking
root in the political life of its country can never be entirely
worthless; it invariably reflects some real need and aim of
some stratum of society, carrying some weight. But precisely
in so far as it is a party, it can only be partly right, can only
reflect certain aspects of political and social life to the exclu-

PREFACE

sion of others. 'Truth,' said Hegel, 'is only in reality as a whole.'
Parties, by definition, reflect only *aspects* of reality. It has
become *à la mode*, in these last decades, for political parties to
make theirs some theory about the essence of life and the law
of development of mankind, and to demonstrate that they
represent this essence and fulfil this law; Fascists and Socialists
of all shades have evolved this habit. But the sociologist ought
to discard these claims *a limine*. If he is not able at least partly
to overcome the limitation of party views, and make some
attempt to see the whole in its complexity where parties cannot see more than a part, then he had better leave his job and
take up the work of a professional party organizer or party
journalist. These are necessary occupations, but they are
different from scientific research. The social scientist is in a
position to make the common claim of the administrator; if
all parties resent his partiality, he may well have been fair to
them all. I have done my best, in the following pages, to
achieve this; though I know well how difficult it is to get
rid of political passion in scientific study, of which it would
be impossible to rid oneself in ordinary life.

The main material of this book is derived from two jour-
neys to republican Spain. I tried to travel to the Franco
camp too, but did not succeed. It is a newfangled habit,
growing with the gradual development of 'totalitarian' States,
to forbid entry not only to definite adversaries, but to all
observers of whose subservience one is not certain in advance.
This attitude brought my work in the Government camp to a
premature end; it thwarted the attempt to study the Franco
camp from the outset.

I ought to acknowledge my gratitude to many people,
both Spanish and foreign, humble and in high office, who
have been helpful to me in the accomplishment of my work.
Among them I owe special gratitude to Miss Rebecca West
and Dr. Audrey Richards for having helped me to get to
Spain, on my first and my second journey respectively. I am
deeply indebted to the friends who saved one part of this
manuscript—and incidentally helped to rescue myself—
from the hands of an all-too-curious police. Dozens of party

xi

PREFACE

officials, members of committees, administrators, officers, and political commissaries have obliged me by giving information about their respective activities, sustaining sometimes with chivalrous patience real interrogatories amidst a turmoil of business. Whatever I have managed to find out I owe to them. I express my special gratitude to Señor J. Miravitlles in Barcelona, Señor A. Arias, then in Madrid, and Señor Hidalgo Rubio in Valencia for having provided me with opportunities to travel through almost all regions of republican Spain. I want to thank, finally, the driver and the guard of the car I had in Andalusia—I do not know their names—who risked their lives to enter the bombarded village of Cerro Muriano in order to rescue me, though I had not asked them to do so in any way. It is one striking example of the sheer incredible amount of self-sacrificing hospitality many foreign observers have found in Spain.

Paris, 9 April 1937.

CONTENTS

CONTENTS

I

THE HISTORICAL BACKGROUND

The Old Monarchy

'La Passionaria', a Basque peasant woman and worker's wife, now Communist deputy and in fact the Jeanne d'Arc of the Spanish revolution, has been more emphatic than any of the more political leaders of the movement in insisting upon its close relation to the heroic feats of the popular rising against Napoleon, in 1808. In fact, the roots of the present movement in Spanish history are deep; they can be followed back, far beyond the origin of any revolutionary movement in the proper sense of the word, into the eighteenth century. We have to go back so far in order to understand what is happening at present.

Spain, after having been the leading power of Europe in the sixteenth and the beginning of the seventeenth century, after having produced a brilliant literature and art in the first half of the seventeenth century, had decayed rapidly and, at the beginning of the eighteenth century, in the War of the Spanish Succession, became the prey of the contending interests of the French on the one side and the British and Austrians on the other. It was at this juncture that the Spanish 'people', as distinct from the nobility and the higher clergy, appeared on the historical stage for the first time since the end of the Middle Ages. Spain was believed to be a thoroughly aristocratic country. The majority of the aristocracy and of the higher clergy supported, in the struggle for the throne, the Austrian pretender, the Archduke Charles. But he was beaten. The lower clergy and the masses were for the French king, Philip V of Bourbon. He succeeded. Only Catalonia, always opposed to Castille, and in silent revolt since the time of Richelieu, took the opposite side. In 1714 Barcelona was taken and sacked by the Castilians, after a heroic defence. Two main facts of modern Spanish history first became clear on this occasion: the profound gap between the upper stratum and the people and the superior power of the latter in a great national crisis; and the antagonism of Catalonia and Castille as one main factor of Spanish politics. The result was the more striking because of the international context in which it happened. The arms of the coalition all over the world had been victorious against Louis XIV, with the one exception of Spain. Still, of the armies resisting Britain and Austria, those operating in Spain were certainly the weakest. In its state of decay and disintegration Spain on its own territory had proved stronger than Britain and Austria together. Its tremendous power of resistance, owing to the fanatical enthusiasm of the lower classes, contrasted strangely with the incapacity of the Spanish State for any positive action whatsoever.

Almost no heed was paid to the fact by the ruling states-men of the time. The national war over, the Spanish State continued to decay, with its leading groups, aristocracy, episcopacy, and the small stratum of wealthy bourgeois intelligentsia. Cabinet wars were undertaken and lost. Reforms, including the expulsion of the Jesuits, were introduced in imitation of France, with very superficial effect indeed. Goya, the glorious painter, imitated the harmless shepherd scenes of Boucher and Fragonard. But when another great national catastrophe made its irruption, Goya, the rococo shepherd, painted the most pathetic, the incredibly fanatical execution scenes of his great tableaux in the Prado. The age of enlightenment in Spain was simply a delusion of a few men of goodwill. It never was a reality.

With the French Revolution and Napoleon, the modern 'bourgeois' world made its irruption into Spain. But the

Spanish people did not want to imitate the achievements of their larger neighbour. Modern administration and 'enlightened' principles were forced upon the country, against its will, by the French, who destroyed the basic institutions beloved by the people. Spain reacted with a tremendous popular revolt.

The French first forced the Spanish into an alliance; then took over the Spanish fleet and led it to destruction at Trafalgar; finally occupied the country (under the pretext of a march against Portugal, occupied by the British), and disarmed and disorganized the Spanish army. All classes helped them in the task of disintegration. One section of the upper classes, the 'afrancesados', welcomed the French as bearers of the age of enlightenment. Another section, the larger one, hated them but did not dare to resist. Finally the mob itself upset the throne. Exasperated by the toleration of increasing French tyranny, they revolted and, in the famous Aranjuez mutiny, forced the king, Charles IV, to abdicate and his omnipotent Prime Minister Godoy to resign. The heir to the throne, Fernando VII, was not recognized by Napoleon; father and son were both ordered to Bayonne to put their quarrel before the emperor, and there arrested. Spain was without a king. Murat occupied Madrid, hoping to win the Spanish crown for himself. To further this aim, he made the last members of the royal family depart for France.

It was at this moment that the Spaniards really revolted. The mob of Madrid, helped only by three young artillery officers—who paid with their lives for their patriotism—rose in an unexpected insurrection, against the express orders of the junta which represented the king in his absence. The rising of Madrid, on 2 May 1808, was suppressed in a frightful massacre. Soon afterwards Joseph Bonaparte, Napoleon's brother, was proclaimed king, and all seemed over. In reality, it had only just begun. The popular rising, subdued in Madrid, spread all over Spain. In July, already, it achieved a famous success. The French general Dupont, marching against Cadiz, was stopped on his way to Andalusia, forced to retreat, and finally surrounded and forced to capi-

3

tulate by the peasants at Bailén. The Spanish general Castaños claimed the glory of the day. But in reality one look at the battle-field, a large open plain of olive-groves, is convincing as to the real situation. It was impossible to surround the French there with a small army. Only a rising of all the villages could bar and did bar the way. Madrid was reconquered, by half-organized forces, in the name of the exiled King Fernando. But in reality there was never a real central government, the first and the second central junta both obstructing the movement as well as they could. It was a popular movement, led by local juntas. This movement had inflicted upon the French their first defeat in many years. It was a turning-point in world history. Napoleon himself went to Spain and reconquered Madrid. But after his departure the rising continued. The British interfered. They found the Spanish soldiers very bad allies indeed and Wellington, after one single experience, was horror-stricken at the incompetence of the Spanish generals and refused ever again to co-operate with them. But the popular rising remained a decisive factor, with its guerilla methods and such extraordinary feats of heroism as the defence of Gerona and the defence of Saragossa by Palafox.

The situation of 1707 repeated itself in 1808. The populace was successful in starting a national war of despair, against the will of the higher classes. This sharp severance between the masses and the higher classes is the real decisive effect of the national wars of 1808–14. In the upper stratum: decay, corruption, political incapacity, as well as complete lack of creative power in any other respect. Below: fanaticism, capacity for self-sacrifice, spontaneity of action, but of action in a narrow, local, prejudiced sense, without constructive capacities on a wider scale. Such was the structure of Spain at the beginning of the nineteenth century, and such it has remained to this day. The content of the political antagonisms has changed, but the cleavage between the two strata has remained and broadened. It is the distinguishing feature of Spain as compared with other countries who regard themselves as more progressive. To put it into one sentence: in

Britain, in America, in France, and in Germany, every popular movement originated in the higher stratum of society and then permeated the masses. In Spain, in these last centuries, no movement in the higher classes ever penetrated deeply the masses. Spain is the country where the spontaneity of the 'people' as against the aristocracy, the bourgeoisie, the intelligentsia, and, in the last decades, the clergy, is most conspicuous. Such a deep severance of the people from ruling groups, such a passing of the initiative to the lowest stratum of society, is always a symptom of deep decay and disintegration of an old civilization. Socialism in more 'modern' countries has accepted wholesale the 'progressive' industrialist outlook of the bourgeoisie. In Spain the masses revolted, and, basically, still revolt against all sorts of progress and Europeanization, and, at the same time, take the lead, in more than one great historical crisis, of the nation as a whole. This one fact shows the profound difference between Spanish and European problems. It makes Spain an unconstructive country in the European sense of the word, and many a self-confident observer of the present civil war has come back full of horror about aimless cruelty and unconstructive slaughter, forgetting that our aims may not be their aims, our values not their values. Spain ceased to participate constructively in Western civilization at the end of the seventeenth century. On the trunk of Western civilization it is the branch which has withered first, after a period of marvellous blossom. Under the repeated impact of those countries which are still progressing, it has passed into a period of disintegration which is far from being at its end. But in the course of this slow process of disintegration the primitive, spontaneous forces of the lowest classes—of which there is so much talk and so little reality in the progressive West—have been set free and started to act, with incredible force, along the line of the most basic reaction of all backward people against their more progressive neighbours; the Spanish masses hated and hate this modern civilization which is forced upon them, and fight it with the fury which only Spaniards are able to display on such occasions.

THE HISTORICAL BACKGROUND

Since then Spanish history proceeds, so to speak, in two stories. In the upper story there is conservatism, liberalism, socialism, all sorts of imported European ideas, an up-and-down of superficial tendencies, superficial victories and defeats, the upshot of which is the disintegration of the higher classes, the State, and the administration. Below, there are the real masses, miserable, subdued, living a life far from the great historical trends of the world, but appearing suddenly, surprisingly, on the days when these forces attempt to disturb them in their traditional existence. Success and defeat in the long run always depend, in Spain, and have done for more than a century, on the capacity of every political and social trend to join with these forces of the depths; if they fail to do so, they are nothing but sounding brass and tinkling cymbals.

During the nineteenth century, and especially in the twentieth century modern capitalism has slowly penetrated the country, from abroad, with a certain participation of the Basques and the Catalans (the latter priding themselves on being the only 'Europeans' in Spain), and very little of the Spaniards proper. The movements of the depths have had to adapt themselves, slowly and partially, to the new mode of life forced upon the country by its stronger neighbours. The history of this process of adaptation is the history of the transformation of the mass movements. But there is no reason to believe that the adaptation will ever become complete. The resistance is very deep indeed, and Spanish republicanism, socialism, and anarchism, as well as 'Carlism' (the particular form of Spanish reaction) are at least as much attempts to adapt modern capitalism to Spanish ideas as attempts to adapt Spain to modern conditions.

The higher, Europeanized, superficial stratum reappeared politically for the first time, after an eclipse of four years, in 1812. Characteristically it appeared at the moment of decay of the mass movement. After four years of horrors unequalled in a war both civil and international, the Spanish peasant was tired and gave signs of falling away from the cause of the fight against the French. At this moment, in order to inspire the movement with a new spirit, the Cortes of Cadiz were

6

convoked. They started to reform the country on European lines. A strange paradox appeared. The European lines on which the country was reorganized were the ideas of the French Revolution; precisely those ideas against which the peasants and burghers had revolted in 1808. But the popular movement, entirely negative as it had been, contained no suggestions as to the political reconstruction of the country. It had only one aim, to expel the French. Other aims could only be borrowed from Europe. The conservatives, the so-called 'serviles', were discredited by their inactivity at the critical moment. The Assembly fell into the hands of the liberals, who legislated to their hearts' delight. Many of the provisions of the Cadiz legislation, such as the administrative division of the country and the taxes on land, subsist till this day. Others, such as parliamentary government, were very soon swept away. The two basic problems, the agrarian question and the position of the Church, were not seriously tackled. The efficiency of the Cadiz system as a whole was not tested. In 1814 Joseph Bonaparte fell and Fernando came back as king. He immediately annulled the constitution of Cadiz and hunted down all those who had partici- pated in its creation.

The following fifty years are a period of continual civil war, usually described as a fight between conservatives and liberals. In reality it was a struggle for power between the Church on the one hand and on the other the one new social force which had appeared in the anti-Napoleonic war: the army. In this struggle the Church very soon began to act as one united force, co-operating in the task of upholding the power it had held in pre-Napoleonic times. A number of liberal priests had participated in the reform work of the Cadiz Cortes. But soon there was no liberal Catholicism left in Spain. The army, on the other hand, was divided against itself. Generally, in the first half of the nineteenth century, it was predominantly liberal, but it gave some of the ablest leaders, such as General Narvaez, to the conservative cause. In consequence, Spanish 'liberalism' has little in common with those convictions which are labelled with the name in

Europe. In Spain it is simply synonymous with anti-clerical-ism. We do not need to follow here in detail the interminable ups and downs of this fight between the 'liberals' and the 'conservatives'. But a few words must be said about the evolution of the two leading institutions, the Church and the army. It is these two institutions which, to-day, play the leading part in the Franco rising.

As in the old Roman Empire, so in Spain in the nineteenth century, the power of the Church increased with the decay of the administration and the decay of the State as a whole. Kings fanatically Catholic, such as Philip II, had known how to hold the Church under their sway. But when, in the beginning of the eighteenth, and again in the beginning of the nineteenth, century the State disappeared the Catholic hierarchy remained the one order to which the masses could rally. It derived an enormous authority from this situation. All through the nineteenth century the hold of the Church over the masses was absolute, in appearance. Its hold over the masses was much more absolute than its hold over the State. The State—whatever that meant concretely in nineteenth-century Spain—had to limit the power of the Church in order to live. In 1837 the Prime Minister, Mendi-zabal, struck a bold stroke against it; he confiscated all its landed property and put it up for sale, after the example given by the French Revolution. The measure was carried out, and broke the power of the 'Carlist' rebellion. (The Car-lists, as is well known, are partisans of the pretender Carlos, the younger brother of Queen Isabel, daughter of Fernando VII, and of his heirs; they have their stronghold in Navarra, a province where medieval conditions continue almost un-changed, and from thence have twice launched an insurrec-tion against the legitimate dynasty. Their slogan, character-istically, was 'The king Christ, and the Holy Virgin'. To-day Carlist battalions are among the best military forces of Franco.) Never since has the Spanish Church recovered its wealth in land. The story of the Church as the largest landed proprietor in Spain is a myth. Only a small part of its *landed* property has been regained. As a compensation, the Church and the various orders accumulated an enormous amount of *mobile* property. The Church, to-day, is not the largest landowner but the largest capitalist in Spain, particularly the Spanish Jesuits. This is part of the explanation of the financial sources of the Franco rising. It is a supremely important element in the history of the severance of the Church from the masses too. Never would the masses have been driven away from a Church fixed upon the land; they were easily led to abandon a Church which was the richest shareholder in the country.

The action of Mendizabal was only the beginning; again and again the State has attempted to limit the power of the Church, lastly under the strongest man of the early days of King Alphonso XIII, the Prime Minister Canalejas. In this struggle for power the Catholic Church degenerated. More and more it ceased to trouble about its pastoral duties, ceased to be interested in the people, and instead became ever more interested in the struggle for privileges, very largely economic privileges. An ignorant, immoral lower clergy, acting mainly as helpers for the local *guardia*, and a haughty, worldly episcopacy; that was on the average the Spanish clergy. In order to understand its position in society one must not think of modern Catholicism such as it exists in Germany, France, Britain, and other modern countries. One must think of the late medieval Church in the periods of its deepest decay, before the Counter-Reformation. Most of the work of the Council of Trent has been undone, in fact if not in words, in Spain during the nineteenth century. Accordingly the Church lost its hold over the masses. At first it was a silent process. So long as the masses continued to live in the old ways nothing seemed to be changed. But when, during the twentieth century, the impact of modern conditions upon the masses became stronger, literacy more general, new problems, such as that of the position of wage-earners, urgent, the Church had nothing, absolutely nothing, to say about that. There are not many contrasts so sharply outlined in our times as that between German Catholicism, which owes all its influence to the genuine, sincere, and able interest it takes in modern social problems, its powerful welfare organizations, its co-operatives and (before Hitler) its trade unions, and the Spanish Church, which tried, occasionally, to imitate all that, but not for any reason except to create better electoral machinery for the conservatives. Accordingly, these attempts in Spain were made only in the last years of the monarchy, when the situation of the Church had become critical. And the masses refused to participate in actions which were obviously not prompted by a genuine interest in their needs, but by subservience to the powers of the day. The profound success of Catholicism in countries where it had little or no political power when it started to take an active interest in the problems of modern life, and its wholesale failure in Spain, where it wielded enormous political power, shows that nobody is to blame for the failure, except the Spanish Catholic hierarchy itself. In the beginning of the nineteenth century it was all powerful over the souls of Spaniards in general. Towards 1930 it had lost all real authority, except in those districts where the clergy had kept close to the masses: Navarra and the Basque country. The one to-day is with Franco, the other with the republic. Both are fervently Catholic. In Navarra the clergy, continuing to live with the people the backward life of a primitive community of freeholders, had no need to adapt themselves to modern conditions. In the Basque country, which to-day is the strongest industrial centre of Spain, the Catholic clergy kept close to the masses from the first in the traditional defence of the Basque language against Castilian centralization. Starting from this foundation, the Basque Church created a genuine co-operative and trade-union movement and genuine social welfare work. As a result, the Basque clergy has kept the true allegiance of its flock through all political upheavals, to such an extent that socialism, communism, and anarchism never got a firm hold over the centre of the Spanish metallurgic industry, Bilbao. It is a clear indication of what Spanish Catholicism could have become had it been equal to its task, or even equal to the simplest duties of the pastoral office.

The Spanish masses have relinquished the Spanish Church, not because they have lost the traditional religious fervour of the Spanish race, but because the Spanish Church has lost it. The desire for fanatical faith, without which the Spanish soul seems unable to live, has found itself other channels, mainly in the guise of anarchism. The Spanish Church, on its side, has largely become a pretext for political action in the hands of officers who have no profound belief; certainly not the great majority of them, by any means. It has remained greedy for wealth and power, however, and in certain conflicts between Franco and the Carlists there appears already a foreshadowing of future fights between the Church and the military dictatorship. This does not imply, of course, that the Spanish Church has linked its fate to the fate of Carlism. Nor is it inconsistent, as will be seen in the diary which follows, with the survival of a good deal of instinctive traditional Catholicism among the masses. But their instinctive belief is infinitely more concerned with images and other religious objects than with the persons of the priests. The Church, the last force of old Spain still left standing erect after the Napoleonic Wars, is now in disintegration. This will mean, inevitably, an enormous increase of power for the army.

The army, on its side, is a more modern force. It has in its ranks many aristocrats, but is not essentially aristocratic. Not only in the insurgents' army are few of the leading men aristocrats. All through the nineteenth century a high percentage of those very generals who got political power came from the lower classes. Prim, the strongest of the 'caudillos' (the military chiefs of political factions) was hardly literate.

The political functioning of the Spanish army is a phenomenon not peculiarly Spanish. The preponderance of the army and the open fight between contending generals for domination over the State is a common feature of declining civilizations which have evolved, in the past, a strong government that later becomes the prey of adventurers. Contending generals dominated ancient Rome in the times of its decay; they dominate China to-day in its disintegration. For more than a century most of the ancient Spanish and Portuguese colonies in the new world have been their playthings. They have presided over the transformation of Turkey. And they have been, for a century, the masters of Portugal and, till these latter times, the real rulers of Spain. Their claim to be the specific bearers of the spirit and the fittest supervisors of the welfare of the nation is wholly unfounded. Their domination is easy to explain. No army ever gets into its head the idea that it could take over power from a well-established régime, with a functioning administration and a generally recognized social hierarchy. It knows, then, that, in spite of its mechanical superiority, it would find the whole nation united against it. But when the administration ceases to fulfil its tasks, when the régime is in disintegration, when there is nobody who can win general recognition as an established authority, then the army becomes supreme. It is then able to claim to rule the country, because it has kept more or less intact the material and mechanical resources of physical power evolved in better days, whereas the finer threads of civil government and spontaneous obedience are already in disintegration. It is a significant fact in the history of civilization, and one commonly observed, that the military organization of a higher society is one of the things most easily copied by backward neighbours. Turkey and Russia had fairly modern armies, from the Western point of view, without being for all that any the more like Western countries in other respects. Similarly, military organization is one of the elements remaining intact longest in times of decay. This is meant in a relative sense. Chinese soldiers are notoriously no good against European troops; but they have proved strong enough to subdue the other political forces of their own country. Both Germans and Italians in the Franco camp, and foreign advisers of many nationalities in the Valencia camp, complain about the incompetence, the lack of training, and sometimes the lack even of ordinary courage, of the Spanish officer. But the Spanish officer, for more than a century, had not to test his ability in fighting foreign troops, but in fighting his Spanish colleagues and the civil population. He proved up to this job. In 1921, however, even the Moors proved a match for him!

The army became the other decisive power in the State besides the Church, when, during the Napoleonic Wars, every other authority was in abeyance. And it continued to be so after the Napoleonic Wars, because the other authorities, the crown, the administration, the aristocracy, were restored formally, but no one could restore their prestige. The one force which had kept its old prestige was the Church, and from this fact resulted by conflict a superficial liberalism in the army. One characteristic feature of this liberalism was that it was directed against the large majority of the population. The Carlists fought their insurrections with few professional soldiers, but with wide popular support, and with a brilliant group of popular guerilla leaders, such as Cabrera. The liberals had never wide popular support for any of their *pronunciamentos*. Moreover, the Spanish army displayed one more feature characteristic of every military dictatorship. Where there is one military pretender there are always several. Once the appeal to sheer force of arms has been made there is always some competing general who thinks he has as much right to rule as his happy colleague. And there is, in consequence, war between military pretenders. Characteristically, this military *fronde* against the liberal leaders of the army did not join the popular movement of the Carlists. It expressed itself in the form of a moderate group against the liberals. Thus the Catholic Church was in the favourable position of having alternately two trumps to play: the Carlists and the moderate generals. The history of Spain from 1814 to 1868 is the history of the interplay, the interminable and sterile alternation of these forces.

In the meantime the social texture of the country changed slowly. Foreign capital introduced railways. Catalonia, in and after the 'forties, reorganized its textile industry on modern lines. The export of certain crops increased. A few Basques created banks with Spanish capital. These newly arising modern forces, of a European character, worked for liberalism. They turned the balance in its favour. The dissolute life of Queen Isabel had its part in upsetting the former balance. She preferred her favourites to the leading generals of the army, who, at a critical moment, joined forces against her. In 1868 all the forces of the Left united and upset the

13

throne. General Prim, the leader of the revolutionary army, made himself master of Madrid.

It soon proved to be a catástrophic situation for everybody concerned. Now, even the formal appearance of a settled order had vanished, and it proved impossible to set another in its stead. The army was very far from wanting a republic. But the generals could not agree about a new candidate for the throne for three years. They finally called in an Italian prince, but when he arrived he was immediately submerged in intrigues and plots. The very day of his landing Marshal Prim was assassinated by a revolutionary. It was symptomatic. A new element, a really revolutionary stratum, had entered Spanish politics in the wake of the struggle of the generals. After a reign of less than two years the Italian prince was completely disgusted with this turmoil. He left the country, and left it without a monarch. A republic was proclaimed, not because any one of the political groups (with the exception of a small layer of 'progressives') really wanted a republic, but because there was no alternative. It is officially known as the 'First Republic', and like the prince, lasted less than two years.

With the proclamation of the republic, chaos swept the country. In the north the Carlists took the opportunity to rise. But, more important, in the south, in Andalusia and in the province of Murcia, the anarchists revolted. It was their first entry into Spanish history, and it had immediate and far-reaching effects.

The Andalusian so-called peasant, who, in reality, has been a serf since late Roman times, tied to the estate, suffered perhaps not less in the eighteenth than in the nineteenth century, but he rose in revolt in the nineteenth century, whereas in the eighteenth he had suffered silently. And yet perhaps this is not quite true. The revolt of the Andalusian serf in the eighteenth century took the form of widespread and indomitable brigandage, which involved the most active elements of the peasantry and was regarded by the masses not as criminal, but, on the contrary, as an enviable, honourable, and even admirable profession. Something of this tradition of brigandage has remained for ever in the Spanish revolutionary movement, not in the sense given to the word in modern Europe, but in the sense it would be used in the tradition of Robin Hood. The link between the old and the new spirit is to be found in Bakunin, the founder of anarchism, who praised the revolutionary brigand as the avenger of the oppressed and the truest keeper of the spirit of revolt. This interpretation must be insisted upon because the important problem of the Spanish *Lumpenproletariat* cannot be understood without it. It is a fact that a not unimportant number of these 'lumpenproletarian' elements have joined the anarchist movement, and form part of its redoubtable terror organizations. In Spain these elements are not covered with the opprobrium that would attach to them in countries civilized in the Western sense, any more than the revolutionary brigand is covered with opprobrium in China, or was so in tsarist Russia. There is a profound difference, in the view of a primitive peasantry, between the man who breaks the solidarity of the peasant community itself by criminal acts and the man who, in seeking his own right against the rich and the mighty by brigandage and murder, helps the common cause of the oppressed. The former, the thief or the murderer who has killed or robbed a peasant, would be unhesitatingly delivered to the police or given short shrift by those he had damaged. The latter will be protected by the poor, throughout his district. This was so at least until far into the nineteenth century. Brigandage has abated since, but other forms of violence more urban in character, such as assassinations and expropriations, have taken its place. The average Spanish peasant and worker has not developed that respect for his enemies' life and property characteristic of the well-policed countries of the West. This mentality was to be felt even among the militia of 1936. The same men who would have shot unhesitatingly a man who had stolen from his comrade a pair of boots saw no harm in ruthlessly sacking the houses of the fascists, and objected little (I know of actual cases) if militia-men put the money they found there into their own pockets. But the blame should not be reserved for the poor alone. The guardia, too, did not conspicuously respect the property, nor even the life, of *their* enemies, who were indeed those very poor that they persecuted for lack of respect for established property rights.

It would be worth while investigating why, at a given moment, old-style Robin Hood brigandage transformed itself into the risings of villages against their owners. The change dates from the 'forties, and is probably connected on the one hand with deterioration of labour conditions and expropriation of communal lands by the aristocracy owing to the change from home consumption to export crops, and, on the other hand, with the creation of the guardia in the 'forties. The 'guardia civil' is a supremely important element in Spanish politics; perhaps the most important administrative achievement of Spain in the nineteenth century. It is recruited on the basis of a very strict selection, and systematically kept apart from the population of the district where it serves. (*Guardistas* never serve in their home district, are not allowed to marry in the district where they serve, and invariably live in barracks.) Thus, the State, which could not count upon its army, secured at least one reliable force which was invariably and integrally at the service of its superiors. At the same time, it was a very efficient police force. But, in consequence of all this, it was separated from the population, hated by the masses, and hating them as a natural reaction; and there is no deeper abyss, no more deadly or constant war imaginable, than that waged continually, every day, between the village, especially the Andalusian village, and the guardia. Anyway, the guardia made an end of brigandage. Instead, the State got risings.

These risings of starving Andalusian serfs, which had continued since the 'forties, came to a head during the complete abeyance of the power of the State in 1873. It was a very serious matter, because at this moment the peasant movement, which had before been local, dispersed, spontaneous, and instinctive, came into contact with the 'First International', and more particularly with the anarchists, who were members of it. This meant that the peasant movement

merged with the incipient movement of the urban proletariat into one popular movement. It was the third rising of
the Spanish people as a whole. But while in 1707 and in 1808
the people had risen against the upper classes in defence of
Church and national dynasty, this time they rose, still against
the upper classes, but in defence of their own immediate interests. It was a result of the still deeper disintegration of the
upper classes and the State during the last five decades. A
new era of Spanish history dates from this rising. It is important to understand its implications.

Joaquin Maurin, the leader and theoretician of the Spanish Trotskyists, since executed by a Franco squad, has created
the theory (repeated since, uncritically, by people who have
nothing in common with Trotskyism) that the predominance
of anarchism in Spain reflects simply the preponderance of
the miserable Andalusian serf over the modern Catalonian
worker. Though this idea is not entirely devoid of a basis in
reality, it is a gross exaggeration. In fact, anarchism had a
foothold in Barcelona before it ever touched the illiterate
serfs of Andalusia. The working-class movement, first as a
co-operative, then as a semi-political, finally as a trade-union
movement, dated, in Barcelona, from the 'forties. It had pro-
gressed, against the strong opposition of the authorities, without a clear theory of its own, but when it came into contact
with the newly founded International and its anarchist faction in the 'sixties, had at once with passion and enthusiasm
accepted Bakunin's faith. The new gospel (for this it was, in a
literal sense, replacing directly the old Catholic faith of the
people) reached Andalusia only through common participation in the popular risings of the early 'seventies. Since then
anarchism in Spain has had two roots, the one peasant and
Andalusian, the other proletarian and Catalan. There is no
reason to give one more importance than the other. The
characteristic feature of the Spanish political situation, and
of the Spanish labour movement in particular, lies precisely
in the close union of these two elements, so widely different in
many other respects.

Marxists of various shades, all of them disliking the preponderance of the anarchists in the Spanish labour movement, have offered various explanations of the fact that anarchism, in Spain, has existed as a mass force since the First Republic, at least thirty years before the socialist mass movement began, and that it was still preponderant, in spite of innumerable efforts to supersede it, at the beginning of the civil war in 1936. All these explanations, at the same time, are depreciations. Nearly all foreign observers are particularly unfair to the anarchists. Those who are Marxists of some description usually come with deeply established prejudices, and most of them do not even try to make contact with the anarchists, but prefer to believe, without the slightest attempt at criticism, everything the Spanish adversaries of the anarchists tell them. Non-socialist observers are naturally prejudiced against the most ruthless and most cruel section of the revolutionary movement. The explanation which follows is not intended to be a 'defence' against these interpretations. The sociologist has not to accuse or to defend; one cannot repeat it too often. He has to understand. Anarchism has proved unable to tackle the decisive problems of the Spanish situation, for reasons soon to be discussed; this is a fact. (Socialism, for its part, was no more able to tackle them; this is a fact too.) Still, a correct understanding of Spanish events depends largely on a correct understanding of anarchism.

I do not think that it is necessary to seek far-fetched explanations: anarchism says, fairly openly, itself what it is. It has fully explained its convictions in the debates with the Marxists. The salient point of these debates is that Bakunin accepted the atheist faith of the Marxists, but not their materialistic interpretation of history. What are the implications? Marx regarded social revolution and socialism as the inevitable result of the economic progress of capitalism. He identified himself, in consequence, to the full with 'progressive capitalism' and all its implications, including parliament and political action within the framework of capitalism. Bakunin, for his part, regarded social revolution and socialism as the result of the revolutionary action of people prompted by the moral conviction of the immorality, the hideousness, the human inacceptability of the capitalist world. The one waited for industrial development and democratic action (without shunning revolutionary means) to bring the hour of the social revolution nearer. The other saw socialism as possible at any moment, provided there was revolutionary conviction and decision. But this conviction and decision, according to Bakunin's idea, could not be put at the disposal of the masses simply by a small group of professional revolutionaries; they must emerge from a revolutionary spirit in the people itself. A closely-knit group of self-sacrificing revolutionaries would be needed to prompt the movement, but would be of no avail without a revolutionary people.

Why did this theory appeal to the Spaniards? First of all, because at its core stood the spontaneous revolutionary spirit of the masses of the people. Such a spirit was not to be found among the progressive nations, where the proletariat had, according to Bakunin, become nice, decent, and subdued, and itself admired the blessings of modern capitalism; in those countries revolution had withered down to a merely political principle. It had left the hearts of the people, only to remain in their heads. Bakunin only shrugged his shoulders about the English trade unions. But with a shrewd appreciation of psychological realities he also distrusted the German movement, with its early successes in the electoral and organizational field; the Germans, he thought, were slaves by nature. He knew them, from 1848, and his revolutionary instinct was not impressed. Revolutionaries by heart and instinct, according to Bakunin, were first and foremost those nations who did not admire the blessings of civilization; who were not in love with material progress; where the masses were not yet imbued with religious respect for the property of the individual bourgeois; revolutionary were the countries where the people held freedom higher than wealth, where they were not yet imbued with the capitalist spirit; and particularly his own people, the Russians, and, to a still higher degree, the Spaniards. How could the Spanish workers and peasants have refused to accept the teaching of a man who believed that the specific mentality of the Spanish lower classes ought to be the model of the labour movements of the whole world?

I do not mean to say that Bakunin won his cause among the Spanish revolutionaries by appealing to nationalistic instincts, though, undoubtedly, never a foreigner spoke more lovingly about the Spaniard. Most of his ideas about Spain contained some essential truth, and here was the point of contact. (By the way, in this particular question, which is of supreme importance, Bakunin, as historical experience has proved since, was completely right as against Marx. Revolution did not come to Britain and Germany, but to Russia and Spain.) The rebellion of the Spanish masses was not a fight for better conditions inside a progressive capitalist system which they would admire; it was a fight against the first advances of capitalism itself, which they hated. The Spanish popular movement is directed not towards overcoming capitalism in the future as a result of and after its complete unfolding, but against its very existence at any stage of its possible progress in Spain. Whatever concessions later decades may have made to the uncomfortable facts of increasing industrial development, the Spanish worker has never submitted at all in the matter-of-fact way of his German and English colleague to the fate of being an industrial worker. Therefore the materialistic conception of history, based on the belief in progress, meant nothing to him; for the Spanish worker is little progressive. This was why the Barcelona engineer could feel one with the Andalusian peasant. In Spain the American mentality that it is a virtue to be exigent is not yet introduced. (In 1936 I still heard a young socialist praise, as the highest quality of the Castilian labourer, that 'he could live on almost nothing'.) The fight against oppression, the mentality of the brigand who leaves his village in order to be free, is still much stronger than the mentality of the trade unionist who accepts hard months of strike in order to become well-to-do. In consequence, violence is neither shunned in others nor rejected if proposed to the Spanish masses. But peaceful trade-unionist action is suspect. In a word, the Spanish labour movement is based on a mentality directed against the introduction, not against the indefinite continuance, of capitalism. And this, in my opinion, is the explanation of the preponderance of anarchism in Spain.

Hence 'freedom' as the central element of anarchist ideology. Its 'libertarianism' (this monster word comes from the anarchists themselves) has been ascribed, alternately, to 'individualism' as a feature of the Spanish national character, and to a misunderstood exaggeration of liberalism. As to the second, one ought not to play upon words. Liberal ideology is something profoundly connected with the specifically bourgeois, and more concretely the puritanical ideology, and worlds apart from anarchism. As to the first, it does not exist in the sense in which it is used as an explanation of anarchism. Neither are the Spaniards simply individualists; they have on the contrary a very strong sense both of co-operation and of hierarchy; nor do the anarchists object to collective action, which is, on the contrary, one of the mainstays of their programme. The pre-eminence of freedom in the anarchist programme is explained simply enough by the fact that in a movement which cares relatively little for material achievements, tyranny is the main objection against the modern industrial system, exactly as it is the main objection against serfdom.

From the specific type of anti-capitalism embodied in anarchism derives, moreover, the feature most remarked by impartial observers, its strange attitude towards morals and law. There is not the slightest doubt that the anarchists have in their ranks not a few criminal elements, and that these elements are regarded with little horror. More striking still, anarchism presents to every observer the puzzle of men obviously prompted by the highest idealism, prepared to sacrifice not only life but happiness for their cause, together with elements which are neither controlled nor have any kind of self-control. To put the same thing in another form: there is certainly no group of the European labour movement in which moral questions are taken so seriously, in which there is such a genuine, serious attempt to make actions square with convictions, and yet this movement has certainly a higher percentage of criminals in its ranks than any other political party. It is significant that the anarchists have consistently refused their leaders regular pay, and forced them to live, either by the work of their own hands, or by the friendly help given them by their comrades; the same movement does not shun, or at least did not shun, expropriations. But here we begin to see the solution of the puzzle. Anarchism *is* a religious movement, in a sense profoundly different from the sense in which that is true of the labour movements of the progressive countries. Anarchism does not believe in the creation of a new world through the improvement of the material conditions of the lower classes, but in the creation of a new world out of the moral resurrection of those classes which have not yet been contaminated by the spirit of mammon and greed. At the same time anarchism is far from being well behaved and pacifist; it has integrated, in its mentality, all the Robin Hood traditions of former generations, and emphatically believes in violence; not in organized conflict only, but in fighting as an everyday means of settling the divergence of views between simple men and their masters. One result of the peculiar type of anarchist anti-capitalism is its emphatic belief in direct action, which mostly, though not always, means violent action.

Two anecdotes may illustrate the contrast between anarchism and European socialism. Years ago I was talking with a British communist, a high official of his party; he praised the attitude of the British worker who would not tolerate any sort of violence. Foreign seamen, when, rarely, they tried to use violence in rows, where invariably run down by the British port workers themselves, he told me. I agreed that it was a charming characteristic, but ventured to ask whether he thought it entirely compatible with the drive towards violent revolution to which his party was pledged. He said he was convinced it would be different 'in an organized fight'. I think he was wrong. Years later a friend of mine was sitting in a café in Toulouse with a group of Spanish workers, when news of the outbreak of the Asturias revolt came in. The Spaniards were exultant about it and started explaining to

some French colleagues: 'You see, that's the difference between you and us. You descend from burgher craftsmen; our
ancestors were brigands.' And they related to this fact the
capacity of the Spaniards to rise in armed revolt against the
established authorities. Whether these particular Spanish
workers were anarchists or not I do not know. But the whole
difference between the European and the Spanish labour
movement, and the whole explanation of anarchism, is in the
antithesis of these two anecdotes.

'Backward mentality, inevitably to be overcome with the
further development of capitalism in Spain,' both liberals
and Marxists will say; they both believe in industrial progress. But the majority of the lower people in Spain care little
whether Europeans find their views backward. They feel,
though perhaps they know it not, that their views are not due
to the backward stage of the factories in which they work—
the pet explanation for anarchism in the Marxist camps—but
are simply one element in the resistance of the whole nation
to the industrial stage of Western civilization. Spain severed
itself from the progress of Western civilization towards the
end of the seventeenth century, and the Spanish people
simply, deeply, and instinctively dislike what has been done
since. This dislike makes itself felt in the distaste for work in
modern enterprises, in the distaste for work in the modern
way of intensive application at all, in the inability to handle
modern machinery, whether technical or administrative or
military or of any other kind; it makes itself felt in the stiff
resistance of the administration, of the landed aristocracy
and gentry, and even of most factory-owners, as well as of the
workers, against innovation; it is to be felt in aristocratic conservatism, in Carlism, in anarchism, in fact in most of the
political movements of Spain. And the belief in the predeter-
mined superiority of capitalism in this struggle is wholly unfounded. The resistance of Spain against modern life is deeply
ingrained. The expanding powers of capitalism, or, in other
words, of the modern industrial version of Western civilization, are doubtful and probably not unlimited. The issue of
the struggle is not settled beforehand. Again and again in our

investigation we shall meet the problem, and recognize the dubiousness of the issue. It is the central problem of Spain.

Anarchism is only the particular aspect this problem takes among the lower stratum of society. Were there no capitalist intrusion whatsoever, there would be no anarchism. Had the spirit of capitalism permeated the nation, anarchism would be at an end. It corresponds to the resistance of the Spanish lower classes against capitalist intrusion. This resistance, in many countries only occasional, instinctive, and devoid of organizing impulse, has in Spain created a powerful movement. This is in itself an indication that the final result of the attempt to modernize Spain is very doubtful indeed.

Only one fact remains to be explained. In general, Catalonia as well as the Basque country have been less refractory against Europeanization than the rest of Spain. How is it, then, that the Catalan labour movement is thoroughly anarchist? The answer, I believe, is to be found in the study of the specific political conditions of Catalonia. Catalonia, in its age-long struggle against Castilian domination, evolved a deep hatred of the one existing authority; the Spanish State. The authority of the Catalan bourgeoisie slowly evolving since the middle of the nineteenth century, was not nearly great enough to take root among the masses. Thus, the lower classes in Catalonia lived for centuries in a natural condition of anti-authoritarianism. The specifically acute revolutionary spirit, the well-developed preference of the Catalan worker for violent rather than for legal means of action is, in my opinion, simply a reflection of the centuries of struggle of the Catalan region against the Spanish administration and police. The Catalan bourgeoisie is not authoritarian either, for the same reason. And it is characteristic that Catalonia as a whole, during one single generation, between 1870 and 1900, has evolved from Carlist to anarchist preponderance. Every sort of violent opposition against the State was welcome to the population.

But we must go back to 1873. The republican government was caught between the Carlist rising in the North and the anarchist rising in the South. It decided first to strike down

24

THE HISTORICAL BACKGROUND

social revolution, and to settle the Carlist question later. Had it decided otherwise Spain in 1873 would have become what it became in 1936. Deciding as it did, it decided the fate of the republic. Before the menace of social revolution, the army immediately buried its superficial antagonism with the Church. They rallied, and after having subdued Andalusia in blood and tears, proclaimed, in the *pronunciamento* of Murviedro, early in 1874, the monarchy, with the old dynasty, and Alphonso XII as king. There ensued some fighting with the Carlists. But the main issue was settled, and the Carlist insurrection was ended by an honourable surrender. What is called, officially, the era of restoration had begun.

The Restoration Period

For twenty-eight years, during the reign of Alphonso XII and the minority of Alphonso XIII, from 1874 to 1902, times were quiet. Under the menace from the depths of society the ruling classes, Church, aristocracy, and army, with a crown whose bearer was a decent man as their point of union, rallied to the defence of the existing order of things. No more *pronunciamentos* then. The generals were no longer alone in the field; there were the masses, which must be kept in subjection. The political expression of this union was the absolute dominance of the 'Conservative' Party, under the clever leadership of Cánovas. It united the old moderates with many of the old Carlists and most of the old liberals. The republicans of 1873, a small faction without real social backing in any group of the population, had divided into two sections. One section under Sagasta, calling themselves 'liberals' now, repented, became monarchist, and, by the goodwill of the conservatives, were granted occasional ministerial office. The other section, under Castelar, pretended to remain true to republican principles, never participated in the administration, but took care never to attempt to put their republican programme into practice. This union of all active classes—the poor had receded into the dark—made times peaceful; in consequence, modern commercial and industrial enterprises had a chance to evolve. The foreigners, the Basques, and the Catalans took the chance. Thus peace itself created the conditions that worked for its breaking by new social forces.

These new forces, in contrast to those which had filled the stage since 1808, were genuinely European, working for the modernization of the country in the Western sense. The first of them was the Catalan bourgeoisie. It had played a hesitant and unsuccessful role during the revolution, but had achieved one thing during the years of chaos: the creation of what was later baptized 'Fomento del Trabajo Nacional', the Catalan union of factory-owners. It preserved this achievement carefully and successfully through the years of restoration of the power of the army and the Church. It was well advised in not using it, at first, to promote regionalist politics. The Catalan bourgeoisie appeared, in the era of restoration, as one more element of peace and order. But it got, in exchange for this important service, a tremendous reward: Spain changed from free trade to protective tariffs, both for wheat and textiles. It was a compromise between the demands of the Catalan bourgeoisie and the Castilian and Andalusian landowners. The chief political result was that the great Catalan bourgeoisie never stood unreservedly on the side of Catalan nationalism. Yet the position in the 'nineties was such as to make the cause of the industrial bourgeoisie appear as something particularly Catalan. There was hardly any industry outside Catalonia. Towards the end of the century the Catalan textile-millowners felt strong enough to claim a share in the government of the country. The 'Fomento' began to take an active interest in political questions, and soon the Catalan Lliga, the party of the great Catalan bourgeoisie, appeared. It claimed regional autonomy, but not independence, for Catalonia, and co-operated continually with the leading Castilian parties. As the representative of this policy, and as the leader of the Spanish bourgeoisie as a whole, Francisco Cambó, from the beginning of the present century, gradually rose to the position of being the leading statesman of Spain. He was president of both the Fomento and the Lliga and moreover president of the Chade (Compania Hispano-Americana de Electricidad), the most important financial company of Spain, and frequently became a cabinet minister. But, repeatedly named as a candidate for the premiership, he never obtained the post, because he was, as a Catalan, unacceptable to the Castilians. It is the misfortune of the Spanish bourgeoisie that its strongest section belongs to a disaffected border region, and not to the centre of the country. No other factor contributes so much to the weakness of the Spanish bourgeoisie; here lies the tragical importance of the Catalan problem. But what else is this than one more aspect of the anti-capitalistic character of Spain as a whole? The one region whose leading classes were thoroughly in favour of Europeanizing the country has always been an outlying and suspected district.

Later than Catalonia the north coast was drawn into the movement towards modernization. After the beginning of the present century new parties appeared in the North, this time genuinely European parties, not parties unjustly claiming European affiliations, as the old liberals did. Among them were the 'reformists', under Melquiadez Alvarez; representatives of the bourgeoisie of Bilbao and other industrial centres of the North; differing in their programme from the Catalan Lliga mainly as centralists differ from regionalists. Somewhat earlier appeared the socialists, under Pablo Iglesias, and with them a trade-union organization of the pacific European type, the UGT (Union General de Trabajadores). It is characteristic that the socialists too had their stronghold in the North, mainly in Asturias, i.e. in a region easily permeable by European influence. The socialists were not only pacific but timid. They were, in every respect, the contrast of the anarchists. And this is only natural. The socialists and the UGT were not against but for the development of capitalism. And what else but timid could a proletariat be, when it was as weak, uncultured, untried, poor as the Spanish workers, unless it was ruthless and violent? The UGT got hold of most of the Spanish miners. The socialists limited their campaigns mainly to the important task of

fighting elections, which had always been shamelessly
'made' by the administration and the local grandees, the
'caziques'. They tried to make them into something genuine,
in order to provide a basis for parliamentary action.

In this task they were strongly supported by both the
'reformists' and the Lliga, who both regarded the breaking
of the political power of the priest, the chief of the guardia,
and the large landowner as a preliminary condition of their
own domination over the State. Soon another ally appeared
in the rejuvenated Republican Party, which now cast off
leaders of the type of Castelar and under the influence of the
Freemasons and the Ateneo (a free university), led by Francisco Giner de los Rios, began to transform into a fighting force. It was backed, mainly, by a section of the Madrid
intelligentsia, eager to rejuvenate the decaying country on
European lines. This new conglomeration, the republican
revival, is closely related to the revival of Spanish literature
at the turn of the century, which was embodied in such personalities as Unamuno, Blasco Ibañez, Joaquin Costa, and
many others.

But the bourgeoisie could be bought off with economic
reforms, the socialists were timid and pacific, and the young
republican writers were no force to be afraid of. Had the
masses not interfered a second time, the coalition of progressive forces might have come to naught. But 1902 marks a
revival of the mass movement, never to stop again. In 1873
the masses had risen as an effect of the disintegration of the
old régime. When the régime was reorganized, they were
easily subdued. With the growth of modern industry, of
knowledge and education, they got a strength of their own;
and they were able to use the growing movement for reform.

The old régime which used to rule through the local
grandee, the priest, the guardia, and with the occasional help
of lawyers, knew of only one method for dealing with serious
problems: cartridges. Naturally, the inability to do anything
constructive to relieve the grievances of the masses, the inability to win over the bourgeoisie to the régime, the inability, finally, to provide for the most urgent national needs,

made the use of cartridges at last inadequate to accomplish the task which faced the Government. This became obvious after the defeat of Spain by the U.S.A. in the war of 1898, and the loss of Cuba, Porto Rico, and the Philippines. The régime began to founder in slow disintegration, its gradual loss of power only interrupted or marked by sanguinary massacres perpetrated by the military.

A series of general strikes and revolts, each invariably on a wider scale than its precursor, shook the country. There was a general strike in Barcelona in 1902; another in 1906; another, on a much wider scale, in 1909. The administration had lost all credit; it had not been able to provide for the conquest of the Rifi tribes in Morocco. It was forced to call conscripts to arms, because the army at peace strength was not up to its task in Morocco. Was it the idea of Castilian politicians that it was better to sacrifice Catalans rather than Castilians in the murderous war in Morocco, or was it sheer inadvertency of a careless administration? Anyway, only Catalan reservists were called to the colours. All Catalonia rose in revolt. Recruiting had to be abandoned, but then the revolt was drowned in blood. Francisco Ferrer, an anarchist educationalist who had next to nothing to do with the movement, but was hated by the clergy whose school monopoly he attacked, was executed in the Barcelona fortress, the Montjuich. There was an outcry all over Europe, and the mass movement had found a martyr. The habit of burning churches, followed occasionally in former risings, became a regular feature of every popular rising in Catalonia after the execution of Ferrer.

The old régime felt weak. It became increasingly difficult to control the urban constituencies in elections. Under the pressure of the rising forces of the mass movement the old parties began to disintegrate and split. The new parties asked for reforms with increasing insistence. After the defeat in the West Indies, political assassinations became a regular feature of politics. Cánovas was murdered, the king narrowly escaped. An attempt was made to introduce reforms. Canalejas, a personality similar and contemporary to the Russian Stolypin, a decided enemy of democracy, but a friend of the modernization of the country, took the helm, but was paralyzed by the resistance of the Church, and assassinated by an anarchist. The régime was driven to desperate methods. In order to frighten the Catalan bourgeoisie into submission the Barcelona police actually co-operated with gangs of *pistoleros*, who, more or less, claimed to be revolutionaries; the police itself directed and protected a campaign of assassinations, whose victims were leading men of Catalan industry and of the Lliga. At the same time the régime tried to form a dam against both Catalanism and anarchism by fomenting Alejandro Lerroux's 'Radical' Party. Lerroux acted as a wild republican revolutionary, but he limited his early activities to Barcelona and there violently opposed the Catalan national movement, which, at the time, was the real danger for the régime. He has always remained suspect, to a large part of Spanish public opinion, because he is believed to have actually co-operated, during his 'revolutionary' period, with the Spanish police. At one time he could be called the 'king of the Parallello' (the chief artery of the lower class districts of Barcelona), but after the beginning of the war his influence was broken by the rising tide of anarchism. Thus the intrusion of modern economic life into a society unable to digest it became, all along the line, an additional factor of disintegration.

The war made disintegration an overt fact, precisely because it gave a strong impulse to the economic development of the country. Being a neutral Spain profited splendidly from the war. Never had business so prospered before. In consequence, both the bourgeoisie and the workers became more urgent in their claims. The régime, moreover, committed the frightful mistake of sympathizing with the Germans, and helping them as much as it could from the fellow feeling of one conservative power for another. The Allies, in consequence, appreciated the need for the rise of opposition movements in Spain. The subdued conflict broke out openly and came to a head through a crisis in the army. Some officers had mishandled a caricaturist who had displayed his wit at the expense of the army. The Minister of

War tried to apply ordinary disciplinary measures against the perpetrators of this act of violence. He came up against the resistance of a body not officially acknowledged, the 'Juntas de Defensa'. This was a sort of clandestine officers' trade union, which had long existed under the nose of the higher army command, or with its connivance, and now acted in defence of a colleague who ought to have been handed over to justice. It became apparent, suddenly, that the army, by the restoration compromise, had been subordinated to the civil authorities only superficially; that it could act in concert and directly against the ministry; that the administration had no executive machinery it could trust. The problem of the army, which had seemed solved during a quarter of a century of apparent 'progress', appeared in its old shape, entirely unchanged. The 'juntas' were formally dissolved. But they got what they wanted; first, the resignation of the war minister, than a big cabinet crisis and a new cabinet after their own heart. This happened early in 1917. Ever since then the secret organizations of the officers' corps have continued to exist, under different names, until, as a secret 'Union Militar', they prepared the rising of 1936.

The insolence of the Juntas de Defensa, in 1917, was too much for the political parties. The cry for wholesale reform, for subordination of the army under the civil administration, for the introduction of parliamentary government, for a constituent assembly, rose in the country. The Government refused to call the constituent assembly, which would have meant the beginning of a new revolution. More than seventy members of parliament, most of them représentatives of the Catalan bourgeoisie, assembled nevertheless in Barcelona as a rump *constituante*, and were enthusiastically greeted by the municipalities of the larger towns of Spain. One month later things reached a climax. The masses rose in the first all-Spanish general strike. It lasted three days, led, not in common but on the same lines, by both socialists and anarchists, with the object of proclaiming a republic. But the bourgeoisie sat still, frightened by the prospect of social revolution.

THE HISTORICAL BACKGROUND

More than one change had to occur before a united front of the lower middle classes and the workers strong enough to overthrow the monarchy, was to come into being. For the moment, the revolutionary movement had reached and over-stepped its climax. The strike of 1917, as its precursors, was drowned in blood. The problems which had not found a solution on the revolutionary road drove towards a solution by means of a counter-revolutionary dictatorship.

But if the immediate practical results of the movement of 1917 were nil, its effect upon the mentality of the masses and of their organizations was immense. In the first place, 1917 had definitely drawn the majority of the country into the orbit of a revolutionary movement. The process of the dis-integration of the old hierarchy, of the devaluation of the old authoritarian values, was almost complete. The Spanish people, which, except for the risings in Andalusia, had stood completely aside during the First Republic, had interfered this time. They could no longer be kept within the frame-work of the old régime. A new régime, fascist, republican, or socialist, must come. Secondly, the political parties had deeply changed their character during, and in the years immediately following, the crisis. The republicans had fought, and in-tended to fight again. The socialists had partly overcome their pacific timidity in their co-operation with the more active and decided republicans. But the deepest transforma-tions ensued in the ranks of the Catalan nationalists and of the anarchists.

The inactivity of the Lliga in the movement of 1917 made it once for all a pro-Government force. Cambó soon began his career as a Finance Minister. But at the same time the Lliga lost its sway over the Catalan masses. It appeared as an agent of Madrid and was treated accordingly. It entered a stage of acute disintegration; for years there was a pullula-tion of Catalan nationalist groups, all of them more advanced than the Lliga, some of them even demanding an indepen-dent Catalan republic. Catalonia, for a decade after 1917, fell back into a state of political chaos. Out of this chaos emerged slowly the Catalan 'Esquerra' (the 'Left'), under the leadership of Colonel Maciá. It beat both Cambó and Lerroux and proceeded to organize the whole of the Catalan lower middle class. To the right a small stratum of industrialists remained true to Cambó and the Lliga, which became increasingly pro-Castilian, increasingly clerical, and was increasingly hated by the Barcelona intelligentsia. To the left, the whole proletariat fell under the sway of the anarchists. The country-side, for the time being, remained inactive. During Primo de Rivera's dictatorship, from 1923 onwards, Maciá tried more than one *coup de main* in Catalonia. He did not succeed at first, but he gradually acquired the prestige which was to make him the leader of the Catalan nation. In these anta-gonisms between the Lliga and the 'Esquerra' and in the final success of the Esquerra it was proved that an industrial region such as Catalonia, with all its markets in Spain, could not at the same time be regionalist and allow itself to be led by its bourgeoisie. The dilemma was solved in favour of Catalan nationalism, against the interests of the economic development of the region. So the Spanish bourgeoisie was beaten even in its stronghold, and with it the cause of the modernization of Spain.

Anarchism, on the other hand, developed in almost the opposite direction. From repeated defeats the anarchists learnt that, in the industrial districts of Spain, they must to some extent adapt themselves to the conditions of life of a modern industrialized proletariat. Out of this process of adaptation emerged anarchism as it is to-day, neither simply the old Bakunist league for the destruction of the sin-ful capitalist world, nor simply one among other labour movements working within the conditions created by modern life and accepting them. The basic convictions of Bakunin have always survived at the core of Spanish anarchism, and, during the civil war of 1936–7 prompted such actions as the wholesale burning of churches, the burning of title-deeds of landed property, the rejection of military discipline and creation of a militia of the Robin Hood type (in the early days), the attempts to 'abolish the state' (also in the early days), and, last, not least, that ruthless anarchist terrorism, which would and did attempt to sweep all the corrupt from the face of the earth. (In this context 'the corrupt' includes all members of Right parties, all large property-owners, all priests, and others.) But beside the persistent original unspecified faith emerged new trends, prompted, mainly, by two leaders of strong personality and shrewd understanding of political life: Salvador Seguí and Angel Pestaña. Seguí, a man of unlimited devotion to the idea, was killed, in 1923, in prison, without trial or investigation. Pestaña, a less disinterested man, spoiled a splendid political career by going too early and too far along the road of adaptation to the European labour movement. He himself had moved entirely away from the original anarchist convictions and, early in the 'thirties, tried to form the anarchist movement into a political party which was to participate in the elections. He produced a minor split, but finally remained isolated and to-day is nothing but an insignificant satellite of the republicans. But, during the first decades of the century, these two men, with the help of others, made anarchism into a force able to act in the framework of modern industrial society. After the failure of the insurrection and the general strike of 1909, they created the CNT (Confederacion General de Trabajo) as an anarchist trade-union centre, opposed to the socialist UGT. Strikes, both for political and economic ends, the movement had known before, but as an incidental feature beside these more important activities of the movement: insurrections and assassinations. Now economic strikes became a regular feature of anarchist policy and contributed considerably in making certain groups of the Barcelona proletariat the best-paid workers of Spain. But in spite of this, the CNT was never an ordinary trade union in the European sense. Not only because the anarchist faith was always kept alive among the membership, but also on account of its special methods. The CNT, in contrast with the UGT, rejected all sorts of social insurance; it did not even keep strike funds, but relied, in strikes, upon the solidarity of those sections of the movement which were not implicated, or upon the sympathy of the public at large. In consequence strikes had to be short, and to be short they must be violent. And they were. Barcelona never knew the peaceful type of strike action which is normal in Europe. It always experienced strikes plus bomb-throwing, or plus riots at the factory doors, or things like those that happened during the last tramway strike in Barcelona, when the strikers set the cars on fire and made them run down the streets in flames; and won the strike with it! Again, the CNT rejected all sorts of agreements with the employers. Strikes ought to lead, in their conception of trade unionism, to the *de facto* application of better wages and shorter hours by the employers, but without any obligation, on the side of the workers, to keep to a settlement for a given time. The state of war between employers and wage-earners must be continual. These ideas are more or less directly adapted from the teachings of the French founder of 'syndicalism', Georges Sorel, who, surprisingly enough, never in his life became aware that his theories had been put into practice in Spain. With the creation of the CNT, with the rejection of absolute negative destructiveness, with the acceptance of a trade-union organization and its discipline, Spanish anarchism transformed itself into 'anarcho-syndicalism'. The strangest thing about it is that it continued to exist successfully under these conditions. Other labour movements, such as that of Norway, have lived through the same attempts to create a trade-union movement based on syndicalist ideas; but invariably, after a time, the trade unions reverted to the typical trade-unionist mentality, to regular settlements with the employers, to the keeping of strike funds and social insurance funds, to completely pacific methods of action. Only Spain makes an exception. The Spanish CNT is perhaps the one genuinely revolutionary trade-union movement of large size in the world. It is proud of it, rightly or wrongly. Anyway, it could not have succeeded had the Spanish proletariat ever undergone that process of 'embourgeoisement' which is characteristic of the industrial proletariat all over the world. But the Spanish world is not bourgeois, and the Spanish proletariat, in consequence, could not be either.

The year 1919, as a result of the experiences of the general strike of 1917, brought a new step forward on the way of adaptation to modern industrial conditions; the creation of the *sindicatos unicos*. These are simply industrial unions, as contrasted with craft unions, and the contrast between the old and the new organization of the CNT corresponds exactly to that being fought out to-day in the U.S.A. between Green's American Federation of Labour and Lewis's Committee of Industrial Organization. The case was complicated, however, in Spain, because federalism, the right of the smallest possible unit to decide its own destinies, is one of the panaceas of anarchism. Now here was a suggestion to form monster unions with iron discipline. But again the innovators succeeded in putting their suggestions through, and again the effect was not to make the movement in the least like the UGT, reformist and pacific. The *sindicatos unicos*, on the contrary, became the horror of the Spanish bourgeoisie. They continued to employ the violent means traditional in the anarchist movement, combining, for instance, strike and assassinations, but, being stronger than the old craft unions, employed them more efficiently. For years Barcelona was thrown into a turmoil of mutual assassinations, not without the interference of the secret police, who, according to the interests of the administration, shut their eyes, alternately, before the assassination of bourgeois and of anarchist leaders. On the side of the revolutionaries, this terrorist campaign united men of the purest heart, such as Durutti and Ascaso, with professional *pistoleros*, an association which has remained one of the weakest points of anarchism, but natural in the framework of the Bakunist faith. *En fin de compte* the CNT became, through all these struggles, an organization which was more than a match for the Spanish administration.

During the same period the political programme of anarchism evolved too. Bakunin's absolute condemnation of the State as such had always been more of a demagogic manner of speech than a serious political conviction. Its practical importance lay in the emphatic rejection of any participation in parliamentary life, which, he and his followers believed, must inevitably lead to the 'embourgeoisement' of the politicians.

Still, Bakunin had welcomed the Paris commune of 1871, which, after all, was a central organization of the State, and the Spanish anarchists had created, in 1873, communes after the example of Paris, in Murcia, Alcoy, and Cartagena, which resisted the regular troops for months. But all these somewhat uncertain and wavering opinions about the State coalesced under the impulse of the Russian Revolution of 1917. In its first, Soviet stage, when the dictatorship of the Communist Party over the Soviets had not yet become apparent, when the other socialist parties had not yet been terrorized, the G.P.U. not yet created, the Spanish anarchists exultantly welcomed the Bolshevist revolution, and accepted the programme of the Soviets as theirs. They watched the evolution of the Russian revolution, the antagonism between the Soviets and the party dictatorship, and, finally, they joined with the Russian anarchists, with Machno and the Kronstadt sailors, in this programme: Soviets without political parties, Soviets without communists. The Soviet tradition itself is near the popular feeling of Spain. It has its counterpart in the national tradition of the 'juntas' or local revolutionary 'committees' which have arisen, in Spain, in every revolutionary emergency. Such a net of 'committees' arose all over the country in July 1936, and the anarchists intended to transform it into the politically ruling power of Spain.

Finally, in 1925, after the death of Seguî, when Pestaña showed a tendency to co-operate with the dictator Primo de Rivera, the FAI (Federacion Anarchista Iberica) was founded as a counterpart against possible 'reformist' tendencies in the movement, and to keep it close to its original rebel faith. Since then only members of the FAI can hold positions of trust in the CNT. The FAI itself reflects exactly the queer phenomenon that Spanish anarcho-syndicalism is as a whole. Intended to group all those elements who are not simply CNT trade unionists but convinced and active anarchists, it unites in its ranks on the one hand the élite of the anarchist movement, the active guard which has passed through innumerable fights, imprisonments, emigration, death sentences, and which is undoubtedly one of the most idealistic elements existing in the world at present, together with doubtful elements which other groups might hesitate, not merely to entrust with positions of responsibility, but simply to accept as members. But this is the essence of Spanish anarchism. It is a moral and a political conception worlds away from the modern European scene, and all the transformations of anarchism in the last generation, which we have just described, have only brought about a superficial adaptation to the *milieu* of the modern factory, without transforming the old spirit of popular rebellion of exasperated peasants against their oppressors. In fact the modern factory itself is only superficially received into the Spanish community. The engines are there, materially, but the mentality which has created them is foreign to the average Spaniard, and so is the social and political order which goes with them. It is precisely because of the slightness of their adaptation to modern industrialism that anarchism has remained near the heart of the Spanish people, and is the clearest expression of the attitude of the lower classes at the present juncture. And so long as it had only Spanish adversaries to deal with, whether in competition for the allegiance of the masses or in fighting the army, the guardia, and the administration, it was invincible. But it was bound to break down as soon as it got in touch with aeroplanes, tanks, and cannon handled by Europeans, not by Spaniards.

But for a moment we must revert to the aftermath of the crisis of 1917. The process of adaptation which all opposition groups had entered upon after their defeat would make it much more difficult for the Government to win the next round. But the next round was not to come so soon. Before it came, all the adversaries of the Government passed through a stage of weakness. It is during this period that the personality of the king, Alphonso XIII, played an important part. Eager for personal power, he welcomed this disintegration, which gave him an easy chance to divide and rule. He did it astutely, discrediting one weak parliamentary coalition after another; playing with his cabinets, cajoling the army as the one real force in the country. He was well on the way towards a personal régime when, in 1921, a catastrophe intervened. The king had supported one of the generals commanding in Morocco in a campaign undertaken against the express orders of the central command. But he had underestimated the Moors. They were no more, as in 1909, isolated Rifi tribes, but were now under the unified command of Abd-el-Krim, a leader of quite extraordinary gifts. Abd-el-Krim took his advantage, surprised the general, who, on the advice of the king, had acted with much daring and little circumspection, and defeated him completely. In a few hours the Spanish army lost its honour, ten thousand men, an enormous train, and all its conquests of one and a half decades. The outcry in Spain was overwhelming. And the personal responsibility of the king was implicated. He had prompted General Silvestre to disregard the orders of his superiors.

From this moment Spanish political life transformed itself into a network of intrigues, wherein the political parties, now even including important sections of the conservatives, tried to unite in order to call the king and the régime to account, while the king tried to divide them in order to escape. He was well served by the agrarian crisis, into which Spain drifted through the improvement in the culture of wine, oranges, and olives in other countries. Under the pressure of this crisis the *entente* between the textile mill-owners and the large landowners for the mutual granting of protective tariffs broke to pieces. The large landowners tried to use their political supremacy in order to get favourable commercial agreements at the expense of the industrialists. The *entente* between conservatives, liberals, Lliga, and reformists against the king failed. At the moment when the committee formed to investigate the Morocco disaster completed its preparation of a report to the Cortes, the king managed to make the parliamentary system unworkable. With his usual cleverness he now retired into the background and left the stage to the military dictator whom he had chosen. Primo de Rivera took office and dissolved parliament without the slightest attempt at resistance.

The Primo Dictatorship

It was obvious that things could not continue as they had been, because the wound in Morocco was purulent, if for no other reason. The revolutionary attempt to regenerate the nation had failed in 1917, the constitutional method had failed between 1917 and 1923. Things were not yet ripe for a new rising of the revolutionary forces. Hence dictatorship was obviously the one remaining way out of the crisis. The army having defaulted in its primary duty of defending the territory of the Spanish crown, the administration having sunk to the level of co-operating with professional gangsters against decent citizens, the political parties having lost all prestige in a sea of sordid and unavailing intrigues, everybody welcomed the dictatorship. Even in the ranks of the CNT there were, for the first time, waverings, which led by reaction to the creation of the FAI. Primo de Rivero started his job as a dictator under the most favourable auspices that ever inaugurated a dictatorship. His programme was contained in two sentences: destroy the old political parties, and reorganize the State by modernizing the country. In the six years of his dictatorship he did as much to achieve the second task as could possibly be expected. What elements of modern European life there are to-day in Spain mostly date from the time of Primo; the republicans are loath to acknowledge it. But wherever there is a splendid road (and there are many), a modern inn in a small town, a new breakwater at some important port, a modern barrack or a modern prison, in nine out of ten cases it will have been constructed under Primo's administration. The dictatorship was able to secure the foreign loans needed for this work of construction. And at first it had the enthusiastic support of the industrial bourgeoisie. (Cambó had been deeply involved in the plot, preparing the *coup d'état*.) Neither was the dictator unaware of the need for giving the urban proletariat something more than prisons and cartridges in order to make it co-operate. For the first time in Spanish history a constructive effort was made to solve the 'social problem'. Compulsory collective bargaining was introduced, in order to secure acceptable wages for the workers. The UGT was only too glad to accept this unexpected gift; it was recognized, officially, as a partner in collective bargaining, and, while all the other parties were persecuted, the socialists were tolerated. Caballero, after Iglesias's death their recognized leader, and then by no means a revolutionary, entered the service of the labour ministry. In 1925 the Morocco problem was solved. Abd-el-Krim was defeated (in co-operation with the French), and then roads were built through the hills and the country thoroughly pacified. Altogether it was the greatest attempt ever made to transform Spain into a modern country, comparable only to the similar attempt of Kemal Ataturk in Turkey.

For the moment everybody was relieved. But soon it was precisely the modern character of the régime that began to raise violent opposition, and caused Primo to fail. Even a strong and, on the whole, benevolent dictatorship was not able to overcome the intrinsic revulsion of the Spaniard against the modern version of Western civilization. And Primo did not have at his disposal the power both Kemal and Mussolini had, to help him to overcome the resistance of the forces of the old world.

Primo's régime fascist? Had it, or could it gather, the totalitarian power characteristic of fascism? By no means! Firstly, Primo had no fascist movement, nor a large and enthusiastic party of all classes, behind him. From the first to the last moment he was in power, he was passively tolerated by a population which, after all, appreciated good government, but saw no reason to help it. Moreover, Primo's régime was not only up against the profound Spanish apathy that confronts constructive effort; it contained within itself elements absolutely incompatible with the winning of mass support. A progressive dictatorship such as his must rely, in the first place, on the bourgeoisie and the progressive intelligentsia. But Primo had to foregather with their two natural enemies, the army and the Church. He was a creature of the army, had made his *coup d'état* with the army, and could not exist without it; worse, he had not acted as the recognized chief of the army, or as a general covered with glory and authority would have acted. He had simply been commander of the Barcelona garrison, and for his *coup d'état* had got the *placet* of the other generals, not altogether without hesitation on their part. From the point of view of the army he was simply in the position of innumerable predecessors who had made successful army *pronunciamentos*. Under these conditions he had the allegiance of his army colleagues. He might lose it, and in fact did lose it, under other conditions. He was never strong enough really to subdue the army. There was insubordination, and the formation of secret political groups to pursue sectional ends, among both the higher and the lower ranks of the officers' corps. This old cancer of the Spanish body politic remained unchecked under Primo, as before and after his time. So Primo had to cajole the army. But he could not cajole the army and the bourgeoisie at the same time. In order to keep the allegiance of the former he must offend the latter. It was no use for him to confide the Ministry of Finance to a supremely gifted young man of the Spanish bourgeoisie, Calvo Sotelo; no use to pump subsidies into business. He was bound to undermine the political position of the bourgeoisie, and the bourgeoisie was well advised not to renounce all power of its own, and so put itself into the hands of one out of such a number of generals. The antagonism became overt over the Catalan question. The army was fiercely Castilian, anti-Catalan, centralist. (It had very few Catalan officers.) The dictatorship was stronger than any previous régime. In consequence, Catalan regionalism was persecuted more ruthlessly than ever before. That went so far as to prohibit Catalan national dances and national songs; teaching in Catalan was strictly forbidden; the university of Barcelona was ruined. But Catalan regionalism was the one possible political programme of the Lliga, the strongest group of the Spanish bourgeoisie. Without it, it could have no support from the masses. In this dilemma the enthusiasm of Cambó and his followers for Primo cooled down. Caught between its industrial interests, which were one with those of the dictator-

ship, and its political interests, which were diametrically opposed to those of the army, the Lliga wavered, hesitated,
finally broke with the régime, but only after having lost what
credit it had left among the Catalan masses. The chief result
of the Primo régime, then, was to uproot the strongest section of the Spanish bourgeoisie politically, while fostering it
industrially. And even this industrial policy was hampered by
the jealousy of the Castilians, and in consequence of the army,
against any help given to Catalonia.

But it was worse with the progressive intelligentsia. In
Catalonia they were automatically driven into a position of
furious opposition as a result of the persecution of everything
Catalan; from this policy only the Esquerra profited. But it
was hardly better in Madrid. For the dictatorship had to rely
on the deadly foe of the progressive intelligentsia, on the
Church. It had to insist upon conformity, at least temporarily.
Any permission of free discussion would have meant the resurrection of the superficially dissolved old political parties
and with it the end of the dictatorship. But it was impossible
for a régime based on the army and the support of the crown,
and shunning revolution, to enforce ideological conformity
against the Church; so it had to be enforced along the lines
of the Church. In other words, the universities had to be
muzzled. The Ateneo, for the first time in its existence, was
closed. The leading intellectuals rose in fury against the
Government, many of them preferring voluntary exile to life
in Spain. And from Paris Unamuno started his redoubtable
campaign against the dictator.

Once the rift had opened, it widened automatically. The
administration was forced to employ the old illegal and unwarrantable methods of police persecution. The refugees
made these methods public; an increasingly efficient organization spread their tracts at home; indignation grew among
the educated classes. Uncertain of the firm support of the
bourgeoisie and too weak to govern in direct opposition to it,
the Government had to try to win it by concessions; but these
concessions clashed with the promises given to the trade
unions. In the end the situation became so muddled that the

Government roused the distrust of the employers at the same time as opposition against all collaboration with the Government was growing within the UGT. Following its plan of modern reform, and in order to create a counterpart to the forces of the conservatives (who disliked the régime, which had destroyed their political machinery), the Government made a very modest attempt at agrarian reform. The large landowners had no wish to sacrifice the tiniest bit of their wealth. They started a *fronde* against the Government, making full use of their important personal connections with both the Church and the army. The army itself began to be unreliable. That was the beginning of the end. Sanchez Guerra, the leader of the conservatives, who had chosen voluntary exile, landed in Valencia and tried a *coup de main*. He was arrested, put before a court martial—and acquitted. The Government had to recognize that it had the army against it, and resigned. The end of Primo, who had started as a sincere rejuvenator of the country, was hardly different from that of many another *caudillo* who had risen by the army and been overthrown by the same army.

A comparison with Italy and Turkey, which both solved the problem Primo failed to solve, will throw some light upon the reasons of his failure. In Italy Mussolini succeeded because he had behind him a sufficiently strong mass movement and a sufficiently strong section of the bourgeoisie and the progressive intelligentsia to be able to push the forces of the old landed aristocracy, the army, and the Church into the background. In Turkey Kemal succeeded because the army had no competitor, and, once set upon the road of reconstruction out of sheer patriotism, could put it through without serious resistance. In Spain Primo was caught between the contending forces of the army and the Church on the one hand, and the bourgeoisie and the intelligentsia on the other. In Spain a programme of reconstruction must be carried out against the Church and the army, as in Italy, but without the forces Mussolini had at his disposal. In one word, Primo tried to create a new order of things with the unchanged forces of the old order, and naturally failed. The strongest forces, army and Church together with the aristocracy, were unwilling to reorganize the State. The forces willing to Europeanize the country, bourgeoisie and part of the intelligentsia, were far too weak to accomplish the task. In consequence the task itself failed of accomplishment. The country was driven back to its traditional mode of life, and, as this could not last, it advanced towards revolution.

The chief result of the Primo régime was the ruin of the Spanish bourgeoisie. During the last two years of the dictatorship the currency had been depreciated, the budget was unbalanced, the level of production began to fall; the world economic crisis did the rest. It hit Spain more severely than any other country. What was worse, the political structure of the bourgeoisie had been shattered, as well as the old political parties of the aristocracy. The 'pact of San Sebastian' was the reward of this policy.

In the autumn of 1930 the socialist leaders met the republicans and the Left Catalanist groups, notably the Esquerra, in San Sebastian, and there agreed on a plan of revolutionary action. It was felt that the king, deeply discredited by his objectionable parliamentary policy, by the Morocco disaster, by the fall of the dictatorship he had fostered, would be defended by nobody. Hence the next revolutionary upheaval would lead directly to the creation of a democratic and parliamentary republic. The leaders of the UGT promised to put their unions under the orders of joint committees of all revolutionary parties, in case a general strike were needed. The other parties, in their turn, granted the demands of the UGT as to social legislation and the secularization of the State. The Catalans got a promise of regional autonomy.

There was no real resistance, from this moment, to the republican drive. Nobody wanted to defend the monarchy any more. Sanchez Guerra, leader of the aristocratic conservatives, was careful not to take sides in the struggle. The military lay very low. Discipline was still strong enough to subdue a small republican rising in December 1930. But politically there was no way out. The monarchy had no way open but a return to constitutional methods, but the Left parties refused to participate in the elections of new Cortes under the monarchy. As a compromise, the last monarchical government organized elections for the municipalities, in which the Left parties agreed to co-operate. These took place on 12 April 1931.

The polls demonstrated a series of facts of primary importance for the future. The revolutionary movement had hardly yet reached the countryside; the peasant was untouched; which meant, after all, that it had no deep roots in Spain as a whole. The countryside still obeyed the *caziques* and the aristocrats and voted monarchist. But, on the other hand, both the administration and the bourgeoisie had lost all hold upon the country. With two or three exceptions, all the provincial capitals voted for the united list forwarded by the coalitions of those parties that had signed the pact of San Sebastian. The monarchy had been optimistic; the result came as a terrible shock. The results in Barcelona were decisive. There everybody had expected a success of the Lliga; the Esquerra came in with an overwhelming majority. A few hours later Maciá proclaimed the independent Catalan republic. The only possible help lay in the military. But the generals saw no reason to defend Alphonso, whom they had learned to hate. Many of them, Franco, Goded, Cabanellas, most of the leaders of the 1936 revolt, were more or less in the republican plot, feeling the weakness of the monarchy and scenting splendid opportunities for a rule of the sabre in the coming republic. After the election General Sanjurjo, the commander of the guardia, went to the king to tell him that the guardia would not shoot upon the people. Nobody was left to defend the king. He issued a pathetic proclamation that he resigned in order to spare the country civil war; in fact, he was not the man to spare the country anything; he would not have found a single unit to defend him. The republican committee took over automatically and without bloodshed, on 14 April 1931; Azaña, the chief of the republicans, became Prime Minister; the socialists joined the Government, which contained several Catalans. A few months later, at the elections for the Constituent Cortes, the parties of the pact of San Sebastian came in with an overwhelming majority.

46

THE HISTORICAL BACKGROUND

The Second Republic

Intrinsically the new régime was weak. It had both aristocracy and bourgeoisie against it, on the Right. On the Left it
had against it the CNT, the strongest organization of the
lower classes, which wanted to use the opportunity to drive
forward towards social revolution. It was backed only by the
radical intellectuals and by the weaker and more moderate
section of the labour movement. It had won, not by its own
strength, as did the great revolutionary movements in Britain,
France, and Russia; not in the trial of insurrection and victory on the barricades; but simply by the complete abeyance
of the forces of the old order, by the complete disruption of
every link uniting army and administration with the monarchy. Both the army and the civil service, and perhaps even,
after some hesitation, the Church and the aristocracy, would
have tolerated the republic, had it not changed anything except the form of government. Unfortunately, it was impossible to leave things as they were. The republic had arisen out
of deep crisis and intolerable conditions. Something must be
done to overcome the disintegration of economic life and administration. Besides, the radical intellectuals were full of
ideals, and the masses were pressing behind.

From the first day the republic was torn between opposing
tendencies. The story which, during the first republic, made
the progressives a laughing stock was repeated of the Republican Party in the Second Republic. It ought to be a complete
rejuvenation of the country, but, by God, it ought not to be a
deep upheaval. Intellectuals such as Señor Ortega y Gasset
made impressive speeches in the Cortes, and accused mankind and fate because these speeches had little effect. But at
the same time the basic problem of Spain, the agrarian
question, was tackled with inexcusable timidity. It was
perdition for the republicans, in 1931 as in 1873.

The republicans were no socialists; neither were those who
called themselves 'socialists'; they were, under Caballero's
leadership, fully satisfied for the time being with the demo-

47

cratic republic and social reform. And much could be said to prove that their attitude was sound. But if a democratic republic was to exist, it had to get rid of the independence and the claims to power of the Church and the army, and this could only be achieved by breaking the power of the landed aristocracy and getting the sincere allegiance of the yet untouched peasantry. Abolition of *de facto* serfdom, splitting up of the *latifundia* in the South and the Centre, legislation securing humane conditions of land tenure for the tenants of the North and the East, and a sweeping diminution of rents on land, would have been a minimum programme to give the republic a solid backing in the countryside. The bourgeoisie, though not touched immediately by these measures, would probably join hands with the aristocracy in fighting them, because it would be afraid that expropriation would spread to industrial property. But the Government, provided it was strong, need not allow that extension; and it would be strong when backed by the support of a numerous peasantry, who, by agrarian reform, had become individual proprietors. The republicans would have been able to put the agrarian reform through, in the rush of the first months, without much resistance. Once put into effect, it would have constituted a solid basis for a democratic republic with tendencies far from socialist, as it has procured a solid basis for such a régime in France. Later, the bourgeoisie, reassured about their own property, could have been induced to collaborate with the republic. On the other hand, the Government would inevitably be caught between the Scylla of the CNT and the Charybdis of the army unless it managed to get a solid backing of its own by thorough agrarian reform, which, at the same time, would have involved a thorough Europeanization of the country. Here was one more opportunity to adapt Spain to modern Western civilization so much admired by the leading Spanish intellectuals. Again the opportunity was lost.

Instead of putting agrarian reform before everything, the Government immediately got itself into trouble with the Church about religious matters. The creation of the Secular State was the pet idea of the radical intellectuals, and at the same time an easy way of escaping for the moment the urgent problems of economy and administration. Moreover, the CNT raged in the towns and burnt churches. The Government introduced legislation to separate Church and State. When, many months later, after the ecclesiastical question had created a Government crisis, a split in the republican camp, and an attempt at armed rising in Navarra, the Government at last turned to the agrarian question, the reaction had rallied again. Now the agrarian problem, which could have been solved peacefully in April and May, could only be solved with blood and iron. The civil service, deeply implicated with the interests of the large landowners, sabotaged the reform, and the only way left to make it effective would have been to appeal to the peasants to take their claims into their own hands; which would have meant social revolution. The republicans were far from wanting that. Exactly as in 1873, but with more violence, the republic had awakened the masses of the peasants, who, without the invitation of the Government, tried to speed up matters by revolting against the guardia and the landowners. All over the country ran a wave of peasant risings. They merged, in a disquieting manner, with proletarian risings in all the larger towns of Spain. The workers, too, had expected the republic to introduce a new régime to their advantage, and, as they got nothing without a fight, they tried to take their cause into their own hands. Under the leadership of the CNT, Spain was filled with combined risings of workers and peasants. The Government had little hesitation in deciding how to deal with them; it called for the help of the guardia and the army, and thus put itself into their hands. Things had reached the same point as they had reached in 1874, with the one difference that the movements of the Left were now much stronger, and aristocracy and Church much weaker than then.

The republicans, together with the socialists, drove matters to a climax by exasperating the forces of the old order just when they were forced to accept their protection. They had exasperated them through their Church legislation. They could not help granting Catalonia regional autonomy (as promised in San Sebastian) after an enormous lot of wrangling, but that again exasperated the army, the guardia, the civil service, the aristocracy, the Church, and in general the partisans of the old order. Superlatively insensitive to the tactically appropriate, they started to react against this irritation just when they were weakest, by introducing a reform of both the army and the civil service. It was certainly true that the abuses in both cried to heaven; that there were three times as many officers and civil servants as were needed; that both the administration and the army were unable to fulfil the primary requirements of efficiency; still, it was a strange policy to pass bills pensioning and dismissing thousands and thousands of officers and public servants at a time when the republic was at their mercy for defence against the risings of the workers and the peasants. In the summer of 1932 General Sanjurjo, who had secured the peaceful entry of the republic, rose in insurrection against it at Seville. The insurrection failed, mainly from lack of serious preparation, but the Government was not strong enough to obtain a serious condemnation of the guilty general.

In the meantime the opportunists bided their time. Lerroux, naturally, had been enthusiastic for the republic in the early days of 1931. When the tide turned, he went into opposition with his 'radicals'. At the same time the Right made a serious effort to reorganize. Under the leadership of Gil Robles, the Accion Popular was founded, a party trying to imitate the German Catholic Party, to be not exclusively the party of the clergy, the army, the caziques, the aristocracy, and the bourgeoisie, but, as much as possible, the party of Catholic masses too. Robles merged his new party with other groups of the Right into one electoral block, the CEDA (Confederacion Electoral de Derechas Autonomas), and with it gloriously won the elections in the autumn of 1933. The time of the domination of the Left was over. The Right did not need to take power by a *coup d'état*. It had won it by the legal method of the polls.

The elections showed the intrinsic weakness of the republican forces. Their success of 1931 had been largely due to surprise and to the lack of resistance from the Right. By 1933 the peasant masses had been discouraged by the agrarian legislation of the Government and by the guardia massacres. The countryside, which, for one moment after the proclamation of the republic, had awakened politically and gone wildly to the Left, had fallen back into apathy and followed again the lead of the local caziques, who ordered them to vote for the CEDA. In the towns the republic had been a deep disappointment for the proletariat. The slogan of the CNT, abstention from the vote, got the widest support. Owing to anarchist abstentionism, the Lliga won against the Esquerra even in Barcelona. Large groups of small owners in the towns, together with a considerable number of civil servants and intellectuals who had voted for Lerroux in 1931 as a partisan of the Left, voted for him now as a partisan of the Right. The introduction of the female vote did the rest. This vote was almost wholly illiterate and much more under the sway of the priests than the male vote. It was the complete breakdown of a position which had been mainly artificial and incidental. The Spanish republic seemed at an end. After the dictatorship the forces of the Left had tried and proved miserably unable to reorganize the country.

But the alternative now imposed by the elections proved equally unavailing. It was, in fact, the worst alternative possible. For Gil Robles and his CEDA, in contrast to Primo de Rivera, did not make a sincere attempt to reform the country with due respect to the forces of the past; they simply represented the union of all those forces which wanted to maintain the past order of things, unchanged and unreformed. Some modern-sounding talk was only for the ears of voters. The real forces behind Robles were the forces which had ruled Spain before Primo, even before 1917, which, after having got rid of the unpleasant sting of both the progressive dictator and the progressive Left, enjoyed returning to the old gang, the old corruption, the old inefficiency and immobility. The policy of the Right coalition was simply to abolish everything the Left had done, and to leave it at that. The separation of Church and State was repealed. So were the laws of administrative reform. The reduction of the army officers' corps was reversed, the army increased, and made practically independent of every other force. The agrarian reform, which had never been effective, even in the extremely moderate sense in which it had been passed in 1932, was revised in such a way as to make it wholly illusory. Remained Catalan autonomy, which, in spite of the success of the Lliga, had such a strong backing in the Catalan region as to be at first unassailable.

The new Cortes had started with a government of Lerroux and the Radical Party only, supported by the CEDA. It was known that an openly Catholic government might mean a big outbreak, and the reaction wanted to strengthen its positions before meeting it. Robles was shrewder than Azaña in the sense that he knew when to do what. In September 1934 he felt strong enough to join the Government, taking for himself the Ministry of War. It was the signal for the wholesale abolition of all the achievements of the republic. The republican parties wanted to resist. In October 1934 they rose in revolt but failed. It was the famous Asturias revolt, which was of such wide significance for the subsequent history of Spain. In order to explain it we must go back some months, and study the changes introduced into the Spanish Left by its failure to rule the country.

Among the republicans these changes reduced themselves to the final alliance of Señor Lerroux and his 'Radical' Party with Robles (Lerroux has since declared for the Franco camp), and to a small split inside the 'Radical' Party, which brought Señor Martinez Barrios (now President of the Cortes) and his Union Republicana back to the Left. But the changes in the labour camp were more profound and of deeper significance.

From the very beginning the CNT had regarded the UGT as an extremely unwelcome competitor, as a danger to the revolutionary purity of the labour movement, and considered the split in the labour movement as a danger to its power. In fact, the working class of Barcelona was with the anarchists, while the miners and some of the engineers of the North coast, Asturias, and Bilbao, were with the UGT. The UGT

THE HISTORICAL BACKGROUND

was stronger than the CNT in Madrid, while the CNT dominated, more or less, the labour movement in the East and Andalusia as well as in Barcelona. The forces were not equally divided—the CNT was probably somewhat stronger—but the UGT had quite enough strength to make united action of the proletariat all over Spain dependent on its consent. And this consent was never obtainable. As is natural in backward countries with a backward proletariat, there was no middle line between violence and timidity. The extreme reformism of the UGT was as abhorrent to the CNT as what the socialists called 'anarchist criminal methods' were abhorrent to the UGT people. The gap between the two branches of the labour movement had greatly widened since 1926, when Caballero became an official of the Primo dictatorship and tried to use the legal privileges granted to the UGT by Primo to harass individual anarchists in the factories with all sorts of direct and indirect pressure. Things went a trifle better, from the point of view of working-class unity, between the fall of Primo and the proclamation of the republic. As soon as the republic was proclaimed they became worse than ever. The socialists, now defended and sometimes ordered the use of the guardia against strikers and rioting peasants, mostly led by anarchists, and they were held responsible, by these same anarchists, for all the blood shed in the suppression of the mass movements of 1931 and 1932. The result of all that was that all contact between the socialists and anarchists had completely ceased when the socialists lost office after the elections of 1933. The anarchists, making no bid for socialist support, rose in armed insurrection against the newly formed Lerroux Government in December 1933. They were easily beaten, and retreated from the political scene, disgusted with all political parties from Robles to Caballero, and more firm than ever in their anti-political faith in 'direct action'. In the meantime a big swing to the Left took place among the socialists. They realized that Robles was only biding his time and that, as soon as he took office, he would try to destroy them completely, by law or by violence. Influenced by the double failure first of Primo and then of Azaña and the republic; by the deep discontent among the rank and file of the movement, and by the disastrous results of the surrender of the German socialists in March 1933 to the violence they refused to fight against; and, last, not least, stimulated by the example (though little less disastrous) of the socialist rising in Austria in February 1934, Caballero suddenly changed his mind and decided that, after all, there seemed to be something in Marxist revolutionism. He got the passionate support of the rank and file when he renounced, formally and emphatically, the old policy of alliance with the Left 'bourgeois' parties and led the socialists along the road of preparation to resist the attack of the Right by violence. The change of party policy was not effected without serious disagreement among the leaders, complicated by the acrimonious enmity between Caballero and his second in command, Indalecio Prieto. But finally the change was effected, even Prieto not opposing it absolutely. It is significant of the real Spanish situation.

The turnover of the Spanish socialists to revolutionism has been likened to similar movements in other countries, especially in Austria. In reality, I believe, it is unique. In Austria, in February 1934, there fought a group of some hundreds, or at the utmost a few thousand, *Schutzbuendler*, that is to say, members of the military defence corps of the socialists, who were completely unable to draw the masses of the Austrian proletariat even into a general strike, still less into an armed fight. In Spain, once the slogan of armed resistance was issued, it found an echo, not only in the words but in the hearts of great numbers of the working class; it roused them to a practical response. This difference is not due to a better economic position of the Spanish workers. On the contrary, if anything, the iron and copper mines of Spain, the strongholds of Spanish socialism, were worse hit by the world economic crisis than even Vienna. Nor is the difference due to better preparation. Who knows Spain knows that 'good preparation' is a contradiction in terms if used together with the word 'Spain'; in fact, the Austrians were very well prepared indeed for a rising, whereas the Spaniards were hardly prepared at all. Nor was the menace to the Spanish labour movement greater than that which had faced both the Germans and the Austrians; on the contrary, the impending Robles régime was something much less intolerable for the socialists than Hitlerism. Remains the one difference that the Spaniards saw the fate of the German and the Austrian movements before their eyes. This did, in fact, influence the leaders; but it would be an exaggeration of the broadness of the average Spanish miner's international outlook to believe that foreign examples prompted the passionate response of the rank and file to the leaders' change of policy.

In the apparently sudden change of Spanish socialism from extreme reformism to a policy of armed aggressiveness is reflected the same peculiar national mentality of the Spaniard which, in a slightly different form, reflects itself in anarchism. The use of arms is traditional in Spanish politics; the code of lawful and peaceful settling of civil affairs has never really entered the consciousness of the Spanish people. This had been less apparent in the socialist movement than in anarchism, partly because it had become a group of the less violent elements; partly because intellectuals and trade-union secretaries played a larger part in the Socialist Party; partly because it dominated in those districts which were for geographical reasons most permeable to European influence. Still, in a decisive hour the Spanish socialist worker was as ready as his anarchist colleague to settle it arms in hand; and this without caring for the fact that both the original Lerroux Government and the later Lerroux-Robles coalition Government had a clear well-established legal majority in the Cortes; a Cortes not derived from the managing of elections; for these elections, which had brought the Right into power, had been held under a government of the Left. But, basically, the socialists had as little a legalist outlook as the anarchists, and they had overcome their timidity with their sudden and overwhelming rise in the last decade, and had been exasperated by the loss of power so splendidly conquered and for a time so joyfully held.

The socialists tried, for the purpose of insurrection, to unite all forces of the Left. But in that they failed. Azaña and the republicans flatly refused. The anarchists, embittered by the past policy of the socialists and their own defeats, had fallen back into a narrow sectarianism. The one important group ready to join was the Catalan Esquerra, now, after the death of Maciá, under the leadership of Companys. And the small Communist Party, which had hitherto more or less co-operated with the anarchists, supported the socialist attempt.

Shortly after Robles had joined the Government the socialists started the rising, in the first days of October 1934. But it was doomed to defeat from its first hours because in Madrid and in Barcelona it was a miserable failure. In Madrid the labour movement had been under the personal leadership of Caballero, and the Madrid UGT certainly tried to do its best. But Madrid has never been a working-class centre; it is the town of the radical intelligentsia. Since the republicans failed to support the movement, it was subdued immediately. In Barcelona the Catalan Esquerra, caring little whether the Madrid Government was legal so long as it was inimical to Catalonia—as, indeed, it was—rose. But the anarchists held the working men back—they explained, afterwards, that they had reason to believe that the Esquerra would immediately put down the anarchists after having beaten the Castilians. Without anarchist support the revolt broke down, almost without resistance. Companys was arrested and sentenced to death, a sentence commuted to life-long imprisonment; and Catalan regional autonomy was abolished. In the other centres, where the lower-class element was mostly republican and the working-class element anarchist, there was not even an attempt at a rising; nor was there any in Bilbao and the Basque country, where the Basque Catholic regionalists still hoped to get regional autonomy from parties of the Right.

There remained Asturias, where the UGT was supreme and rose in a revolt more heroic than any working-class rising since the days of the Paris commune. So great was the power of the revolt that not only the communists but even the local anarchists joined. Local leaders, unknown beyond their district, rose suddenly to national importance, among them Dolores Ibarrurri, called La Passionaria. For a fortnight the province held out against the Government. It governed itself by a sort of Soviet system. The Robles Government was unable to find reliable and efficient Spanish troops, and finally subdued the rising with Moors, foreign legionaries, and by air-bombing. The Socialist Party was defeated. But its splendid resistance in its strongholds made this one of those defeats which sow the seeds of future victory. In a military sense, the Robles Government had won. It was much too narrow-minded to see that the events in Asturias had given its opponents a tradition combining the pride of an army in its previous feats of military glory and the pride of a Church in its religious martyrs. Moreover, a few atrocities of the Reds were avenged in a sea of atrocities of the reaction. And as the agents of the reaction on the spot were mostly Moors and foreign legionaries, the 'nationalist' Government roused against itself the national besides the social fury of the lower classes. Finally, while something like 30,000 prisoners were kept in jail for eighteen months after the revolt, hopeless of release, the spirit of the Asturias rising was also kept alive among all the poor and burdened of Spain.

The Government of the Right, in order to overcome the Asturias tradition, had to put something very strong and constructive in its place. Instead, it believed the thing was settled and did nothing, except mechanically to undo the legislation of the first two years of the republic, and to persecute and imprison its partisans. Moreover, the last years had been meagre of spoils for the upper classes; it was good to have fat years again. The Lerroux-Robles coalition treated the State as a milch-cow for the governing clique; the 'radical' Lerroux group much more so than the Catholic Robles group. Anyway, the corruption was worse than under the rule of the Left —which means quite a lot—and broke out in nauseating public scandals. As usual with Spanish governments, the coalition of the Right was at the same time weak and overconfident. When a minor Government crisis obliged them to appeal to the polls they met the electorate more with menaces than with arguments.

On the other side the change had been very considerable

indeed. Asturias had transformed the socialists into something different from what they had been. Armed revolt and the ensuing persecution had completed the process initiated by the formal renouncement of the policy of government participation. The careerists, these bloodsuckers of every parliamentary party in Spain, had left the socialists, who had no more splendid jobs to offer. Moreover, the union of the Left forces, unattainable before Asturias, was increasingly realized after it. The republicans, who had refused to co-operate in the revolt, naturally agreed to participate in the electoral fight against the Right. But they went farther, and identified themselves so far with the socialist policy of the last two years as to appear on joint lists with them; this electoral alliance between the socialists and the republicans was the 'Frente Popular', the Popular Front. It was well understood that the individual parties and groups sharing in this alliance would be free again once the elections were over. The communists joined in too. It was their second step to the Right, in accordance with the general sweeping turn to the Right of the Communist International since the middle of 1934. First, they had changed from co-operation with the anarchists to co-operation with the socialists, now, in defiance of their old principles, they even accepted co-operation with the republicans. From their point of view, it was certainly sound policy. But they were as yet too insignificant for their moves to be important; the Popular Front would have won even without them; and their claim to have 'founded' the Popular Front in Spain is unfounded.

Another change had wider significance. The anarchists dropped their sectarian attitude, reluctantly, explaining that nothing had changed; but in reality it was a very big change. The success of the Right in 1933 was largely due to their electoral abstention. Now, under the pressure of the Asturias tradition and of the sweeping demand of the masses for united action, actuated, moreover, by the consideration that their own numerous comrades in jail could only be liberated by a success of the Left, they consented to renounce the slogan of electoral abstention and—without themselves launching parliamentary candidates—to bring their following round to vote for the Popular Front.

In Madrid it seemed to be a close contest between Left and Right, but it proved to be a sweeping victory for the Left. Madrid, traditionally, had been a republican town almost since the beginning of the century, and had voted Catholic only in 1933, at the moment of the deepest decay of the Left. The victory of the socialists in Asturias was a foregone conclusion. But their success in two out of the four provinces of Galicia, a thoroughly reactionary region, was a great surprise. The Basque provinces, naturally, voted for the Basque regionalists, which then seemed a success of the Right but soon proved a success for the Left. The Right, during the two years of its government, had lost precisely those regions where it formerly had, not only the administrative power to manage elections, but real mass support. But the wholesale victory of the Left was decided by the dropping of anarchist abstentionism. It gave the Left a majority in all the Catalan and one Aragonese province, in all the provinces of the Valencian region, and in by far the larger part of Andalusia. The Right retained its hold only in those districts where the elections could still be 'made' by the administration and the caziques, Extremadura, Old Castille, La Mancha, and those parts of Andalusia where anarchist influence had not yet penetrated, notably the province of Jaen. Some of these districts later showed, by the furious resistance of the peasants against Franco, what their electoral results had been worth.

16 February 1936, the day of the elections, meant again a sweeping change for both Left and Right, and for Spain as a whole. The Right, which had so miserably failed to make something of its success of 1933, tried now seriously to reorganize. It did not accept for one moment the verdict of the elections, any more than the socialists had done when the polls had decided against them in 1933. They considered a *coup de main*, but then decided to wait because reconstruction of the Right must precede revolt. Gil Robles, in consequence, was removed from leadership of the CEDA, and Calvo Sotelo, the former Finance Minister of Primo, took over the helm,

with a definite policy to merge and consolidate all elements of the Right under his leadership. In that he had considerable success. The army immediately prepared a rising and nego-tiated for foreign help. In the political field, the young fascist group, Falange Española, under the leadership of Primo's son, began to rise; it seemed to promise a rejuvenation of the Right, where Robles's party had only been a feeble repetition of the Conservative Party of the *ancien régime*.

The Left took office again. But it was no longer the same Left. Many of the elements that had joined it in 1931, and among them intellectuals of world-wide fame such as Una-muno and Ortega y Gasset, had either retired from politics or gone over to the Right. The republican camp was smaller now the socialists refused to join the Government. There was some argument about it, between the Right wing of the Socialist Party under Prieto and the Left wing under Cabal-lero (Prieto, through two of his lieutenants, carried the As-turias organization with him, while Caballero held Madrid), but finally the new-born Marxist orthodoxy of Caballero ob-tained. The republicans had to take office alone, with Azaña as president and Casares Quiroga as Prime Minister. For them the work of the revolution had been mainly achieved by the laws of 1931 and 1932 about the secular state, Catalan regional autonomy, and the administrative and army reform. They immediately put these laws into force again. But this time they did not get away with it so easily. In 1931 only the anarchists had risen against this limited programme; the socialists had shared in the governmental repression. In be-tween, not only the anarchists but the socialists too had fought, arms in hand. The Government must do something to satisfy the seething masses. But it attempted the dilatory policy of 1931 over again, unchanged: again there was delay of the agrarian reform, again the guardia began shooting in-surgent peasants. Only now the popular resistance was much stronger, feelings more bitter, claims more decided. In certain districts the peasants began to take the law into their own hands and to divide the large farms of the aristocrats between them.

It is difficult to predict what might have happened, had the movement proceeded unchecked. But there is much evidence to suggest that nothing particularly important would have happened. The republicans had not changed at all: many words, few achievements. Casares Quiroga, who had the reputation of being a 'strong man' and, in July, proved to be a very weak man indeed, had taken, jointly with the premiership, the Ministry of War, in order to purge the army of all officers either incompetent or subversive. He denied that any acute danger existed—perhaps not with deep conviction— but anyway he did nothing to meet the rising danger of military revolt between February and July. He had sent General Franco, who, in February, had almost publicly prepared a *coup d'état* against the new Government, as commander to the Canaries. The republicans did not want a thorough agrarian reform and were unable to introduce a thorough administrative and military reform. The socialists, though more radical, had not now become any the more active for that. They had settled down in an attitude of 'principled' abstention, backing the Government with their votes, but refusing to share in it. They would certainly still decline to lead a mass movement against the republicans and probably be unable to push the Government forward, either from without or from within. The rising masses, then, could find support among the anarchists only, or, in other words no more support than in 1931. The anarchists, it is true, had become somewhat less doctrinaire since 1931, but certainly—events since July have amply proved it—not to such a degree as to try to involve the socialists in revolutionary mass movements of any kind. In fact, these mass movements would be somewhat more violent than in 1931, but would, probably, fail in the end from lack of adequate leadership and because of local and regional isolation.

In February 1936, as in October 1934, as in April 1931, the masses had united against something; against the old régime which they hated as a tyranny. But the elements of a constructive policy were lacking, now as then; more conspicuously lacking, in fact, than they had been under Primo. The republic had failed to Europeanize the country. It had marked a step back from the level attained under Primo in this direction. Both Left and Right had co-operated to bring about this retrogression. There was no reason to believe that things had changed profoundly in these last two years.

But all that was not put to the test. Instead, the political fight, carried on with immense bitterness, evolved into a series of assassinations. As a reprisal against the assassination of a republican police officer, a group of shock police killed Calvo Sotelo, the intended leader of the insurrectional movement of the Right. This sped things up. The generals got frightened that, while the Government was treating them with velvet gloves, uncontrollable elements from among the masses of the people might not allow them to live long enough to rise against the republic. They decided to rise immediately, though the change of date upset all their preparations. On 17 and 18 July they rose, convinced of immediate success.

They got a big surprise. The Left had been in rapid disintegration while it was ruling unchallenged. But once the Government of the Left, upon which workers, peasants, and the 'small people' in general had set their hopes, had been attacked by armed force, the people rose, as it had never risen since 1707 and 1808. The ruling group disintegrated immediately. Casares Quiroga broke down. Martinez Barrios took office, and saw himself between the alternative of arming the workers or surrendering to the generals. He and his Minister of the Interior, Sanchez Roman, resolutely refused arms to the trade unions, which implicitly meant surrender to Franco. But the socialists, who had been incapable of one single constructive step in the last five months, still knew how to fight. By the menace of immediate insurrection in the streets they forced Martinez Barrios to resign. An almost unknown republican, Giral, took office as the third Prime Minister on the one day of 19 July. The Prime Minister did not matter much, for the moment. The UGT got arms, in Madrid, and with it the proletariat became the one real power. It was enormously helped by the attitude of the military. General Fanjul, commander at Madrid, was in the military plot, but thought it better to wait and see how things would move elsewhere. In consequence of his double play between his friends and his enemies he gave the workers the few hours they needed in order to arm themselves. They used their time well, and then surrounded, attacked, and took the military barracks. General Fanjul was captured, and, a few weeks later, executed after a death-sentence passed by a revolutionary court.

In Barcelona the military, under the leadership of the very able General Goded, put up a better show, but in this wildly Leftist town they met with stout resistance. The Catalanists alone, in 1934, had mostly run. The Catalanists united with the CNT in 1936 fought heroically. The guardia, which in the rest of Spain had gone over to the insurgents wherever it could, held firm in Barcelona. So did the two republican police formations, the *asaltos* and the Mozos de Escuadra, so did the air-force. The police formations gave the untrained workers a backing and competent leadership; both together, in two days' street-fighting, put down the revolt, captured Goded (who, later, was shot like Fanjul), and conquered the town. The real power fell immediately into the hands of the CNT. In the next few days half Spain was reconquered from the insurgents. Neither the anarchists nor the socialists took Government office. But they alone retained real power in their respective strongholds, and exerted it through the defence committees created in the days of the street-fighting.

The rising of the generals had achieved what socialists and anarchists themselves would never have achieved: in half Spain and in six out of its seven largest towns it had played power into the hands of the revolutionary proletariat. The problems were: Could they hold it? What use could they make of it? Would they be able to find a more constructive solution of the problems which had tortured Spain for a century than their predecessors?

II

A DIARY IN REVOLUTION
1936

The following diary represents the transcription, into comparatively readable English, of German catchword notes taken during my first journey in revolutionary Spain, and scribbled into various note-books. The method of direct presentation of the transcription of original notes, with only the inevitable adaptation to publication—has not been dictated by aesthetic considerations; far from it. From the point of view of literary attractiveness a transformation of my notes into a continuous account of my journey, a sort of book of travels, would certainly have been preferable. There was only one consideration which argued in favour of the method here adopted, but this one decisive: in a matter so controversial as the Spanish civil war every presentation that departed from the observed facts themselves, to however slight a degree, would open the door to doubt. The form of a diary, giving my day-to-day observations, was the one which offered the best chance to stick close to the actual facts. Nothing has been done, for this reason, to smooth out contradictions. When I have observed contrasting facts I have presented them as I saw them.

There have been excluded from publication in this diary those of my original notes which were of a purely personal character; incidents of no significance whatsoever, which would have only tired the reader; and confidential information which I had no right to publish; occasionally, in

64

order to avoid unnecessary prolixity, I have condensed identical repetitions of identical observations in my notes into one statement.

Pure mistakes of fact, corrected by later and more accurate information, have naturally not been reproduced. But mistaken generalizations have not been dropped. There are a number of such generalizations in this diary. I have been careful to distinguish them clearly, wherever they appear, from the description of the facts. They are quite distinct from my own final conclusions about the present problems of Spain, which are contained partly in the tale of my second journey, partly in the introductory and the concluding chapter. The generalizations contained in this diary are thus sometimes self-contradictory. They simply represent the impressions the author got from the situation at a certain moment. In themselves those impressions are certainly not interesting for anybody except for the author himself. Still, I decided not to leave out the notes containing them. In the first place, these notes give a better idea of the viewpoint from which the material here contained was collected. Nobody in an event such as the Spanish civil war would simply collect facts without drawing inferences as to the probable course of events, the strong and the weak points of the contending parties, and similar things. But in forming opinions, the observer inevitably takes sides, in however detached a way. To remove the marks of these opinions would mean to pretend to an objectivity which nobody can attain, and to mislead the reader, instead of putting him into a position to judge for himself. The latter aim is best achieved by clearly separating the presentation of facts from the presentation of the author's opinions.

But there is something more than that alone. As already remarked, the author's impressions and, I believe, the impressions of every observer have changed with the course of events, as those events have gradually unfolded the real driving forces behind them. These changing impressions, in consequence, reflect hopes, illusions, and disappointments produced by the day-to-day surface of the events themselves. Less than any other social situation can a revolution be understood by the description of dry facts only; half of its significance lies in the general ambience and atmosphere in which it moves. This atmosphere, unless reproduced with the creative power of an artist—which, unfortunately, involves an artist's subjectiveness—can best be conveyed through the medium of those impressions, hopes, mistakes, and disappointments it creates in the sympathetic observer. I would go so far as to say that the rising, transformation, and decay of these illusions is half of the history of the revolution itself.

5 August, 6 p.m., in the train from Port Bou to Barcelona.

In spite of many rumours to the contrary, the French train, as usual, crossed the frontier and went through to Port Bou. And there things, far from being unpleasant, as everybody had foretold, were peaceful to an almost ludicrous extent.

In the train from Toulouse I had made the acquaintance of an Englishman who was going to Spain as delegate of one of the British socialist organizations. He knew no Spanish, so I offered to act as his interpreter and we decided to travel together. We were received, at Port Bou station, not by an armed guard pointing his bayonet at our breasts—as I had almost expected after all the silly rumours in London and Paris—but by a porter, offering to carry our luggage with as much politeness and doing so with as much laziness as one could possibly expect from a Spanish porter in peace-time. We had to wait for hours, which also was no new experience to me, knowing the country in normal times—and there, in the hall where we were waiting, sat dozens of peasant women, chatting peacefully and not even mentioning the revolution. There were the usual armed guardias, and in addition a few armed workers; young boys in their civilian clothes. One of them was chatting with us when he was called away, not to perform any specifically revolutionary duty, but in order to find a drink for a crying baby.

Still, there were signs of critical events, and of problems both political and social. From a previous journey in Catalonia I knew that the Catalans, though usually knowing

66

standard 'Spanish' (which, in reality, is the dialect of Castile) fairly well, hate to talk it. If talked to by foreigners in Spanish, they were in the habit of replying in French—or, rather what they believed to be French—or, worse, with a curse in Catalan which no foreigner understands. So had it been under Primo. Now, every question in Spanish got an answer in Spanish, and when I repeatedly asked people in the station how it was that they now spoke Castilian without reluctance the reply invariably was that they had no reason now to hate it, since Catalonia had been granted its rights by the republic in 1931.

Another change, more important, dated only from recent days. When our passports were examined, we were faced with a queer distribution of administrative power, a practical outcome of the civil war. The Barcelona police, as we had already been told on the French side of the border, had ordered the frontier police at Port Bou not to admit any foreigners, even with regular visas. I knew the civil servants who controlled passports at Port Bou from previous crossings; they had been at their post for many years, first under the orders of the Madrid Ministry of the Interior, and now, since 19 July 1936, under the orders of the Catalan Regional Government, the 'Generalitat'. For with the defeat of the Spanish military in the streets of Barcelona, the executive power of the Madrid Government in Catalonia had disappeared, and all administrative powers of the central Madrid Government, even that of controlling the Spanish frontier, had passed automatically into the hands of the Catalan Regional Government. But the change did not stop there. Even the Catalan 'Generalitat' had obviously no power to put its orders through. My English companion had his documents as a delegate from a socialist organization, and I had a letter of recommendation from a fairly well-known Spanish socialist. When the officials at the passport-control told us that they could not admit us, we showed these credentials, with the result that the police officials at once declared our case out of their competence. We had to go to the 'committee', which seemed to retain the real power of decision in cases of a political character.

There were, in fact, two committees in Port Bou, one for the railway station, the other for the town. The first was composed of representatives of both the CNT (anarchist) and the UGT (socialist) railway union in equal numbers; the latter consisted of one representative respectively of every pro-Government party existing in the town. This composition of the committees on the basis of complete parity between the parties concerned derived from a decree of the Catalan Generalitat, identical in content with a decree of the Madrid Government. It had been religiously obeyed; in consequence, the composition of the committees did not give any indication as to the balance of power between the individual political parties on the spot.

We went to the offices of the town committee, which had taken its seat in the building of the *ayuntamiento* (the municipality), where it was officiating side by side with the old municipal officials and the old local police. Outside there floated a large red flag with hammer and sickle. The atmosphere was not much agitated inside either. A few peasant women, again, waiting quietly for something. Much chatter, little excitement. After five minutes we appeared before the president of the committee (obviously a working-man), presented our credentials, got his permit to pass the border, and, provided with it, went back to the station police, who, with sour faces, stamped our passports. The committee had been stronger than the police. We set off into the country of revolution, then, in one of the most peaceful trains I ever met, carrying first-class and dining-cars, starting and proceeding according to time-table. A few militia-men and guardias in arms went with the train, and a few patrolled the stations. The country-side seemed peaceful, the factories were mostly working.

In the train there was at any rate excited political talk. The guardias, to be sure, were very reserved—they could hardly like the position into which they had drifted, fighting, together with armed workers, against the military. I asked one of them how it was that the guardia had sided with the Left, and got the characteristic reply: 'We had our orders, you know, and we guardias are not political people.' The civilians were less reluctant to talk. There was a group of four in our compartment, eager to tell the foreigners about the days of fighting and about the present situation. One of them was an Esquerra secretary, another an active socialist. Their views, however, were indistinguishable. They seemed to be concerned mainly with one thing, the danger from the anarchists. 'Criminal elements, sacking and burning!' Obviously they had no intention of making the outside of things look smooth to the foreigner. Soon, they contended, an armed clash between the anarchists and the Generalitat (in other words, the nationalist Esquerra) would come. And it was dangerous, because the anarchists were strong. Of the railwaymen they had, according to our companions, something like 50 per cent. behind them. (I wondered whether 50 per cent. of the railwaymen were criminals.) They seemed upset in talking of things to come. Their eyes shone, on the contrary, when they spoke about the 19th of July and the glory of their victory over the generals. What had brought about so swift a success, we asked? Partly it was the fact that General Goded had been captured at an early moment of the revolt, and had consented to order his troops by wireless to surrender. But a large section of these troops had simply dropped their arms and gone home, without any order, as soon as they realized that their officers were not acting under orders from the Government, but in revolt against it. Anyway, the defection of the troops, whether spontaneous or by command of General Goded, seemed to be the chief factor in the defeat of the insurrection.

Barcelona

11 p.m.

Again a peaceful arrival. No taxi-cabs, but instead old horse-cabs, to carry us into the town. Few people in the Paseo de Colon. And, then, as we turned round the corner of the Ramblas (the chief artery of Barcelona) came a tremendous surprise: before our eyes, in a flash, unfolded itself the revolution. It was overwhelming. It was as if we had been landed on a continent different from anything I had seen before.

A DIARY IN REVOLUTION

The first impression: armed workers, rifles on their shoulders, but wearing their civilian clothes. Perhaps 30 per cent. of the males on the Ramblas were carrying rifles, though there were no police, and no regular military in uniforms. Arms, arms, and again arms. Very few of these armed proletarians wore the new dark-blue pretty militia uniforms. They sat on the benches or walked the pavement of the Ramblas, their rifles over the right shoulder, and often their girls on the left arm. They started off, in groups, to patrol out-lying districts. They stood, as guards, before the entrances of hotels, administrative buildings, and the larger stores. They crouched behind the few still standing barricades, which were competently constructed out of stones and sand-bags (most of the barricades had already been removed, and the destroyed pavement had been speedily restored). They drove at top speed innumerable fashionable cars, which they had expropriated and covered, in white paint, with the initials of their respective organizations: CNT-FAI, UGT, PSUC (United Socialist-Communist Party of Catalonia), POUM (Trotskyists), or with all these initials at once, in order to display their loyalty to the movement in general. Some of the cars simply wore the letters UHP (Unite, proletarian brothers!), the slogan glorified by the Asturias rising of 1934. The fact that all these armed men walked about, marched, and drove in their ordinary clothes made the thing only more impressive as a display of the power of the factory workers. The anarchists, recognizable by badges and insignia in red and black, were obviously in overwhelming numbers. And no 'bourgeoisie' whatever! No more well-dressed young women and fashionable señoritos on the Ramblas! Only working men and working women; no hats even! The Generalitat, by wireless, had advised people not to wear them, because it might look 'bourgeois' and make a bad impression. The Ramblas are not less colourful than before, because there is the infinite variety of blue, red, black, of the party badges, the neckties, the fancy uniforms of the militia. But what a contrast with the pretty shining colours of the Catalan upper-class girls of former days!

70

A DIARY IN REVOLUTION

The amount of expropriation in the few days since 19 July is almost incredible. The largest hotels, with one or two exceptions, have all been requisitioned by working-class organizations (not burnt, as had been reported in many newspapers). So were most of the larger stores. Many of the banks are closed, the others bear inscriptions declaring them under the control of the Generalitat. Practically all the factory-owners, we were told, had either fled or been killed, and their factories taken over by the workers. Everywhere large posters at the front of impressive buildings proclaim the fact of expropriation, explaining either that the management is now in the hands of the CNT, or that a particular organization has appropriated this building for its organizing work.

In many respects, however, life was much less disturbed than I expected it to be after newspaper reports abroad. Tramways and buses were running, water and light functioning. At the door of the Hôtel Continental stood an anarchist guard; and a large number of militia had been billeted in the rooms. Our driver, with a gesture of regret, explained that this obviously was no longer an hotel but a militia barrack, but the manager and the anarchist guards at once retorted that not all the rooms were occupied by militia-men, and that we could stay there, at somewhat reduced rates. So we did, and were well cared for, as to food and service.

All the churches had been burnt, with the exception of the cathedral with its invaluable art treasures, which the Generalitat had managed to save. The walls of the churches are standing, but the interior has in every case been completely destroyed. Some of the churches are still smoking. At the corner of the Ramblas and the Paseo Colon the building of the Cosulich Line (the Italian steamship company) is in ruins; Italian snipers, we are told, had taken cover there and the building had been stormed and burnt by the workers. But except for the churches and this one secular building there has been no arson.

These were the first impressions. After a hasty dinner I went out again, in spite of warnings that the streets would not be safe after dark. I did not see any confirmation of this.

Life, as usual in Barcelona, was even more seething after nine o'clock at night. True, the turmoil now abated earlier than in peace times, and long before midnight streets were empty.

Now when I went out the streets were full of excited groups of young men in arms, and not a few armed women as well; the latter behaving with a self-assurance unusual for Spanish women when they appear in public (and it would have been unthinkable before for a Spanish girl to appear in trousers, as the militia-girls invariably do) but with decency. Particularly numerous groups gathered before the fashionable buildings now requisitioned as party centres. The enormous Hôtel Colon, dominating the splendid Plaza de Cataluña, has been taken over by the PSUC. The anarchists, with an eye for striking contrasts, have expropriated the offices of the Fomento del Trabajo Nacional, in the fashionable Calle Layetana. The Trotskyists have settled down in the Hôtel Falcon, on the Ramblas. A tremendous group of cars and motor-lorries, with one or two armoured cars, was standing before the door of their newly acquired offices, and a group of young people in arms was standing about, in excited and eager discussion.

I do not understand Catalan. I was glad to hear German spoken. In this atmosphere of general enthusiasm there is no difficulty in talking to anybody. I soon discover that one of the militia-women in the group is the wife of a Swiss newspaper correspondent, and now I can begin to gather 'stories'. The care to find out whether they are true or not will come later. Let's listen to what people want to say.

A good deal of their talk is of the cruelty of the insurgents, who shoot all their prisoners. Is it the habit of the insurgents only, or among the Government militia too, I ask myself?

A second point discussed, and this with a surprising frankness and *naïveté*, is the problem of foreign help. Among the group I am in conversation with there are already many foreign volunteers, who have come to Spain eager to find a chance to fight fascism arms in hand, after having lived through its unopposed success in their respective countries,

or watched its triumph over a large part of Europe. Among
this POUM group, exactly as among the young people gathering at the doors of the Colon (the Socialist-Communist
Party centre), there are Germans, Italians, Swiss, Austrians,
Dutch, English, a few Americans, and a considerable number
of young women of all these nations; the latter sharply contrasted, by their unconcerned behaviour and by the absence
of any sort of male chaperoning, from their Spanish sisters,
even those who wear arms. All languages are spoken and
there is an indescribable atmosphere of political enthusiasm,
of enjoying the adventure of war, of relief that sordid years of
emigration are passed, of absolute confidence in speedy success. And everybody is friends with everybody in a minute,
knowing that in twenty-four or forty-eight hours one will
have to separate again, when the next transports to the front
send people towards different sectors. Among this crowd, the
question discussed is not whether Saragossa, the next object
of the Catalan troops, will be taken, but when it will be taken.
Still, something like a shadow seems to have fallen over the
volunteer units in this last day or two. The French, they
explain with the frank *naïveté* which is so characteristic of the
whole atmosphere, have promised aeroplanes, and with the
help of these aeroplanes a big attack upon Saragossa was to
be launched in the next few days. But in the meantime the
French had accepted the principle of non-intervention. (I
had known that report, of course, but did not think they had
accepted it in earnest.) And now, they explain, with supreme
unconcern for military secrets, the aeroplanes have not
arrived. Things are more, much more difficult now.

It is interesting to listen to what these Marxists say about
the anarchists. Immediately after the defeat of the military,
they explain, there was quite a lot of looting in the Ramblas,
on the pretence of anarchist action. Then the CNT interfered,
disclaiming any responsibility for these acts; now, the first
thing that catches the eye on the walls of the houses are big
anarchist posters menacing every looter with execution on the
spot. But there are other tales, of a more surprising character.
In sacking and burning the churches, the militia naturally

73

made a considerable loot in money and valuable objects. This loot should properly have gone to the CNT. It did not, however; but the anarchist rank and file themselves preferred to burn the stuff wholesale, including bank-notes, in order to allay any suspicion of robbery. The question of anarchist criminality, settled in such a sweeping manner by our Esquerra and PSUC friends in the train, seems really to be somewhat complex.

On my way home I saw the burning of a church, and again it was a big surprise. I imagined it would be an act of almost demoniac excitement of the mob, and it proved to be an administrative business. The burning church stood in a corner of the big Plaza de Cataluña. Flames were devouring it rapidly. A small group of people stood about (it was about 11 p.m.) silently watching, certainly not regretting the burning, but as certainly not very excited about the matter. The fire-brigade did service at the spot, carefully limiting the flames to the church and protecting the surrounding buildings; nobody was allowed to come near the burning church— in order to avoid accidents—and to this regulation people submitted with surprising docility. Earlier church burnings must have been more passionate, I suppose.

6 August.

It is impossible, of course, under present conditions, to get in touch with Spanish friends of the insurgents, or with members of those foreign colonies which sympathize with them, notably the Germans and Italians. These latter, if they are not refugees sympathizing with the republicans, have left; not a few have been killed in the fighting. But there are, among the members of the neutral foreign colonies, quite a lot of sympathizers with the rebels, who speak fairly openly. I met such a man this morning, and it was revealing to see the other side of the picture.

His first words were about terrorism. Executions, executions, executions: that seems to be the thing which is in the heads of the wealthy, the Catholic, the Right wing, in these days, and it drives them almost crazy. 'The Spaniards are absolutely panicky,' this foreigner tells me. He has a lot of Spanish friends, who are all more or less business people, as he is himself. The shudder about the massacres of these latter days is still in his voice. 'The foreigners are fairly safe,' he says, ' but the Spaniards, the Spaniards'—meaning by Spaniards, naturally, that group of Spaniards with whom he has contact, the people around the Fomento and the Lliga—'hundreds and thousands were killed in the first days. Immediately after the defeat of the military the workers started *to settle personal accounts*.' This expression I had heard once already, and insisted on being told about the exact facts. It turned out that the accounts which were settled were perhaps not so entirely personal. What really happened, it seems, was that priests were killed, not because they were individually disliked by somebody (*that*, in my opinion, is what can fairly be called settling of personal accounts), but because they were priests; the factory-owners, notably in the textile centres around Barcelona, were killed by their workers, if they did not manage to escape in time. Directors of large companies, such as the Barcelona tramway company, known as opponents of the labour movement, were killed by pickets of the appropriate trade union; and the leading politicians of the Right by special anarchist pickets. It is only natural that my interlocutor, who has lost friends, perhaps even close friends, in this massacre, is horror-struck. Perhaps it is as natural that he has obviously lost all sense of proportion. 'What a horror,' he exclaims. 'People killed without trial, without even the allegation of a crime, on the simple acknowledgement of their identity, for nothing but their social position and their political and religious faith, by their personal enemies! These anarchists! These POUM people! These gangsters! The socialists and communists, it is true, are better, and the Generalitat, with the Esquerra, is horrified and terrorized itself.' I venture mildly to hint that it is perhaps not so peculiarly anarchist to massacre. The British Press, and especially those correspondents sympathizing with the fascists, have enlarged in reports on the systematic killing of all republicans, socialists, communists, and anarchists in the Franco camp, from the first day onwards. I venture to suggest that perhaps it is not so much an anarchist but a Spanish habit to massacre one's enemies wholesale. But though he does not deny the facts about the other camp, he is wholly impermeable to the argument.

His information allows of generalizations concerning what I observed yesterday in Port Bou: The 'double régime' between the ordinary administration and the committees which I found there exists in Barcelona too, and seems to exist all over Spain. In Barcelona there rules, besides the old regional administration of the Catalan Generalitat, the new Comité Central de Milicias (Central Militia Committee), composed, on a basis of parity, of all anti-Franco political parties and trade unions, but in fact under the preponderant influence of the anarchists. Its president, as a matter of fact, is not an anarchist; it is Señor Jaume Miravittles, a young man of twenty-eight, member of the Esquerra, former adjutant of Maciá in some of his attempts at *coups d'état*, but originally an anarchist, who has participated, as a youngster, in anarchist terrorism. 'But there is only one real power in Barcelona,' says my foreign interlocutor, 'the CNT.' So far does this go that documents signed only by the regular administration are worthless. A man will do well to bear with him, besides some document from the Generalitat, either a recommendation from CNT headquarters or, better still, a pass from the Generalitat countersigned both by the CNT and the UGT. There is no authority besides the trade unions, and, in Barcelona, the anarchist CNT is by far the strongest among the trade-union organizations.

To my intense surprise I learn that my interlocutor is convinced that Franco will win, and that so are other influential foreign observers; I was to learn, in the afternoon, that this seemed to be more or less the prevailing opinion among all those foreigners who did not positively sympathize with the revolution. Their prognostications are obviously prompted by their sympathies—which my interlocutor expresses without hesitation, though he is hardly a fascist in the home politics of his own country—but he adduces serious arguments to back his opinions. There is a deep cleavage between the Generalitat and the anarchists; there is, moreover, the fact that the raw militia which is sent to the front is undisciplined, untrained, and lacking competent officers. There is, finally, the fact of foreign support for the insurgents, not consisting of individual foreign volunteers only—as is the case with the Left camp—but of modern war material too. Not less than sixty German and Italian planes, according to one rumour, have arrived in the Franco camp in these last few days. What a gap between those considered judgements and the young volunteers: and both sides equally convinced of their inevitable and impending success! Exactly as in 1914! Some of the foreigners go farther in the concreteness of their imaginations. In my hotel there is one charming and distinguished old English gentleman who is full of horror about events, heartily dislikes the anarchists and the revolution in general, but most of all is concerned about the fate of the unhappy country in which he has passed many years and which he loves dearly: What will happen when Franco's troops enter Barcelona? (He does not seem to doubt that they will, fairly soon.) What a massacre will ensue! It will be worse than the one we had two weeks ago. And the anarchists will burn down the whole town sooner than allow the fascists to take it!

Between naïve and enthusiastic volunteers, men and girls, Catalan and foreign, on the one hand, and less naïve people of the business community who, with horror or with pleasure, await the entry of Franco, there is the Generalitat, apparently rather helpless, but not so helpless as to neglect the traditional war policy of lies. Yesterday, according to news reports and the wireless, occurred the fall of Cordova, which to-day proved to be a free invention. To-day, it is the turn of Cadiz, which does not deserve serious consideration. But the people in the streets, and, more enthusiastically even, the militia-men billeted in our hotel, believe it, without, however, really caring about it; Cordova and Cadiz are places so far away as to mean almost nothing to the Catalans. 'The important thing is Saragossa,' I heard people say when discussing the invented news of the fall of Cordova. What a *naïveté* again! Nobody

77

seems to think that the landing of the Moors in the South may be a serious matter. The English papers, before my departure, were full of it, but here hardly any foreign papers are available, and the local Press does not even mention the matter.

In the afternoon, I had my first interview with the PSUC, the unified Socialist-Communist Party. The 'Colon', their headquarters, is a beehive, and on the ground floor is a recruiting office, which makes the muddle worse. Still, after some time we find the foreign Press bureau of the party. Everything is in transition from chaos to genesis; this particular bureau has just been created; my English socialist companion and I are their first visitors and we have all the benefit of it.

The party has arisen out of the union of four political groups, of which the Catalan socialists and the communists (who, in the rest of Spain, have still their independent party organizations) are the most important. This union was already prepared before the revolt, and effected immediately afterwards. It is an important indication of how much the antagonism between communists and socialists has abated, not only in Catalonia, and not even in Spain only; for nothing could be done without the assent of the Communist International. Generally speaking, the communists seem to have had the better of the socialists in the negotiations. They had by far the weaker organization, but have secured the affiliation of the unified party to the Communist International. But the real strength of the PSUC is neither in the old socialist nor in the old communist membership; it lies in the affiliation of the UGT, the socialist trade unions. I question my informants of the Press bureau about the groups which the UGT is controlling in Barcelona. It holds, I am told, the allegiance of about half of the railwaymen, of the banking employees, and of a very large percentage of the State and municipal employees; a few days ago the CADZI, the central union of the private employees, joined it. My PSUC informants are frank in admitting that among the manual workers the CNT is by far the stronger element.

Then briefly we touch on the burning questions of the day.

There are political and militia committees everywhere, representing the parties and trade unions. How is it, I ask, that there are no Soviets proper (as in Asturias, in 1934) formed out of deputies elected directly by the workers in their factories. 'It is because everything turns upon the military problems,' is the answer, which does not sound very convincing to me. One talk with either a militia-man or a reactionary will convince any observer that in Barcelona things are far from turning entirely upon military matters. Or were the wholesale killings of priests and employers and the burning of churches 'military matters'? Perhaps the PSUC would like things to be so concentrated on military matters, but the CNT obviously would not. So I am reduced to inferences. It is the CNT which is in a position to decide whether Soviets ought to be created or not to be created. If there are no Soviets, it is probably because the CNT does not want Soviets. If it wanted them, the UGT could not prevent it. And I muse that after all the attitude of the CNT is explicable by the fact that it holds the factories through its powerful trade-union organization, and that Soviet elections could contribute nothing to its power, but would, inevitably, give every other party a chance to test its strength in the factories. In Russia, too, the communists, in 1917, became less interested in the Soviets when they had a safe hold over the country as a *party*.

What is happening in the countryside? It seems, according to my PSUC informants, that things there are much less quiet than they look if you pass through it in the train. There has been, obviously, the same kind of massacres, mainly directed against the landowners, and, if these were absentees, against their representatives on the spot. 'What has been done with their lands?' I ask. Again the answer lacks definiteness, as it did about the Soviet problem. Every party, it appears, has its own land policy, and only one fact is certain; the large landowners and in general the partisans of the military rising have been expropriated. The anarchists, it seems, favour the creation of agricultural communities somewhat after the model of the Russian *kolchozes*; the villages should work the land in common, both that formerly belonging to the large landowners and the peasants' own land, and distribute the produce out of communal granaries. Their practice would be more 'enthusiastic', more imitative of a kingdom of heaven than in Russia; for the anarchists, where they are in supreme command of the villages, try to abolish money and to procure the products of the outside world through direct exchange with the urban trade unions. This, of course, is an ideal and the anarchists have put it into effect only in a few cases. Still, the PSUC people dislike this playing at Utopia. They themselves are in favour of private peasant property, and, where they have things in hand, try to persuade the richer peasants to give part of their land to the poor, in order to equalize landed property. This ideal also is realized only in a few cases. To me it seems very Christian, but I wonder what sort of 'persuasion' can induce rich peasants to give part of their land to the poor; it seems to me at least as Utopian a policy as the anarchist panacea of abolishing money. 'Why', I ask, 'is there no central decree regulating the whole matter?' The Madrid Government is opposed to that, and the expropriations are made *de facto*, is the answer. Again, I am not satisfied. The Madrid Government has no practical say whatsoever in Catalonia, which was already passing independent decrees about its agrarian problems in 1932. If there is no general legislation, it is because the Generalitat, not the Madrid Government, does not want to make laws about the matter. And this is quite intelligible. Why legislate where there is no power to enforce laws? The anarchists, on their side, perhaps do not feel strong enough to impose their ideals upon all the villages of Catalonia. So things are allowed to drift.

Next question: How will the militia be organized? On this point, which, in fact, is the decisive political problem of the moment, the antagonism between PSUC and anarchists becomes overt. The anarchists are in favour of the 'militia system'. This means, my PSUC man explains, that they organize columns from among their members and sympathizers, under the political control of the anarchist organizations, and paid mainly by the factories which the anarchists control; these columns are commanded by elected political commissaries, who appoint their own officers, purely in the capacity of technical advisers. In this shape, the militia, I am induced to think, must be a powerful instrument of the strongest political group, which, in the circumstances, is the anarchists. And now a few occasional remarks from reactionary foreigners come back to my mind. They spoke about the anarchists having kept not only thousands of rifles, but even cannon, captured in the barracks of the military, which they keep out of town, for an emergency in the course of the revolution. And everybody seemed to expect a second anarchist coup, this time not directed against the fascists but against the Esquerra, with which the PSUC seems to be more or less at one; anyway, two days ago, they sent three of their members to join the Generalitat, whereas the CNT and the Trotskyists continue to abstain from participation in the legal Government.

The PSUC, on the contrary, I am told at their foreign Press bureau, is in favour of the 'army system', as opposed to the 'militia system', and in that are at one with both the Generalitat and the official Madrid Government. What the army system is goes without saying: A regular army, with officers in command and political commissars only as advisers in political matters; the officers not elected but named by the higher commands; the units not grouped together as men of the same political faith, but from exclusively military considerations; the whole at the orders of the legal Government, the Generalitat. In one word, the PSUC want an army at the orders of the Government in which they participate, whereas the anarchists want an army at their own orders. At the same time the PSUC idea of an army reflects both the communist and the socialist tendency towards centralization, whereas the anarchists follow their libertarian ideals. The formation of an 'army' would probably increase the efficiency of the forces of the republic. The formation of a 'militia', though certainly detrimental to the fight against Franco, would favour the next step forward of the social revolution. This time, in contrast to all the problems discussed before, the issue is clear. The depth of the antagonism between Esquerra and PSUC on the one hand and CNT and POUM on the other becomes intelligible. In the evening, surprisingly, the newspapers brought the news that the three PSUC members of the Generalitat had resigned, leaving the Esquerra alone in charge again. What had happened? A conflict between Esquerra and PSUC? I could not believe it. But what else could one believe?

Puzzled, I went out into the streets again; they were seething as ever. Before one of the churches in the Ramblas, now completely in ruins, a group of militia-men is chatting with some women, and they are making fun at the expense of the church and of the clergy. The conversation is in Catalan, yet I am able to grasp its general trend. There are two main themes which call forth that special kind of laughter that expresses both hatred and contempt. The one is the greediness of the clergy: the church of the poor, the church whose realm is not of this world, has proved very clever in securing the best of the pleasures of this world. The second, proffered, of course, with still more laughter, is the alleged objectionable conduct of the priests, who, if you are to believe them, are professionals of chastity. The whole conversation is neither original nor, I believe, in any way revealing as to the deeper motives of the church-burning. But it is interesting to watch, how, in its attack against the Church, Spanish anarchism has taken over and adapted to its own use all the arguments used against the Catholic Church by the Protestant pamphleteers of the sixteenth century. Is the Spanish Church itself similar to the English and German Catholic Church of the Reformation era? A young American business man, whose acquaintance I made late in the afternoon, and who, surprisingly, is very much in sympathy with the anarchists—true, he has lived so long in Barcelona as to become half a Catalan—says things to this effect, comparing the Spanish clergy detrimentally with his French brethren; the latter cultured, devout, sincere, and decent, and the former, on the average, he says, just the contrary.

This young American is an interesting personality in more than one respect, and first of all because he shows, by his own attitude, the enormous sway of the revolution over the souls of people one would not expect to be touched by the revolutionary spirit. The business of this young man is ruined, he says. He has been well to do, and in a few days has lost practically all his wealth, so that he can only just manage to continue to live decently. He has never been involved in politics before. One would expect him to be furious, full of hatred against the revolutionaries. But he is not. He could go any day and start a new life at home, being a first-rate specialist in his trade. But he does not want to. He loves this soil and this people; and he does not mind, he says, the loss of his property, provided there will be instead of the old order of things a better, nobler, and happier commonwealth.

He is full of admiration for the anarchists, who obviously are little less than saviours in the opinion of some and little less than devils in the opinion of others. What is most sympathetic to him is obviously their contempt of money. The communists, he says, the first day after the victory, put in economic claims, such as allowances for the widows of the fighters killed in the defence of the republic. The anarchists did not say a single word about allowances or wages, or working hours. They simply contend that every sacrifice must be made in support of the revolution, without reward. The determinate fact, anyway, is that wages have been increased hardly anywhere since 19 July, least of all in the factories managed by the CNT.

I tell him about the bitter complaints I heard a few hours since at PSUC headquarters, of the lack of discipline and organizing capacity among the anarchists, and he does not deny the charge. True, he admits, this is their chief defect. But he emphasizes, as compensation, their self-sacrificing enthusiasm. It seems that this is what has really brought him to admire them. 'I never thought much of the Catalans as fighters,' he says, 'they usually run away at the first shot; anyway they did so, ignominiously, in October 1934.' This time, to everybody's surprise, it was just the contrary. The officers of the insurgents were the first to be mistaken about the fighting power of the people of Barcelona, and that's why they were so swiftly beaten. The whole difference between 1934 and now is, he explains, that then the anarchists abstained and now they shared in the fight, or, more exactly, were the ones who really fought.' (I wonder, personally, whether it was only the anarchists who fought. The incredible energy of the popular resistance against the military on 19 July, about which everybody agrees, seems rather attributable to the fact that it was a *united* fight of all sections of the population against the secular enemy, the Castilian generals; always before only sections had fought, isolated from the rest of the population; at one time the anarchists, at another the Esquerra, and these isolated sections were invariably beaten. No doubt, this time the anarchists took the largest share in the fighting and derive their present authority from their self-sacrificing heroism.)

He leads me to his balcony and describes a scene he himself watched on 19 July. At the corner of his street stood an insurgent artillery detachment of two guns, dominating the big road upon which his house is situated. On this straight road a detachment of armed workers, under the command of a non-commissioned *asalto* officer, approached the insurgent cannon, which could have blown them up with one shell. But they succeeded in a surprise. They ran towards the guns, their rifles with the muzzle upwards, so that it was impossible to use them. The artillery men, baffled by this inoffensive behaviour, waited to see what would happen next. Before any command could be given, the workers had reached the soldiers, and with passionate words began to exhort them not to shoot upon the people, not to participate in an insurrection against the republic and against their own fathers and mothers, to turn round and arrest their officers. And thus it happened. The soldiers immediately turned round. The whole Barcelona garrison had been told that they were under orders from the Government to put down an anarchist rising. When they saw that they had been misled they dropped their arms, or turned them against their officers who had driven them into the fight. In this particular case, my American friend was explaining, some of the officers just escaped, others were killed on the spot by their men; the guns were immediately turned round and now dominated the street in the opposite direction. Things did not happen everywhere, my friend closed his explanation, in this relatively peaceful manner. At many points fierce fighting was needed before the soldiers left their officers; but that was always the end of the story.

At night I visited a POUM meeting, with Nin and Gorkin as speakers. The meeting was enthusiastic, but not very crowded; the POUM is weak. The speeches were not very interesting. On my way home, a young intellecutal from the POUM, a German refugee with a good Marxist education, explained to me: 'You see, it is quite obvious that neither the Generalitat nor Madrid really want to win; proof of it is the stalemate on the Saragossa front, the refusal of Madrid to send any planes for the bombardment of Saragossa, the hesitations as to the bombardment of Oviedo. They fear that the revolution will evolve, with military successes. They will try to make the civil war a failure, in order to prepare a settlement with Franco, at the expense of the workers.' This is not an official POUM opinion; it only approximately reproduces the trend of ideas among the POUM. That the socialists, communists, and republicans are afraid of new anarchist risings is obvious, but that they should prefer a compromise with Franco seems more than doubtful to me.

I had dinner with a group of militia, who talked about their military training, and I was horrified to learn that all they were taught, before going to the front, was the use of their rifles; no training in the terrain, in digging trenches, etc. Sending young people out under these conditions means sending them to butchery. While we talked, some motor-lorries full of volunteers going to the front passed; there was no singing, no shouting, but their lips were shut in eloquent silence.

7 August.

I spent most of the morning in an unavailing attempt to get passes for my English companion and for myself. The disorder in the Government offices is not a pleasant sight. Nobody seems to know about anything and when you happen to find the man in charge, it takes an hour to get a document of a few lines typewritten. Sick of such incompetence, I managed, in the afternoon, to get an interview at the German section of the CNT (the CNT, or more correctly, the AIT, its international organization, has sections in most European nations). They have their seat in the palatial building of the Fomento de Trabajo Nacional, where Cambó had his private apartments as well as his offices; they keep this building in model cleanliness and order. The reception is polite, even friendly, but in their behaviour there is much more of the traditional *grandeza* of the Spanish aristocracy than was the case at the PSUC; in every word they say these people of CNT headquarters display an inner conviction that now they are the real masters of the country, that it is of their own free choice that they are not yet masters officially, and that, in consequence, they can allow themselves the luxury of friendliness, but need not court anybody.

The young German I am talking with is obviously not a man used to political diplomacy; he says what he thinks, and with the *naïveté* so characteristic of many people in these days he admits more than he ought to from the point of view of propaganda. His information concentrated on two aspects, the one concerning the past, the other the future. To be true, it was I who forced the discussion of the past upon him. The conviction had grown on me in these two days of my stay in Barcelona that the change in anarchist policy as compared with only a few years ago was a very big one, and I wanted to know what the anarchists themselves thought about it. How was it, I asked my young man, that the anarchists, anti-parliamentarians and opponents of every sort of government, did not launch the slogan of electoral abstention in February 1936, and did participate in the armed defence of the Esquerra Government in July? An awkward question for him, and the answer ran on lines only too well known from other labour movements. It seems that socialism and anarchism have that in common with catholicism that, whatever their change of attitude in practice, the dogma is never allowed to change. My German anarcho-syndicalist did not deny that the facts I alleged were true, and he did not attempt to deny that there was innovation in them. But, of course, it was innovation on the lines of the old principles of anarchism. In February they had allowed their followers to vote for the Popular Front only in order to free their own comrades in jail; and in July they had fought, not for the defence of the legal Government, but in order to move swiftly towards the abolition of the State. This sterile scholasticism was brought forth with a nice display of genuine conviction. I dropped the subject, convinced, on my side, that it is useless to argue about the dogma with the faithful unless one shares their faith. The discussion of the future promised to be more interesting.

And it was, because it contained a full confirmation of everything I had heard about the intentions of the anarchists, and at the same time put it into an intelligible context. The eyes of the CNT leaders are fixed upon the Saragossa front. They make their policy dependent upon the turn things down there would take. As long as Saragossa is in the hands of the insurgents, they have obviously no intention of attempting a change of régime; as soon as Saragossa is taken, it will make all the difference. At present, he explains, the anarchists do not consider wholesale abolition of private property. They have introduced *comunismo libertario*, i.e. full community of goods and abolition of money, in certain villages where they are supreme, but have no intention of forcing it upon the peasants at present. Neither do they intend wholesale socialization of industry. On the contrary, wherever the owners of factories and shops are available, they force them to continue to manage their business. This does not matter very much in the large factories, whose owners generally are not available, but it matters a lot—as every look about the streets confirms—in the small shops and factories. Neither do the anarchists attempt, at present, to do away with the Generalitat and to create instead a régime exclusively based on the committees. All they do for the time being is to make preparations for more complete change later. These preparations consist in the local introduction of *comunismo libertario* where there is no re-

87

sistance; in the organization of the management by the CNT of those factories whose owners are not available; in the development of CNT control in the other factories; in the creation and extension of the militia; and, last, not least, in the strengthening of the political committees and the gradual extension of their sphere of action, to make them able, at the decisive hour, to take over power without much difficulty. And I am given to understand that the fall of Saragossa—which he seems to think is near—will bring the decisive hour. 'Then', he explains, 'we shall consider a policy nearer to the fulfilment of our maximum programme, i.e. the full abolition of the State (meaning by that the replacing of the Generalitat by the committees), even if other parties resist our aims.' In one word: before the fall of Saragossa, only preparatory steps; afterwards, a revolution to abolish the double régime and make the CNT supreme. The surprising thing about it is the limitation of the outlook to Catalonia. These people know that at present a second revolution would sever them from Madrid and catch them between Madrid, Franco, and foreign intervention. But why in the world the fall of Saragossa should make all the difference I am at a loss to understand.

What about the resignation of the three PSUC members of the Generalitat? It appears that they have been forced to resign because their attempt to join the Government had been prompted by the desire to cross precisely those 'preparatory moves' of the CNT which my informant had just mentioned. The PSUC wanted to relieve the Generalitat from the stigma of being a government of 'bourgeois nationalists' only, and attempted to strip the CNT of the claim to be the one legitimate representative of the working-class as against the bourgeois Government. Joining the Generalitat, they could proclaim the Generalitat to be a joint government of both the nationalist Esquerra *and* of the trade unions. That is precisely why the anarchists claimed, in the form of an ultimatum, the immediate resignation of the PSUC ministers, and threatened to leave the central militia committee if their claim was not granted. This latter step would have meant immediate civil war in the streets of Barcelona; the Generalitat could not govern without the connivance of the anarchists as expressed by their co-operation within the militia committee, which, in its turn, co-operates with the Generalitat. And as the PSUC are trade unionists, but far weaker than the anarchists, and cannot genuinely claim to represent the Barcelona working class, they had to give in to this pressure, and resign. Nothing can be done, at present, without the consent of the CNT.

8 August.

This morning I visited one of the collectivized factories, workshops of the general bus company. Success or failure of the revolution will depend, to a large extent, upon the ability of the trade unions to manage the expropriated factories. In Russia socialization meant at first, and for a long time, hardly anything but wholesale disintegration of industry. How is the situation in Spain?

Undeniably, the factory which I saw is a big success for the CNT. Only three weeks after the beginning of the civil war, two weeks after the end of the general strike, it seems to run as smoothly as if nothing had happened. I visited the men at their machines. The rooms looked tidy, the work was done in a regular manner. Since socialization this factory had repaired two buses, finished one which had been under construction, and constructed a completely new one. The latter wore the inscription 'constructed under workers' control'. It had been completed, the management claimed, in five days, as against an average of seven days under the previous management. Complete success, then.

It is a large factory, and things could not have been made to look nice for the benefit of a visitor, had they really been in a bad muddle. Nor do I think that any preparations were made for my visit. Still, one must certainly not generalize from this one experience. There are many facts which make this particular concern a privileged one. Firstly, and speaking quite generally, Catalonia is not Spain; the Catalans as a whole are a people with a keen sense of business, and the managing committee (composed entirely of former workers) discussed with me the various aspects of financial management with an interest characteristic of the Catalans, but which would be strange with true Castilians. These Catalan workers have actually started their management with the introduction of cuts in expenditure, and there is nothing they are more proud of. Secondly, this factory is run by engineers, who all over the world are one of the most intelligent sections of the working class. What would happen in the textile industry in Catalonia?[1] Thirdly, the CNT was careful to select, for my benefit, a thoroughly anarchist factory, without any competition between CNT and UGT. The new management had been formally elected, when work was resumed, by the workers themselves; but in fact it seemed to be the old factory committee of the CNT, which was an established authority among the men long before the civil war. It must be easy for such a management to make itself obeyed. The technical side of the work of the bus company is easy. After all, Barcelona has no urgent need of new buses and much the most of the work done is simple repairing; the mechanics, whether CNT or Esquerra, are ready to co-operate, and the factory, in consequence, is rid of the problem which was so catastrophic in Russia: the obstruction of the higher technical personnel. Being mainly a repair shop, this particular factory needs little raw material, and is thus free from what is the biggest difficulty of the Catalan industry at present. There is much talk in the town of serious difficulties with the raw material for most factories. Finally, the bus company is in a privileged position as regards finance. It gets its income from bus fares, which come in almost exactly as in peacetime. There is no problem of marketing its product.

But if it would be hasty to generalize from the very favourable impression made by this particular factory, one fact remains: it is an extraordinary achievement for a group of workers to take over a factory, under however favourable conditions, and within a few days to make it run with com-

[1]Back in London, I heard bitter complaints about the mismanagement of the textile industry and the destruction of its machinery. Here again, probably, one ought to abstain from hasty generalizations.

plete regularity. It bears brilliant witness to the general standard of efficiency of the Catalan worker and to the organizing capacities of the Barcelona trade unions. For one must not forget that this firm has lost its whole managing staff. I had the opportunity to look at the wages and salary list, which showed that the president, the directors, the chief engineer, and the second engineer had all 'disappeared' (which is a mild way of saying that they have been killed). It meant economies for the factory, the members of the committee explained calmly, exactly as the suppression of pensions to private friends of the former management and the fixing of a maximum salary of 1,000 pesetas a month (the wages of the workers had not been increased since socialization). Ruthless cruelty in the civil war went together, in these people, with a keen business sense, an attitude characteristic of the Catalan.

In the afternoon I acted as an interpreter in a confidential conference of my British friend with a leader of the PSUC. So much can be said, that the leaders of the PSUC are perfectly well aware of what the anarchists intend after the fall of Saragossa, and are much perturbed by this prospect. Their dislike of the anarchists is at least as great as the anarchist's dislike of them, and is by no means a product of the events of these last days. To break anarchist domination in the Barcelona trade-union movement seems to be their chief aim. In the meantime, conditions seem to be pretty bad. A few days ago the three leaders of the UGT minority among the port workers were killed by the anarchists, and though the CNT has officially disclaimed responsibility and condemned the crime, nobody believes that there is any certainty that such things will not happen again.

Anarchist violence is not limited to their special enemies. Yesterday the POUM was the object of anarchist attack. A group of POUM militia had assembled with their arms in a building for one of their regular gatherings, when anarchist motor-lorries arrived, machine-guns were placed before the doors of the POUM meeting, and its participants disarmed under this pressure, the anarchists openly declaring that they saw no reason why the POUM should be allowed to increase its armaments and so threaten the domination of the CNT. A protest has been lodged by the POUM with the Militia Central Committee, but the *fait accompli* was unchangeable.

9 August.

This Sunday morning I listened to an anarchist mass meeting in the 'Olympia'. Being late, I did not get into the building; many thousands of people stood outside listening to the loud-speakers. There was no loud enthusiasm, but silent and concentrated attention with occasional expressions of assent. The speakers protested emphatically against the plan of the Madrid Government to reorganize the old army, and defended the anarchist 'militia system'. They expressly rejected the Russian authoritarian system; Spain ought not to imitate the Russian Revolution. Garcia Oliver, the actual leader of the Barcelona organization, admitted the stalemate at the Saragossa front, first excused it by the inevitable slowness of the reorganization of industry for the production of ammunition, but then went on: 'Now, comrades, we do not talk about the six-hour day or the eight-hour day or even of any fixed number of working hours. How many hours have we to work now? As many as are necessary for the victory of the revolution.' There was a dead silence when these words were uttered, and it is difficult to say whether this silence indicated support or opposition. Definitely, Oliver has a way with him to tell the masses unpleasant truths. But *Solidanidad Obrera*, the anarchist daily, did not repeat this sentence in its report of the meeting.

In the afternoon I went to the Tibidabo, a suburban country resort which was, in the early days and probably still is, the scene of many nightly executions. But on this Sunday afternoon it was crowded with peaceful people, both young and old, who enjoyed themselves without, apparently, thinking of the horrors either of war or of revolution. Below, in and outside the port, lay the men-of-war of four nations under their eyes.

10 August.

I spent the whole day at various offices but finally succeeded in procuring documents and a car to take me to the front.

11 August.

In a narrow street a car was manœuvring hectically among an excited crowd. Inside sat four armed militia-men, and a fifth man in his shirt-sleeves, collarless, pale as death, with one of the militia-men holding a revolver against his head. Evidently an arrest, with impending execution.

I went into one of the better shops of the Ramblas in order to buy some toilet articles, but the owner explained to me that for some reason he is not allowed to sell them on Monday morning. 'But I am going to the front,' I tell him, and immediately he sells me what I need, with a genuine expression of enthusiasm. Still all these Ramblas stores have suffered heavily from the revolution.

Catalonia and the Aragon Front

This afternoon, at 1 p.m., after days of waiting and delays, I finally started for the front in a car of the militia central committee, with an armed driver and one armed guard. We are three in the party, the Barcelona representative of the *Paris Flèche*, Mr. John Cornford, a young British communist, and myself.

Really the Catalonian countryside is not so calm as it looked from the windows of the train. At most villages all the entries are barricaded and heavily guarded day and night. The guards are picturesque and look as if they were cut out from a Goya painting: peasant clothes, very often not too clean, but adorned with red or red-black neckties; they are distinguished from ordinary mortals by red badges with the stamp of their organization, or of the local committee; bandoliers full of cartridges hold their jackets together. Thus they sit on the road, or more often crouch behind a competently constructed sand-bag barricade, levelling their shot-guns at the car, or waving them wildly. These shot-guns are the best

93

thing about them. The most modern must date back to the Napoleonic Wars and have been kept as a family treasure. Whether they go off in an emergency I cannot tell. The guard invariably stops our car and then starts the scrutiny of the documents: the car's 'pass', the passengers' passes, the permits to carry arms, the Press cards of visiting journalists, and sometimes they even claim to see the party cards of the guards and driver. Going through this procedure more than twenty times a day is nerve-racking, but it is done decently, and in most cases without unnecessary delay. The villagers evidently had not tired of performing this duty through many weeks, with more care, it is true, in industrial villages than in peasant communities. The latter are sometimes without barricades and even without guards.

In practically every village there is a political committee, invariably composed on the basis of the regulations of the Generalitat, which prescribes parity of representation for all political organizations and trade unions. As to mass support, the anarchists predominate in the province of Barcelona, whereas in the province of Lerida the POUM is by far the strongest party. This is due to the fact that Maurin, their most popular leader, is a native of Lerida.

All the villages and small towns which we passed through, though passionately guarding their own territory, have not sent a single man to the front. The main recruiting for the militia is in Barcelona.

In the old decaying townlet of Cervera there had existed a theological seminary. I question one of the village guards, a good-looking boy of certainly not more than sixteen, about it, and he answers with the happiest smile on his face: 'Oh! They've gone—and how they've gone!' Churches are burnt without a single exception; only their walls are standing. This has mostly been done by order of the CNT or the passing militia-columns. Hardly anywhere in this region has there been actual fighting between the rebels and the partisans of the Generalitat.

There are surprisingly few indications that we are approaching the front. The road is intact and there is less traffic than in peace-time. A few motor-lorries with provisions and still fewer with ammunition are passing towards the front, and others are coming back empty. We did not meet a single ambulance car.

Lerida being the meeting-point of all the roads serving the southern part of the Saragossa front, I expected it to be a centre of activity. But there is very little. Thirty or forty cars and motor-lorries are parked in the *plaza* and some of the militia are to be seen in the town; there cannot be more than a few hundred of them altogether. Many of them crowd into the offices of the civil governor, and there talk excitedly and enthusiastically of Buenaventura Durutti, the anarchist leader, and his column; he and his men are the popular heroes of the Catalan war, to the detriment of all the other Catalan columns. Durutti has the reputation of being a sort of avenging angel of the poor. His column is known to be more ruthless than any other in shooting the fascists, the rich, and the priests in the villages, and the glory of its self-sacrificing advance towards Saragossa, careless of heavy losses, is told all through the militia of Catalonia. Some of the guards in the governor's offices have served under him. With a naïve smile, which has nothing of sadism about it, but rather expresses the satisfaction of a child at a good piece of fun, they show me their dum-dum cartridges, which they have made out of regular cartridges by an incision at the top. 'Prisonerssss...' one man tells me, meaning by that that a cartridge is ready for every prisoner. So that is civil war in Spain. I am inclined to think it is not different in the Franco camp. Only, on both sides, neutral Press correspondents must remain silent, if they do not want to get themselves into serious trouble.

It is not easy to find a dinner, as meals are rationed; this is really the first sign that we are approaching the front.

In our unsuccessful search for food we meet a party sitting in front of a café and eating tortillas. They are obviously foreigners, and kindly invite us to share in their meal. They are very reluctant to disclose their nationality, but as soon as I sit down with them I recognize one of them from news-

paper photographs as a Russian Press correspondent. Even
had his photograph not been in the newspapers his secretive-
ness would not have been much use; everybody would have
recognized him as a Russian from his accent and the few
Russian words which he occasionally exchanged with his
companions. But he seems to be under the delusion that nobody outside Russia has any knowledge of Russia. For some
unknown reason he seems to believe that this secrecy is part
of the job of a revolutionary on all occasions. Our conversation again turns on the anarchist problem. We agree that the
anarchists are swiftly moving away from their anti-authoritarian dogma towards revolutionary dictatorship. 'But then',
he says, 'they must leave their organization and join the
communists.' He obviously does not conceive the possibility
of the anarchists, either leaders or rank and file, evolving
towards a new attitude without entering the fold of the Communist International.

We start again through the night and rapidly approach
the front. There are fewer villages now, and in consequence
fewer guards. If an enemy patrol penetrated through the
advance guards, at the front, it could cut the communications
and intercept the traffic without any opposition. At Fraga,
already in Aragon, we stop for the night.

12 August.

In Fraga we stayed in the same hotel as Major Farrar,
second-in-command of the Catalan forces. He is a regular
army officer, had been dismissed by the Robles Government
in 1933, and then made commander of the *mozos de escuadra* by
the Generalitat. These *mozos de escuadra* are a police corps
specially selected for the purpose of protecting the Catalan
Government. At their head Farrar fought in the Catalan
insurrection against Madrid in October 1934, and was condemned to death after the defeat, a sentence afterwards commuted to lifelong imprisonment. He was released in February
1936, again made commander of the *mozos*, fought in Barcelona in July 1936, and then took over his present charge.
He belongs to the Catalan Esquerra and stands next to

Durutti in popularity. In conversation he explains the stalemate at the front: 'But we are in the middle of a social revolution.' This frank admission of the fact of social revolution is
not a usual attitude outside the anarchist ranks. After very
few words he drops the conversation, and turns to clamour
loudly for food, which could not possibly have been served so
soon. With him are a number of adjutants. They are sitting
at one table and conversing gaily, but obviously this whole
important section of the Catalan staff had no communication
with the front during the whole evening and night, either by
telephone or by messenger. Had anything happened, Farrar
would probably have remained uninformed for many hours.
But he gives the impression of a man of great physical
courage.

In Fraga we are directly behind the front line; all food is
rigidly rationed and so are lodgings. The direct intervention
of Farrar is needed (and very courteously granted) to procure
food and a bed for each of us against the infuriated resistance
of the innkeeper, who is obviously suffering from much unpaid billeting. He became more amenable when he realized
that we were willing to pay for our accommodation.

The village bar is full of peasants. The appearance of three
foreigners naturally is a big event. They immediately start
telling us proudly about their feats. Most of them are anarchists. One man with a significant gesture of the fingers
across the throat tells us that they have killed thirty-eight
'fascists' in their village; they evidently enjoyed it enormously. (The village has only about a thousand inhabitants.)
They had not killed any women or children, only the priest,
his most active adherents, the lawyer and his son, the squire,
and a number of richer peasants! At first I thought the figure
of thirty-eight was a boast, but next morning it was verified
from the conversation of other peasants, who, some of them,
were not at all pleased with the massacre. From them I got
details of what had happened. Not the villagers themselves
had organized the execution, but the Durutti column when
it first came through the village. They had arrested all those
suspected of reactionary activities, took them to the jail by

A DIARY IN REVOLUTION

motor-lorry, and shot them. They told the lawyer's son to go home, but he had chosen to die with his father. As a result of this massacre the rich people and the Catholics in the next village rebelled; the alcalde mediated, a militia column entered the village, and again shot twenty-four of its adversaries.

What had been done with the property of those executed? The houses, of course, had been appropriated by the committee, the stores of food and wine had been used for feeding the militia. I omitted to ask about money. But the big problem was the land and the rents which the landlords had previously received from their tenants. To my intense surprise, no decision had been taken about this matter, though it was more than two weeks since the executions. The only certain thing was that the land of the deceased continued to be worked as it had been previously: those parts which had been let were still worked by their former tenants, and those formerly managed as an estate and cultivated by agricultural labourers were still functioning in the same way; only instead of the squire it was now the committee which employed the necessary labour. As to the rest, there was only vague talk: the committee would eventually receive 50 per cent. of the old rents, the other half being remitted, and half of the expropriated lands would be distributed among the poorer peasants, while the other half would be managed by the committee as collective property of the village. Evidently in this village the agrarian revolution had not been the result of passionate struggle by the peasants themselves, but an almost automatic consequence of the executions, which were themselves but an incident in the civil war. Now most of the peasants were bewildered by the new situation. One of them, among many others, simply said: 'What do I know? They will give an order about it.' I ask: 'Who will give an order?' 'Oh, how do I know? There will be some government,' he replied. This threw a new light upon the vague replies I had got the day before in other villages when inquiring about land expropriation and rent abolition.

We drove northward, to the aviation camp of the Sara-

98

gossa front, which I visited twice, at noon and at night. There were no anti-aircraft guns, and when I asked about it some of the pilots agreed that it was surprising that the rebels, for no conceivable reason, had omitted to raid it. At night I saw enemy signals given from places not far off, behind the Government lines. In my presence the men discussed how awkward it was that these signals appeared every night, but nobody thought of sending a patrol to investigate. A small troop of rough militia arrived that night, in the gayest spirits, and was quickly and efficiently quartered on the aviation field, in tents, in a very orderly manner. For most of these boys it was their first romantic experience of camping, and they thought very little of the more serious aspects of campaigning which might follow.

Why had the aviators, in contrast with all the other troops, remained faithful to the Government? Pilots, after some years of service in the ordinary regiments, were individually selected for aviation training, and thus the links of regimental *camaraderie* which have been the basis of so many compact risings of the Spanish military against various governments were severed. Moreover, as one of the pilots emphasized, they are selected for technical ability, and that often seems to go hand in hand with a tendency to the Left. After all, modern industrialism does not go well with the Spanish type of Catholic education, and machine-mindedness in Spain, especially among the routine-ridden Spanish officers, must still be something almost revolutionary. This pilot was a liberal patriot without any socialist leanings, and I asked him what he thought of the social upheaval going on around him. 'That will be as it must be', was his answer, 'now we are fighting in common against the fascists.' But one of his comrades, asked the same question on another occasion, bluntly replied: 'To disaster.' His fellows, although they seemed to agree, hushed him up. Evidently these liberal officers are caught between their allegiance to the republic and their dislike of the anarchists, and are almost in despair about it.

And now we came to the real front. We nearly missed it, it

was so tiny. Driving north on the road to Huesca we were stopped at the last moment by a guard on the road; otherwise we should have driven into rebel country without noticing it. As it was, we climbed a hill to the village of Alcalá de Obispo, and then to our surprise found that we were in the front line itself. Up to a mile behind the lines there was nothing to suggest its existence; then we had seen one shell bursting in the distance, but did not hear any sound. Neither was there a 'front' with trenches or with an outstretched line of troops. The 'front' consisted of a concentration of perhaps three hundred men in the village of Alcalá, with a few advance-guards half a mile ahead. There was no contact with the next militia column, which was stationed in a neighbouring village some miles away. Seeing this, I remembered with some amusement the foreign newspaper reports of sanguinary battles, which we imagined were being fought between tens of thousands of men.

It took me some time to realize that I was actually in an artillery bombardment. But when there was a shout of 'Take cover' I noticed that something was happening. From Monte Aragon, one of the chief forts of Huesca, the rebels were shelling what they believed to be the Catalan lines. Fortunately their idea of the position of these lines was entirely erroneous and they were aiming with great exactitude at a spot half a mile from Alcalá, where, as the officers explained, there was nothing but sparrows. A large group of Government soldiers was standing erect on the exposed side of the village, watching the fun. Every single time we heard the singing of a shell we receded a few steps, but were quickly reassured by its bursting in the wrong place.

The day before, the Catalan troops had had to evacuate the village of Sietamo under a well-aimed artillery attack, but scouting does not seem to be the strong point of the insurgents, and they had not yet found out the new positions. On the Catalan side artillery observation is hardly better. About six light field-guns were placed in front of the village, and occasionally fired without any adequate direction; two howitzers were placed behind the village but the observer, most incompetently, stood on the church tower almost in front of the guns, and I do not think that the shelling did much damage to the enemy. In this column there was not one single casualty that day, despite an all-day bombardment.

Unfortunately my visit was interrupted because our French companion took a photograph, merely on the strength of permission from an officer, without applying to the political committee of the column. As a result we got only a five minutes' interview with this committee, and were then sent away immediately. All I could learn was that this column is composed mainly of POUM militia, but partly also of regulars who, both officers and men, have remained faithful to the Government. They were distinguishable from the militia by their uniforms, and by their enormous and obvious indifference to the whole affair. In contrast to the militia they had no political commissars, but were represented in the committee of the column by their commander. As I had been told in Barcelona, the officers in the Catalan columns act only as technical advisers to the committee, which has the final power of decision.

We tried to find another column where we would be more favourably received, but the car broke down, and we got stuck in the village of Seriñena.

13 August.

We have been stuck in Seriñena for twenty-four hours, first to my disgust and then to my increasing satisfaction. It was a fight to get *vales* (chits) for our meals and lodging, each meal having to be claimed separately from the local committee. Regular provision is only made for inhabitants and the militia, but we were invited, after some discussion, to take our meals in the common refectory of the militia, and so we got to know many of them.

After a pleasant chat with the head of the local committee, an anarchist baker, we left the refectory late at night for our *fonda*. As we were leaving the guard at the entry of the refectory told the president of the committee something, and he invited us to follow him to the Plaza, where a few days ago the church had been burned. There have been executions in Seriñena, as everywhere else. Among the total of about a dozen victims was the notary-public, whose house and offices, immediately behind the Plaza, contained all the documents relating to rural property and many other financial matters. Now these documents, together with all others found in his offices, were being burned in a huge bonfire in the middle of the Plaza, so that no valid written evidence of former property rights will survive. The flames rose higher than the roof of the church, and young anarchists went on carrying more material from the notary's house, which they threw upon the flames with triumphant gestures. A number of other people silently glared into the flames. It was by no means just a matter-of-fact destruction of some unwanted documents, but an act carrying for its participants a deep significance as a symbol of the destruction of the old economic order.

What was the reality corresponding to this symbolic act? Evidently the burning of documents concerning rural property would have concrete meaning only if the private ownership of this property itself was being abolished at the same time. Nothing of the kind had been done. The local committee under anarchist guidance had abolished rents and expropriated four large estates with the agricultural machines belonging to them. Peasant property, with the exception of the property of those executed, had not been touched, but many of the notary's documents must refer to it. Something else, however, had been achieved! In contrast with Fraga the peasants had not just stood bewildered before the achievements of the revolution, they had utilized them. In conversation the expropriated machines were mentioned again and again.

I had become suspicious of much of the talk about the agrarian revolution, and was doubtful whether the peasants were really using these machines, as some of them said they were, or were only vaguely hoping to do. But I was convinced of the reality of the improvement by my own eyes. In the morning I picked up the first two anarchist youngsters I met in the streets and asked them to show me the threshing machines. They led me to a group of granaries outside the village. In front of them stood four of the expropriated machines, threshing enormous heaps of wheat. At every one of them a group of about ten peasants was at work. One could see, even from their clothes, and they confirmed it in conversation, that they were all peasants (not landless agricultural labourers); together they were threshing the wheat of one of them; they were going to move the machine the next day to another granary, to thresh the wheat of the next member of the group. Work was swift, faces were shining, and as far as I could judge the handling of the machines was competent. A village mechanic was available for repairs. All evidence pointed to the lack of compulsion in this arrangement for the collective use of expropriated machines; there were other granaries where people worked with their out-of-date tools and were frank to admit that they did not want to work the machines; most of these belonged to the older generation. The committee intended to use the machines for threshing the harvest of the expropriated estates, as soon as the peasant collectives had finished their threshing, and to use this harvest as a wheat store for the militia, to be stored in the church.

To sum up: as in Fraga so in Seriñena there was a numerous politically indifferent element, and an active anarchist nucleus, mostly of the younger generation. In Fraga this nucleus, under the influence of the Durutti militia column, had helped to kill an enormous number of people in the village, but they had achieved nothing else. In Seriñena a similar nucleus was left to its own devices, for ahead lay not an anarchist but a POUM column, and relations between the anarchist village and the POUM militia were far from good. But in spite of this, with much less killing, the anarchist nucleus had achieved a considerable improvement for the peasants, and yet was wise enough not to try to force the conversion of the reluctant part of the village, but to wait till the example of the others should take effect.

One important result of this was that the relations between the peasants and part of the village intelligentsia were decidedly good. In the streets of Seriñena, for the first time in many days, I met a man dressed in bourgeois clothes; he was surrounded by a large group of peasants and talking with them in a friendly and animated way. He looked like a higher Catalan official, but turned out to be the village veterinary surgeon. Obviously he was not afraid of maintaining his bourgeois appearance. Later on I met his daughter, a nurse in the hospital which had been improvised in the village for the militia. She was evidently serving there more competently than the volunteer nurses from Barcelona, and was very proud of her service for the revolution. There seem to be many intellectuals who, though Catalan nationalists in their political opinions, wholeheartedly collaborate with the anarchists; others, like the aviators I met, are more reluctant.

The hospital seemed quite decent for an improvised establishment. It was under the charge of the local doctor, but when I visited it only four out of sixteen beds were occupied by patients suffering from disease. The adjacent hospital for wounded had only one case. Anyway, this war is not producing many casualties; only the massacres in the hinterland are.

14 August.

By the afternoon of the 13th our car was at last completely repaired, and we reached Leciñana, the centre of the larger of the two POUM columns on the Saragossa front. We were received with great friendliness by its leader, Grossi, and offered every chance to see what was going on. The position here is the same as in Alcalá; a few hundred militia crowded in the village, a few advance-guards ahead, but no contact with the next village, occupied by Catalan troops. Grossi took us at once to the advance-guards. They were posted about half a mile ahead of the village, on a group of hills. In the heat of the afternoon the staff officers did not want to walk. I myself thought it would have been a safer way than to drive up to the advance-guards, but we went in two cars through the open, dusty plain and so quiet was the front that there was not the slightest danger in doing so under the eyes of the enemy, although they hold the next village and could easily see the cars. Some of the advance-guards are hidden behind rocks, some have dug themselves shallow trenches, without barbed wire. Every picket has a machine-gun, camouflaged with branches. They had not been relieved for five days (!) but their life was not altogether uncomfortable; they had their mattresses with them in their trenches! Leciñana had been taken by a night surprise attack last week and very little fighting had occurred since.

Back in Leciñana, Grossi put the relief of the advance-guards into effect. The whole column, consisting of four *centurias* (hundreds), was summoned to the Plaza, and Grossi addressed them with a short speech from a balcony, saying that things must be put in better order, and that the advance-guards should now be relieved. One hour later he himself led the relief and stayed out with them for a whole night. The gathering in the Plaza was more picturesque than military. There was not the slightest sign of military discipline, not even a serious attempt to form orderly ranks. There were very few uniforms, but a multi-coloured mosaic of the most varied costumes which would have been a delightful sight for an artist, less delightful for an officer. What is worse, there is evidently not the slightest attempt to get this incoherent mass organized, disciplined, and trained. There would be ample opportunity for this, as the zone behind the front provides an ideal training ground, and the militia-men, in the long intervals between operations, have nothing to do and are desperately bored. Grossi is of a type somewhat crude, but *au fond* very appealing, and certainly he possesses the personal allegiance of his column. He is evidently courageous and, being an Asturias miner, is an old hand at revolution, and knows how to handle the masses psychologically. But he is deficient as an organizer, and has no conception of the job of warfare. There is obvious rivalry between him and his military adviser. This is a very common state of affairs, which of course results in a considerable amount of disorder. Soldiers, lacking any reasonable occupation, squatted about in the tavern.

There we found, among the militia-men, the one militia-woman of the column. She was not from Barcelona, but a native of Galicia, had been married before to an *asalto*, and then divorced him, and she had now followed her lover to the front. She was very good-looking but no special attention was given her by the militia-men, for all of them knew that she was bound to her lover by a link which is regarded among the revolutionaries as equivalent to marriage. Every single militia-man, however, was visibly proud of her for the courage she seems to have displayed in staying in an advanced position under fire for many hours with only two companions. 'Was it an unpleasant experience?' I asked 'No, solo me da el enthusiasmo' ('To me it is only inspiring'), replied the girl with shining eyes: and from her whole bearing I believed her. There was nothing awkward about her position among the men. One of them who was playing an accordion started *La Cucaracha*, and she immediately began the movements of the dance, the others joining in the song. When this interlude was over, she was again just a comrade among them. The whole position of this isolated girl among a crowd of men was the more remarkable because of the complete isolation of the militia-men from the village girls, who in accordance with the strict Spanish tradition refused even to speak to strangers. Some of the nurses were less strict in their moral principles.

I passed the night in the deserted house of an enemy of the Government, with some foreign volunteers. The house was in a horrible condition. All the cupboards were broken, and their contents—linen, books, clothes, religious objects, children's toys, etc.—had been roughly thrown on the floors all over the house, giving it the appearance of having been sacked, though no actual sacking seems to have occurred. It was uncomfortable for the militia-men themselves, but they did nothing to tidy things up. This lack of order in their quarters must be an element of demoralization.

A DIARY IN REVOLUTION

The morning was rather an exciting one. First a militia-man was fired on and a nervous but unavailing search was made throughout one section of the village. The militia-man believed, rightly or wrongly, that he had been fired at by a hidden 'fascist'. Then three enemy planes flew overhead, and the whole column, together with half the village, crowded most inopportunely to the Plaza to watch them. Grossi, having returned from his night watch, ordered out the machine-guns, but they had nothing to do, as for the first time for many days the rebels did not bomb the village, but only flew over it. As far as I could make out, their previous daily bombardment had been utterly ineffectual. In the village there was only the mark of one hit, and one would not have recognized this as the mark of a bomb without being told, it was so shallow. Obviously the enemy bombing material was of very poor quality. But a peasant had been killed a few days before by a bomb, while quietly harvesting in no-man's-land, and the women still wept for him: 'Oh, señor, what a terrible war! They have killed one of our men in the field.' This was the one casualty which had occurred in Leciñana for many days.

There was a group of deserters from the rebel camp in Leciñana. They were all regular soldiers who had been caught up in the revolt during the period of their military service, and all of them had been socialists or anarchists before becoming soldiers. There seemed to be many such deserters all over the front, all of them previously belonging to some revolutionary organization. Ordinary prisoners were everywhere shot immediately. The deserters had to run this risk in order to live up to their political convictions; when they arrived in the Government lines they had to establish their identity as members of an anti-fascist organization. The deserters talked at length about the rebel leaders' distrust of the regular soldiers, and their reluctance to bring them into the front lines. No pressure, however, seemed to be exerted in the rebel camp to force soldiers to participate in religious services.

On the way back we passed through the village of Alcubierre, which had been taken by the Catalans, then retaken by the insurgents, and taken again by the Government forces. The rebels, after having recaptured it, had, I was told, shot all the most active anarchists and socialists—eight to ten altogether. It was about the same number as had been executed by the Government forces during their occupation.

We arrived in Barcelona late at night, with the exception of Mr. J. Cornford, who had enlisted in Leciñana.

15 August.

My English socialist companion had visited the front at the same time with another party and had been, among other places, at Tardienta, where the PSUC column has its head-quarters. He there got a story of horror, which it is difficult to believe, but which, nevertheless, seems to be true. When the PSUC militia took Tardienta and performed the usual exter-mination of 'fascists', they got a considerable amount of money, jewels, and other valuable objects into their hands. They sent a well-guarded car with these objects to Barcelona, in order to deliver them to the authorities. The guards, it seems, had only their personal documents with them, but no certificate as to the treasure they were carrying. Anyway, at the next crossing of the road they were stopped by a POUM guard, their car was searched, the explanation of the guards about the content not accepted, the guards delivered to the next POUM column, and shot summarily, as robbers. The coffins, to make the measure of horror full, were sent back to the PSUC column at Tardienta, where they got a solemn burial. Trotskyists against Stalinists!

My companion, who is not precisely a friend of the anar-chists, had visited the Durutti column and came back utterly disgusted. Undeniably they had advanced farther than any other column in the direction of Saragossa, without sparing their lives, trusting in the unlimited reserve of recruits which the anarchist proletariat of Barcelona can put at their dis-posal. Finally the central command under Colonel Villalba summoned them to stop this waste of human life, and after much wrangling Durutti was induced not to advance farther.

So far the tale of my socialist friend. I cannot help being somewhat sceptical as to his conclusions. From what I saw myself at the front the other columns had no exaggerated desire to sacrifice themselves, and there were practically no losses whatever. In this way the Catalans would never get into Saragossa. Possibly Durutti may have sinned in the opposite direction, but then it was necessary to find a middle line between useless sacrifice and ineffectual timidity. From the point of view of the whole front, the fanatical push of the Durutti column was certainly an asset, if rightly used.

But what my companion had to tell about the *policy* of the Durutti column was really unpleasant. It seems that amidst the general enthusiasm of the peasants for the republican cause they have found the strange secret of how to make themselves hated. They had to leave the village of Pina for no other reason but the silent resistance of the peasants, which they were unable to overcome. It seems that they had been so ruthless, both in requisitions for the militia and in executions of both real and pretended 'fascists', that they very nearly provoked a rebellion of the village. Neither had the executions yet stopped. They are, it is said, a more or less regular feature of the activities of Durutti's men. My friend had been invited to watch one, as if it were a pleasant sight.

Having seen the front, I am surprised at the lack of realism in the calculations of all political groups. They are all based on the approaching fall of Saragossa, whereas, in reality, nothing seems to be farther off than that. In consequence, the POUM seems to me unfair to charge the Government, in private talks, with a treasonable intention to handicap the operations. If they were afraid of what the anarchists might do after the famous fall of Saragossa, it would only be natural. But it is obvious that nothing of the sort will happen, not because of treason in high quarters, but from sheer inefficiency and incompetence all along the line. It would need the heroic efforts of a group of very able officers and politicians to overcome all the patent defects of the militia, and none such are available. But if POUM distrust and anarchist enthusiasm are both unjustified, so are the anxieties of the PSUC and the republicans, which are equally based on the assumption of big successes in the near future. Reverses will come, not success, if nothing is done to mend existing defects. To overcome them, all parties must co-operate. But before that the socialists and anarchists must overcome their mutual hatred, and the anarchists must drop their anti-authoritarian dogma. Will this happen? Perhaps it will, under the pressure of patent failures; the anarchists have changed much already.

16 August.

A Sunday at the beach, which is crowded with happy people not thinking at all about what is going on around them. Only these places, formerly so fashionable, have lost all their previous *cachet* and the *milieu* is everywhere thoroughly proletarian.

17 August.

Really, people are sometimes surprising. Representative members of the PSUC express the opinion that there is no revolution at all in Spain, and these men (with whom I had a fairly long discussion) are not, as one would suppose, old Catalan socialists, but foreign communists. Spain, they explain, is faced with a unique situation: the Government is fighting against its own army. And that is all. I hinted at the fact that the workers were armed, that the administration had fallen into the hands of revolutionary committees, that people were being executed without trial in thousands, that both factories and estates were being expropriated and managed by their former hands. What was revolution if it was not that? I was told that I was mistaken; all that had no political significance; these were only emergency measures without political bearing. I alluded to the attitude of communist headquarters at Madrid, which described the present movement as a 'bourgeois revolution'; an indication, after all, that it was a revolution. But my PSUC communists did not hesitate to disavow their headquarters. I wonder how it is that communists, who, all over the world, for fifteen years have discovered revolutionary situations where there were none, and done tremendous mischief by it, now do not recognize revolution when, for the first time in Europe since the Russian revolution of 1917, it is really there. Rightly considered, the PSUC will have to give up as many queer ideas as the anarchists before there can be an understanding. Still, the success or failure to come to such an understanding will decide the fate of the revolution. The Spanish revolution, unlike the French and the Russian revolutions, cannot decide its problems by armed fight between the revolutionary factions, not at present at least. Franco is too strong for that, and any open rupture in the revolutionary camp would bring him immediate victory. This is what at present keeps antagonistic groups such as the communists and the anarchists together. But they are doing their level best to make a muddle of things.

A communist deputy and member of the party central committee in Madrid, Jesus Hernandez, had given an interview to a French non-socialist newspaper (*Paris Midi*, if I am not mistaken) covering the anarchists with opprobrium, saying openly that after the defeat of Franco the communists would make short work of anarchists (though it is much more likely to be the other way round, given the present balance of forces), accusing them of preferring to stay behind the lines and kill innocent people, etc., etc. One of the anarchists in my hotel, a Frenchman, a professional terrorist and not precisely a pleasant type, when getting the news, started telling a journalist, death in his voice: 'Cet homme qui a écrit ces saloperies ne doit pas vivre, ne va pas vivre; où qu'il aille on va savoir le trouver. Nous allons nous débarrasser de ces salauds,' and much more in the same tone, with an expression in his eyes not leaving any doubt as to his determination.

18, 19, and 20 August.

Feeling exhausted, I took a short holiday at Sitges, formerly the most fashionable Catalan beach, but now a rather derelict place. Sitges, in ordinary times, lives mainly by rich tourists; its vineyards have been ruined by pests. The atmosphere was accordingly tense, more unpleasant, in fact, than I had found it in any other village, though on the surface things looked very quiet indeed. A few weeks before the civil war the Generalitat had installed a new public library in a pleasant public building, and now the reading-room was crowded with eager young people, obviously children of the less wealthy section of the population, both boys and girls, who protested violently against the disturbance my few words of inquiry to the attendant brought to the room. But these were remnants of a happier past.

Scores of villas had been expropriated and lay derelict now. What had become of the proprietors? Their womenfolk, I learnt on my return to Barcelona, had been forced to do low work, such as laundry, for the militia, a proceeding unique, I believe, in all Spain. It is very much to the credit of the Spaniards that the womenfolk of men who have been imprisoned or shot are hardly ever molested. Here it was different. I personally had no difficulties during my stay, but when I left my luggage was searched at the station by a militia-woman, in a clearly hostile manner; she seemed to want to do my things as much damage as she could. Again, all over the rest of Catalonia, the habit of searching luggage at the stations had been abandoned after the first days.

One afternoon there was a burning of religious objects on the beach, which again was a sad performance. The committee had ordered everybody to deliver objects of worship, such as images, statues, prayer-books, talismans, to be burned in public. There the women went, carrying their petty objects of devotion, most of them with obvious reluctance, many a one taking a last adieu, with a sad look at what had been, perhaps, an object less of religious value than of family pride, a part of the familiar daily life. There was not the slightest sign that anybody was enjoying the proceeding, with the exception of the children. They looked on it all as first-rate fun, cutting the noses of the statues before throwing them into the bonfire, and committing all sorts of mischief. It was disgusting, and obviously very unpolitic. Such an act would be likely to awake rather than to destroy the allegiance of people to their Catholic faith. I do not think that all the revolutionary committees are making decrees about household objects of worship.

One night the sound of heavy firing was clearly to be heard from the direction of Majorca. But the fishermen who stood about at the beach refused to admit that they had heard anything, obviously fearing they might get themselves into trouble by some careless word. Thus, not only the rich people were terrorized, but the poor as well. And the worst of it was that there seemed to be very little improvement for the poor. These fishermen had still to serve their masters; nothing had been changed in the fishing trade. The committee seemed to exhaust itself in all sorts of petty tyrannies. It is an exceptional case, I believe, owing to the fact that in a place like Sitges the revolution cannot find a backing among the majority of the population and must inevitably fall into the hands of a group of people of doubtful integrity or ability.

21 August.

Stayed the morning in Barcelona. An English militia-woman of the POUM tells me about Tosas, another Catalonian seaside resort, where she had passed a good deal of time before and during the civil war. The burning of religious objects had been performed there, as in Sitges, on the instigation of anarchists from a neighbouring village. She had got the impression that the peasant women disliked giving up their religious objects, but that afterwards they went away convinced that now Catholicism had come to an end; she heard them saying things like: 'San Jose ha muerto' ('Saint Joseph is dead'). The next day the village itself abolished the greeting *A Dios* (With God)—'because now there is no more God in heaven'. There were two priests in the village, one fanatic and strict, the other lax in every respect and especially with the village girls. This latter one the village had hidden from arrest since the beginning of the revolution, while the 'good' priest, hated by the whole village as an ally of the reactionaries, had tried to flee and broken his neck by falling from a rock. In Tosas, as in other places, the peasants did not know what to do with the expropriated land of the executed enemies of the Government.

In the afternoon I went to Valencia in an ordinary train, which ran first and second class and a dining-car, and arrived punctually.

Two days in Valencia.

This is the history of the revolt in Valencia: the local commander, General Molta, took a procrastinating attitude, waiting for the result of the revolt in other places before committing himself. The Madrid Government sent to Valencia a *junta delegada* of three members, headed by Martinez Barrios, the president of the Cortes, and one of the chiefs of the Right wing of the Popular Front, to take over the administration. Martinez Barrios first tried to negotiate with General Molta, without making the local UGT and CNT a party to these negotiations. Molta and Martinez Barrios had a link in common; they were both freemasons; and Martinez Barrios counted upon this as an asset in the negotiations. But so did Molta. Valencia was already surrounded by districts which had put down the revolt; Molta had little chance of winning a fight by force, and negotiations were at that time certainly more to his interest than to the interest of his adversaries. After some days Martinez Barrios went back to Madrid, with the conditions of an agreement suggested by Molta. The general, instead of being summoned to obey at once, had been treated as a man entitled to negotiate in his own right. What were the conditions he put to the Government? They have not been made public, but according to one version they aimed at nothing less than the resignation of the present Government and the formation of a government of mediation between Franco and the republic, of which Molta (a general actually compromised in the military plot) and, according to this version, Martinez Barrios, should be members. Whether these were the suggestions brought back to Madrid by Martinez Barrios or not, anyway nothing came of them. Ne-

gotiations between Madrid and General Molta dragged on
and in the meantime the revolutionary movement developed
rapidly in the town. CNT, UGT, and the local republicans
formed a Comité Ejecutivo Popular, created a workers' militia, and refused to take account first of the negotiations, and
then of any orders from Madrid whatsoever. Martinez Barrios, when he returned to Valencia, found the situation completely changed. The Comité Ejecutivo Popular openly refused to acknowledge his authority. While he attempted
again to come to a peaceful settlement, the Comité put an
ultimatum to the troops. After that some of the troops were
allowed to leave their barracks and go home, and the remainder of the garrison, after some more wrangling, was defeated in force by the militia. They stormed the barracks, the
men offering little or no resistance, and most of the officers
were massacred. Martinez Barrios had to leave Valencia, and
went to Albacete, a small town between Madrid and Valencia, which had been reconquered by the republicans a few
days before. In Barcelona they talk now of Valencia as 'the
town where the workers rule'. It seems that there exists in
Valencia a sort of local proletarian dictatorship as the result
of the breach between the local committee and the Central
Government in Madrid.

22 August.

The idea I got in Barcelona about the situation in Valencia
was entirely wrong. Constitutionally, Valencia might almost
be, to-day, an independent Soviet republic. But socially it is
much less 'Soviet' than Barcelona, and remains a thoroughly
'petty bourgeois' town. There are far fewer armed militia
than in Barcelona, less expropriation and workers' control of
shops, fewer red flags and more banners in the Spanish and
Valencian colours. More cars belong to some regular State
administration than to workers' committees and unions.
There are more fashionable, well-dressed people in the
streets; and there is a significant number of beggars too,
whereas in Barcelona there are almost none, on account of
the newly created assistance committees. Valencia has not

passed through a social upheaval like that of Barcelona, but only through a short struggle with the garrison which, for local political reasons, has led to a sort of regional independence. And that is all.

What are the local forces of the revolutionary movement? They seem to be weaker, in every respect, than in Barcelona. In Valencia only can one understand, by comparison, the importance of Catalan nationalism, of the Esquerra. In Catalonia, through the Esquerra, the lower middle-class people, the shopkeepers, the artisans, the intellectuals, participate in the movement; for them the fight against Franco is the fight of the Catalans for their national claims. In Valencia there is a regional movement too, claiming administrative autonomy for the three provinces of the Valencia region and equality of rights for the Valencian dialect with the Castilian language. But it is a weak movement. In consequence, the whole stratum of merchants of all sorts (which is supremely important in a town like Valencia, where there is much commerce but almost no industry proper), remains indifferent or hostile. In the rich *huerta de Valencia*, with its orange-groves and rice-fields, its well-organized irrigation system, inherited from the times of the Arabs, and its wealthy peasantry, the position seems to be even worse for the revolutionaries. The *huerta* is not inhabited by a miserable population of *de facto* serfs, amenable to the orders of a few caziques; yet in the February elections many villages voted heavily for the Right, and from the shrugging of the shoulders with which questions concerning the *huerta* are answered one gets the impression that it is still a disaffected district.

Among the elements which support the revolutionary movement the anarchists are undoubtedly the strongest. They dominate the port, but are equally preponderant among the other transport workers, the building workers, and the manual workers in general. The UGT, as in Barcelona, controls the white-collar workers; it definitely controls the railways too. Socialists and communists have separate organizations here; that is in contrast to their arrangement in Catalonia, but in accordance with the rest of Spain. But both

116

the communists and their Trotskyist adversaries, the POUM, are weak. The UGT members, as far as they are interested in politics, follow the socialist lead. The republicans have a certain amount of allegiance among the lower middle class, but are split into Spanish centralists and two groups of Valencian regionalists.

By far the most difficult local problem is the attitude of the communists. All the other sections of the movement collaborate fairly well. The anarchists here are more moderate than in Barcelona, and, though they shun every idea of merging with the socialists, are ready to co-operate with them. The socialists are very much to the Left; and even the republicans seem to be on friendly terms with the anarchists. I visited most of the party headquarters and listened to a large public meeting of all parties of the Popular Front; it was obvious that everybody was at odds with the C.P.

When I went to communist headquarters and entered the secretary's room my eye was caught by an enormous picture of Stalin and a smaller one of Kiroff. Besides these there were two posters with the slogans 'Respect the property of the small peasant' and 'Respect the property of the small industrialist'. The secretary at once began to complain about the attitude of all parties represented in the executive committee, except his own. 'The *junta delegada*', he says, 'was the authority appointed by the president of the republic, and the anarchists won't understand that they have to obey; they want regional independence.' The socialists would not be so bad if there were only the followers of Prieto (the leader of the Right wing), but unfortunately there is now Caballero and his group, and these people, after having been reformists for many years, have now turned into wild revolutionaries without limits to their aims. 'But after all you will have firm support among the republicans?' I ask. 'Don't think that,' comes the answer, 'they are continually wavering towards the anarchists; but now we have interfered, and instead of their former representative on the executive committee there is now a man who is firm against them.' 'So you have no support whatever?' 'I tell you there were moments when we

stood quite alone here in defending the orders from Madrid.'
While we are talking a man rushes in announcing that the
anarchists have just forcibly requisitioned a motor-lorry belonging to the communists. The secretary dashes to the telephone, rings up anarchist headquarters, and starts an excited
argument, which puts an end to our conversation. Again, as
in Barcelona, I wonder what has driven the communists so
far to the Right as to be more moderate than the republicans,
and to be at one only with Martinez Barrios, who is just
within the fold of the Popular Front.

If the communists are weak in the towns, they seem to have
some peasant support, as a result of their policy of protecting
the individual property of the peasants against anarchist attempts at collectivization. From the communist regional
committee I got an introduction to the co-operative of rice-
growers. Nothing has been changed in this organization
(which is compulsory by law for all the rice-growing peasants
of Spain) except that the former committee has been removed and a socialist put at the head of the new one. They
hope to get better conditions for the sale of rice, now that all
the rice-mills, thirty-three in number, have been expropriated by the trade unions; negotiations with them will be
easier than with the former mill-owners. But if the mill-
owners have been pushed aside, it is different with the wealthy peasants. They tell me themselves that the smaller farmers are reluctant to attack the richer ones, because the
latter are in charge of the administration of the irrigation co-
operatives and to upset this complex organization of irrigation in the least degree would mean disaster.

The impression I got in this conversation with the committee of the rice co-operative was fully confirmed next day by a
trip I made under anarchist guidance into the *huerta*. There,
of all the existing political organizations, the anarchists are
undoubtedly the most active. But they are visibly failing to
secure the support of a large section of the village population;
there is much more political indifference (which probably
covers political antipathy) than in either the Catalan or the
Aragonese villages. There have been many executions, but in

this wealthy district the very idea of shooting *all* the wealthy peasants would be inconceivable. There is no doubt that the peasants here are not in favour of the anarchist drive towards collectivization. In the village of Silla a few members of the local committee in my presence started an argument with my companions from anarchist regional headquarters about it; they not only regarded it as a matter of course that the peasant's land should remain intact, but considered that even the expropriated land of the executed fascists ought not to be collectivized, but distributed among the peasants. This, to be true, was their view of the matter. In fact, wherever I inquired about it, I found that nothing had been decided as to the land of the enemies of the Government, and the peasants were as uncertain—and almost as indifferent—about the matter as in Aragon. In the meantime, the UGT—which has a certain amount of allegiance among the agricultural labourers—cares for the working of the expropriated land, without paying the workers higher wages for their work than before. But at least, one young communist said, contracts with the workers are kept to-day, and that makes all the difference in the world.

The gap between ideals and reality is sometimes grotesque, in Spain, and people are completely satisfied with their own good intentions without bothering to put them into effect. In the village committees the anarchists seemed usually to take the lead, and among other achievements they prided themselves upon the abolition of private commerce in the harvests. All crops were now sold direct to the trade unions, I learnt, and I was inclined to admire this extraordinary feat of organization. My curiosity, in one case, went so far as to ask for an interview with the man who was charged with the commercial handling of the main crop, which in this instance was wheat. And then came disappointment. There was no such man; thus there was visible dismay on the faces of the committee members when I asked to see the man who did not exist. After a few minutes they decided to admit that the crops were handled exactly as before, by private merchants. In fact, the problem of the handling of export crops such as the Valencia oranges is far beyond the capacity of small villages. But if the ideals of *comunismo libertario* could not be put into practice, at least it was nice to talk about them.

In the borough of Gandía, for the first time in Spain, I was threatened with being shot. I was discussing agrarian problems with the local secretary of the UGT when a messenger came in and asked me to see some gentlemen waiting for me outside. There were four of them wearing a sort of uniform unknown to me, with stripes on the sleeves. They at once proceeded to cross-examine me in police manner about my intentions, and when I explained that in this particular spot I wanted to study the agrarian revolution, they retorted that there was no agrarian revolution in Spain, that my research was dangerous, that Spain was not interested in being known by foreigners now, and that if I wanted to bring news home it was quite enough for me to tell England that the whole people was united and obeyed orders from the Government; I ought to leave Gandía immediately unless I wanted to be 'eliminated'. I told them I was there with a car of the Press department of the Comité Regional Ejecutivo, and would they care to come with me to supervise my departure? They did not want to do this—very wisely. And I did not leave the town. I soon found out that these people belonged to the Seguridad, in other words the ordinary police of the old régime, and of course they had acted upon their own responsibility. But it was difficult to convince my anarchist companions of this, their firm belief being that only communists could behave in such a nasty manner. Even my observation that communist militia-men would not wear stripes did not convince them; communists, they said, imitated enthusiastically every sort of military decoration. I do not believe that this is so, but it was characteristic of the mutual hatred between communist and anarchist.

In the afternoon I attended, in Valencia, a mass meeting of the Popular Front (to which neither the anarchists nor POUM belong). There were about 50,000 enthusiastic people there. When La Passionaria appeared on the platform enthusiasm reached its climax. She is the one communist leader who is known and loved by the masses, but in compensation there is no other personality in the Government camp loved and admired so much. And she deserves her fame. It is not that she is politically minded. On the contrary, what is touching about her is precisely her aloofness from the atmosphere of political intrigue: the simple, self-sacrificing faith which emanates from every word she speaks. And more touching even is her lack of conceit, and even her self-effacement. Dressed in simple black, cleanly and carefully but without the slightest attempt to make herself look pleasant, she speaks simply, directly, without rhetoric, without caring for theatrical effects, without bringing political *sous-entendus* into her speech, as did all the other speakers of the day. At the end of her speech came a pathetic moment. Her voice, tired from endless addresses to enormous meetings since the beginning of the civil war, failed her. And she sat down with a sad waving gesture of her hands, wanting to express: 'It's no use, I can't help it, I can't say any more; I am sorry.' There was not the slightest touch of ostentation in it, only regret at being unable to tell the meeting those things she had wanted to tell it. This gesture, in its profound simplicity, sincerity, and its convincing lack of any personal interest in success or failure as an orator, was more touching than her whole speech. This woman, looking fifty with her forty years, reflecting, in every word and every gesture, a profound motherliness (she has five children herself, and one of her daughters accompanied her to the meeting), has something of a medieval ascetic, of a religious personality about her. The masses worship her, not for her intellect, but as a sort of saint who is to lead them in the days of trial and temptation.

24 August. In the train from Valencia to Madrid.

In the corridor of the train I met two young anarchists I knew, from Barcelona. They were on an errand of their organization. I travelled third class while they were going first class, on free tickets procured by the anarchist organization. We had a meal together in the dining-car, and then they invited me to their first-class compartment. I could not help remarking on the change in their station in life, but they only laughed about my criticism of their becoming 'bourgeois'. After all, the change has not gone very far yet. Although they sit in a first-class compartment, they still wear their working men's suits, and one of them had brought his rifle with him and put it into the luggage rack. Opposite sat a couple very different from my companions, obviously not travelling on a free ticket; they were probably well-to-do Valencia shop-keepers, and the woman was scared to death by his handling of the rifle, though there was actually not the slightest danger. When he noticed her nervousness, he boyishly began to demonstrate the handling of the rifle; as he loaded and unloaded it, the couple on the opposite bench became more and more desperate. But there was no real enmity between the two camps, the old and the new upper class, which here met in such a queer and amusing way.

We approached Madrid from the South, through the arid plain of La Mancha. Work on the wheat harvest, which would normally be finished in July, is going on in the fields at full speed. We talked about the miserable condition of the peasants of La Mancha, when suddenly, in the north-east, not far away, a blue mountain ridge appeared. 'Is this the Guadarrama?' I asked, and was told that it was. In a flash I realized that Madrid is in constant and imminent danger, that it might be taken any day, if the insurgents break through the Guadarrama front.

25 August.   *Madrid*

Our arrival at the Atocha station, late yesterday afternoon, was not in any way remarkable. There are no taxis, exactly as in Barcelona, but, exactly as everywhere else in revolutionary Spain, there are porters. And the tube and other public transport organizations are working normally. But food is evidently a more serious problem here than anywhere else, and the hotel-keepers, for this or other reasons, are much more nervous than elsewhere. My first attempts to find a suitable boarding-house were unavailing; obviously it was difficult for the managers to find food for newcomers; nor did they want to take in a newcomer whom they did not know. But at last I found a satisfactory room in a Swiss boarding-house. The manager, although he makes innumerable complaints about all sorts of difficulties, gets as good and rich food for his guests as anybody could desire.

The streets here make quite a different impression from those in Barcelona, but between Madrid and Valencia the difference is only of degree. In Barcelona begging has practically disappeared; in Valencia it was visible; in Madrid it is obtrusive; in this respect nothing seems to have changed. The begging of many children in the cafés is especially repellent. It does not seem to be the consequence of destitution by the civil war, but simply an ingrained habit. Occasionally one might tell a boy that there are now places for poor people to get food without paying, but he would pay no attention, and continue begging. If begging has remained the same, so has, to a certain extent, its antithesis, luxury. Certainly there are fewer well-dressed people than in ordinary times, but there are still lots of them, especially women, who display their good clothes in the streets and cafés without any hesitation or fear, in complete contrast to thoroughly proletarian Barcelona. Because of the bright colours of the better-dressed female element, Madrid has a much less lugubrious aspect than even the Ramblas in Barcelona. Cafés are full, in Madrid as in Barcelona, but here they are filled by a different type of people, journalists, State employees, all sorts of intelligentsia; the working-class element is still in the minority.

One of the most striking features is the stronger militarization of the armed forces. Workers with rifles, but in their ordinary civilian clothes, are quite exceptional here. The streets and cafés are full of militia, all of them dressed in their *monos*, the new dark-blue uniforms; most of them do not wear any party initials on their caps. We are under the sway of the liberal Madrid Government, which favours the army system as against the militia system favoured by Barcelona and the anarchists. What initials there are on the uniforms generally do not indicate allegiance to one or other political party, but membership of a particular trade-union branch. The anarchists, of course, wear their CNT-FAI on their hats, but from this 'spelling plebiscite' it is evident that they are a minority in Madrid, though not an entirely negligible one. On the whole, the military element looms much larger in the streets of Madrid than in those of Barcelona and Valencia. We are nearest here to the most difficult and dangerous of all the fronts, the Guadarrama.

Churches are closed but not burned here. In the afternoon I went to Nuestra Señora de la Florida, to see the Goya frescoes; the church was locked, but the keeper unlocked it on my behalf and showed me them. True, this church has been out of service for a long time; but another church, in the immediate vicinity of this one, has been requisitioned for the use of a district militia committee.

Most of the requisitioned cars here are being used by Government institutions, not political parties or trade unions. Here the governmental element is much more in evidence than in Barcelona, where the socialist, anarchist, and trade-unionist element was more obvious. A striking example of the difference is that here in Madrid an ordinary police permit to sojourn is sufficient; it would be useless in Barcelona. There does not even exist, in Madrid, a central political committee.

Very little expropriation seems to have taken place. Most shops carry on without even control, let alone expropriation. The hotels had militia billeted in their rooms, and some of the most elegant ones, such as the Palace Hotel, the largest hotel in Europe, are still, and are intended to remain, in the hands of working-class organizations. But gradually the billeting of militia in hotels seems to be subsiding. The manager of my boarding-house told me that last night he had served a group of militia-men for the last time; from to-day on they will be fed in some militia refectory, and in future no militia are to take their meals in his house or at his expense.

The banks wear inscriptions similar to those in Barcelona, declaring them to be under Government control. Only a few with their headquarters in rebel territory are declared requisitioned. In fact, in all Spain, banking is one of the trades least hit by expropriations.

A DIARY IN REVOLUTION

To sum up, Madrid gives, much more than Barcelona, the impression of a town in war-time, but much less the impression of a town in social revolution. Were it not for the new militia uniforms, the self-confident behaviour of the ordinary militia-men in the cafés, the lack of private cars, and the occasional posters speaking of control and requisitioning, one would hardly notice any social upheaval.

Perhaps the peaceful impression is deceptive; at least there is terrorism behind the scenes. The conversation of the day is the terrific massacre which happened yesterday. It was provoked by the news of the massacre perpetrated by the insurgents after the capture of Badajoz. They are said to have driven some 1,500 prisoners to the bull-ring and there to have shot them wholesale with machine-guns. The official censorship (of whose unintelligent and obstructive attitude all foreigners bitterly complain) did not allow the news to appear in the papers, in order, as they explain, to avoid an outbreak of popular vengeance. (This was hardly an intelligent policy, as the news soon spread through the whole town, causing both consternation and fury.) The thing was made worse by a revolt of the political prisoners in the *carcel modelo*, the modern prison. There were some 3,000 of them, because the Madrid Government makes a practice of not simply shooting or releasing suspects, but keeps them in prison and attempts detailed investigation. This practice is much milder than that prevalent in Barcelona, where investigations are extremely curt, and, when unfavourable to the suspect, lead immediately to execution. But in this case the value of the more lenient procedure was doubtful. The prisoners revolted, set fire to their mattresses, and attacked the guards with the burning bundles. They did not overcome the guards. But the news of the prison revolt went through the town together with the news of the Badajoz massacre; crowds gathered in front of the model prison, clamouring for the immediate wholesale execution of all political prisoners. Some leaders of the Socialist Party arrived, and tried to calm the excited masses, but with little success. A popular court was formed on the spot, and had a number of leading Right-wing politicians (among them Señor Melquiadez Alvarez) and many others executed. Further mischief was prevented by the declaration of the Government that an official revolutionary tribunal would be created immediately. This last measure throws some light on the practice followed by the judiciary up to now. Many of the judges are with the rebels, or have been dismissed, as unreliable, by Government decree. The same applies to the political police. For the reduced forces of the police and the judiciary to cope with the enormously increased demands of the civil war was quite out of the question. In consequence thousands of prisoners remain in the prisons, waiting for investigation and trial of their cases, or, rather, waiting for the time when the insurgents take Madrid. So the complete breakdown, or rather the complete absence, of any revolutionary judiciary naturally makes for the shooting practices of irresponsible groups, which seem to be fairly numerous in Madrid.

26 August.

One remarkable aspect of the streets becomes more conspicuous with time: the changed position of women. Young working-class girls in hundreds and perhaps thousands are walking up and down the streets, and are especially to be seen in the elegant cafés of the Alcalá and the Gran Via. They collect for the 'International Red Help', an organization 'in favour of the victims of class war', here mostly working for the wounded and for the relatives of the victims of the civil war; it was sponsored originally all over the world by the Comintern, but is run in Spain by socialists and communists jointly. There is no collecting either in Barcelona or in Valencia, whereas the couples of girls (they never go alone; walking through the streets completely unchaperoned would still be unthinkable for any decent Spanish girl), well dressed in working-class fashion, who ask everybody for a contribution, are almost a nuisance in Madrid, or at least would be were they not so pleasant to look at. They enjoy it enormously; for most of them it is obviously their first appearance in public, and now they are even allowed to talk to

foreigners and sit down at their ease in the cafés for a chat
with the militia-men.

The revolutionary tribunal, which is starting its activities
to-day, will limit its trials to such cases as fall under established civil or military law; this means that practically only
cases of mutiny will come before it. But there is an enormous
number of other cases: priests, nobles, and innumerable
people of the Right wing who have taken no part in military
activity but have either been caught conspiring against the
Government or are suspected of having done so. All those
cases are outside the competence of the revolutionary tribunal. In the first days of the rebellion the anarchists suggested that every single member of a Right-wing party should
be shot; they have the lists, and there are 42,000 members of
Gil Robles's Catholic Accion Popular alone. They have been
convinced of the inexpediency of this cruel folly, but no one
thinks of limiting executions to such cases as might be con-
victed of high treason by way of regular trial. What happens
is that investigation committees of the three proletarian
groups in Madrid, communists, socialists, and anarchists, co-
operate. Each of them has a list of suspects, and when they
arrest one they ask the two other parties their opinion. If
they all agree, then the man is either executed or released. If
they disagree, closer investigation ensues. It is certainly a
rough and ready manner of dealing with an insoluble problem.

For insoluble indeed it seems to be. This, at least, seems to
be borne out by another story. On 19 July the newly formed
militia put down the military revolt in Madrid by storming
the Montana Barracks. Then, after five hours of heavy artillery action, followed by a successful attack, the militia went
back to the centre of the town, and was acclaimed by a large
crowd. When they reached the Puerta del Sol, a largely reactionary district, they were suddenly fired at from the windows on all four sides of the square. The *asaltos* immediately
ordered the crowd, men and women, to crouch down on the
pavement, and actually prevented a panic. These Spaniards
find street fighting perfectly natural. Anyway, there they had

to lie on the pavement, under fire from all sides, for many minutes, until the *asaltos* had entered the houses and cleared the snipers from the windows. So it went on in many parts of the town for many days.

Such an outbreak would be bad enough, but worse are the numerous well-confirmed stories of espionage, treason, desertion of officers, storing of arms by the sympathizers of the rebels, signalling to the enemy, and so on *ad infinitum*. Some at least of these tales must be true, and they recall scenes of the French and Russian revolutions, when also the revolutionaries felt surrounded by enemies from every quarter and had to strike in the dark, because there was no time to make sure.

All the air of Madrid is full of stories of terrorism, much more than in Barcelona; and this, as far as I can judge, not so much because the actual amount of terrorism is greater here than in Catalonia (though the proximity of the Guadarrama introduces a specially irritating element) as because in Catalonia the job of exterminating the enemies of the Government is done swiftly and ruthlessly, whereas in Madrid the insufficiency of the administration and the lack of political unity make for friction, uncontrollable individual extravagance, and cruelty, and, last, not least, for an enormous amount of gossip.

One well-confirmed story throws light upon an unexpected aspect of fascism. In an hotel a Spaniard suspected of co-operating with the rebels was arrested. He himself got off by the unreputable but humanly intelligible device of denouncing some of his friends, and was soon released. Not for long, however: his friends in their turn denounced him, with convincing proofs, and he was again arrested, and executed without much delay. But then came a surprising finale. The group of militia who had performed the investigation and the execution were afraid of distressing his widow, actually so afraid as not to dare to tell her. So they went on for more than two weeks pretending her husband was alive, that he had been confined to his native village, and other similar stories. The actual result must have been augmented torture for the family, but the motive was undoubtedly compassion for the widow, who, they said, had nothing to do with the guilt of her husband. The husband appears to have really been guilty of co-operation with the insurgents; at any rate the executioners were genuinely convinced of that. The conception that men ought to be killed for their political opinions, but not women for the opinions they share with their husbands, brothers, and fathers, seems fairly prevalent.

Settling of personal accounts by denouncing a personal enemy as an adversary of the Government was one aspect of terrorism continually mentioned by foreigners in Barcelona, but hardly ever proved in a concrete case. But to-day, in Madrid, I learned of a case which really falls under the heading of the settling of personal accounts in the worst meaning of the expression. A patient denounces his doctor, to whom he owes some money. Fortunately the arrested doctor hits upon the right interpretation, asking his interrogator, 'Has not X denounced me?' and when the answer is in the affirmative explains the whole story. The denouncer was arrested in his turn, could not deny the existence of the debt in question, and then in the course of a short investigation revealed how completely unfounded were his accusations; he was shot at once. But the case is probably not unique, and the issue not always in favour of the innocent.

From these stories of horror I fled to more peaceful and attractive things: in the afternoon I went to the Prado. A group of young anarchist militia-men were walking through its large rooms. They had certainly not seen a museum in their lives, and were staring, puzzled, at the paintings; they had set out to conquer the privileges of bourgeois education, but found it more difficult than they expected. Still, they not only displayed that good behaviour in unwonted circumstances which is one of the conspicuous merits of the Spanish national character but felt that they were amidst things to be admired and reverenced; probably knew dimly that it was something very beautiful indeed; they spoke with subdued voices and went with light steps; only it was all so puzzling.

129

A DIARY IN REVOLUTION

27 August.

Headquarters of the UGT, significantly enough, have not been removed, in the Barcelona manner, to some outstanding hotel, but are still in a narrow and sombre building in the Calle de Fuencarral. A small staff continues to work there, but there is much less life than in either the CNT headquarters or the militia committee in Barcelona. Still the socialists dominate in Madrid, and especially the personal group around Largo Caballero, the UGT president. But in spite of this commanding position, the group around Caballero complains bitterly, and about many things. First and foremost about the republican Government. No socialists participate in it, and they maintain that that means complete inefficiency; and the unfavourable news from Extremadura suggests they are right. According to them, the Government does not do anything, organize anything, foresee anything, but is in everybody's way if something has to be done. There are special complaints about the interior régime of the ministries. Most of the State services, they say, are quite unreliable; a number of State employees are actual traitors; but the liberal ministers are not to be got beyond a sham expurgation of the administrative staff. To-day *Informaciones*, the personal organ of Indalecio Prieto, a moderate socialist, complains that in the Home Office the reading of a socialist newspaper is still frowned upon. The Ministry of War had actually not gone so far as to organize a central staff; there is no unified control of military operations, no organized delegation of authority; even the transfer of a group of militia from one commander to the next needs a personal decision of the minister himself; and even then probably no one at the front will take any notice of it. The prevailing feeling is that this cannot go on, and that the liberals are either unwilling or unable to do better.

While the socialists feel prompted to take government and responsibility into their own hands, yet important considerations make them shrink from such a step. Some, of whom Araquistain is the most important, do advocate an immediate

130

change of régime, but to their view two strong arguments are opposed. The first is voiced by the Right wing of the Socialist Party, led by Prieto and Galarza, and carries weight because supported by the leaders of the Asturias miners: they ask for the maintenance of friendly relations with international democracy, which, according to them, are dependent on keeping the present character of the régime. As long as the present Government continues, the democratic countries might regard the Madrid Government as a legal government unlawfully attacked by the military. But when the socialists take power, transform the old administration thoroughly and set out in the direction of a proletarian republic, then the argument that they are acting in defence of the legal government might be regarded abroad as a fraud. In consequence Prieto and his friends suggest the inclusion of a few socialists and communists in the Government, but with Giral continuing as Prime Minister and most of his colleagues keeping their portfolios. This attitude is backed up by the communists, who, here as everywhere else in Spain, represent the extreme Right wing of the labour movement, and consequently co-operate with the Right-wing socialists rather than with Caballero.

Caballero violently opposes Prieto's views. His group stands for complete socialist domination as soon as possible, and abstention from participation in the Government as long as that is not possible. It is the classical attitude of orthodox Marxism, to which Caballero has been converted late in life, after thirty years of extreme reformism. To Prieto's suggestion Caballero objects, on the ground that such a coalition, still under republican leadership, would not be able to perform the purge in the administration, the military reorganization, and the ruthless control of all economic activities, which, together, are the primary conditions for the winning of the war; and an inefficient participation of the socialists would only compromise them and give the anarchists a grand opportunity. Besides these substantially important divergences, there is a remarkable amount of personal antagonism. Each group has its own daily newspaper; *Claridad* is Caballero's organ, and *Informaciones* Prieto's. The official organ of the Socialist Party, *El Socialista*, has lost most of its importance through this fight of the two contending factions.

Comment on the communists is especially bitter in the Caballero circle. The Soviet Union does not help us at all, they say, no more than France or England; all they do is to intrigue in our politics, strengthening every tendency towards the Right wing of the movement, and they do that for reasons of Russian foreign policy, which is anxious not to jeopardize the Franco-Soviet pact by too revolutionary an attitude in Spain. These critics do not deny, however, that the communists have organized good military troops, especially the famous Fifth Regiment, which has more than once saved the Government positions in the Guadarrama. The socialists, for their part, are proud of some of the UGT formations, notably the railwaymen's battalion and the armed train of the Northern Station.

One big problem for Caballero is naturally the anarchists. They are his old enemies, as he is theirs, and the feelings of his group towards them are nearer fury than resentment. One does not get the impression that the big change in the anarchist camp is appreciated here; to them it appears much more as a defeat than as a transformation. They think that the anarchists, after the sacrifice of their non-authoritarian pet convictions, and under the pressure of circumstances, will 'just have to follow our lead'. But at present the problem of whether the anarchists will follow the lead of the socialists is academic, because a furious struggle is on. There is a serious shortage of rifles at the front, and the anarchists are said to be holding up 5,000 rifles in Madrid, so as to keep their own organization armed for all emergencies. Whether this is entirely true I do not know, but certainly the anarchists are well-armed and do not conceal the fact, justifying their attitude by their distrust of the revolutionary reliability of all other sections of the working-class movement, should a big crisis arise.

In the meantime everybody is looking anxiously to the front, where things are obviously not as they should be. Caballero and Del Vayo drive out to the Guadarrama nearly every day, and seem to be immensely popular among the militia in consequence.

28 August.

One of the most bitter complaints is about the supplies of ammunition. Not only have all hopes of help from the French and Russian governments so far been disappointed, not only is the construction of a new armaments industry in Valencia and Catalonia proceeding at tortoise pace, but experts have resentful feelings about the failure to make use of such chances of buying munitions abroad as do actually and undoubtedly exist.

Other specialists have far from rosy views about the economic situation. There is, of course, a lack of raw materials; there is sometimes a lack of qualified personnel; but more disastrous even than these is the intense reluctance to accept that expert advice which is urgently needed. As a result, not more than 30 per cent. of industry seem to be under State control in the areas actually governed by Madrid. (Catalonia, Valencia, and the north coast excluded), while in Catalonia the State and the trade unions control 70 per cent. of industry. But sometimes one strikes upon brilliant achievements in unexpected quarters. In the Palace Hotel there is a home for derelict children. They have a rapidly improvised boarding-school under the direction of one foreign educationalist, who has had specialist experience with difficult children, and a staff of Spanish women teachers. Boys between eight and eighteen are lodged, fed, and taught in this school; girls have a similar establishment in another building. Some of them have previously been boarded in ecclesiastical schools and have become homeless by their sudden dissolution, others have lost their parents through the vicissitudes of the civil war. Most of them are not natives of Madrid. Many of them have fled, alone, from the insurgents who entered their villages, and have either come themselves or been brought by the militia to this home. The Government is already alive to the danger of a *bezprizorny* problem arising in Spain—that problem of vagabond children which was at one time so very serious in Russia. I saw some of these children arriving in tears, during lunch, and I saw them immediately taken care of by the staff and by their older comrades. The teachers told me that tears were the regular thing to begin with, but that after one or two days the children felt quite at home, and I could see that that was true. The really extraordinary thing about it seemed not so much the quick adaptation of the children to an improvised organization, which, in many respects, could not help being defective—after all they were children of poor workers and peasants, and everything in their new home must have been like paradise for them: the abundant and good food, the rooms in the Palace Hotel, the friendly and attentive attitude of the staff, and, for those coming from the countryside, the brilliant streets of Madrid themselves. But much more remarkable was the lack of maladjustment among these boys, who, all of them, had passed through some kind of ghastly experience, and some through a real inferno, such as seeing the execution of their parents and then escaping on a lonely flight towards the unknown. And yet, in one or two days, with the help of a little kindness and some soothing words from teachers and comrades, they seem to settle down without much difficulty. The head of the staff, who had previously had a lot of experience with working-class children in large industrial centres, was much surprised herself, and had, she said, even under quite normal conditions never met such a crowd of well-adapted children.

The fact, I think, helps to throw light upon one important aspect of the Spanish revolution. I had been surprised, again and again, at the absence of pathological excitement among the masses, even in such acts as the burning of churches and images, and in the course of discussions about terrorism. I had soon learned to discount all the stories circulated by a certain type of newspaper, of the torturing and burning of nuns, and things of this kind. But there was not much evidence even of the excitement one would quite naturally expect from masses in revolution. Another striking aspect of the Spanish revolution is the absence of any deep upheaval in sex life. Something in this line does of course occur, but much less than during the Great War in any country, and nothing at all to compare with the complete dissolution of standards of sexual morality in the Russian Revolution. As for the participation of some women in the fighting, it has always been traditional in Spain. To a surprisingly small degree is the Spanish civil war a psychological crisis. And these children, who, amid the worst horrors, keep their mental balance, are part of the explanation. The Spaniards, amid their terrible ordeal, keep quiet and poised as individuals, because they are basically healthy.

29 and 30 August.

Two days of lengthy preparation for going to the front. The atmosphere is lugubrious. The insurgents are attacking heavily in the Guadarrama, and in Extremadura they have captured Oropesa and are proceeding against Talavera. The junction of the forces of Franco in the South and Mola in the North is a fact, and nobody knows what will happen next. I decided not to go to the Guadarrama, which has been seen and described by practically every correspondent. Things have come to a stalemate there, as on the Saragossa front. I shall make for Talavera, where a decision is obviously approaching.

Political nervousness is rapidly growing. Many people are convinced that things can no longer be allowed to drift in this way, and that Caballero must take command. Among the 'political' people, opinions about his capacities are divided; some of them jeer at the description of him as a 'Spanish Lenin', which part of the Press had readily bestowed upon him. But others have unlimited confidence in him, and he is certainly very popular among the masses. Again, whatever his personal capacities, the acceptance of power by the socialists would at least mean a serious attempt to reorganize the ranks, whereas the republicans are obviously drifting towards disaster without making any effort to avert it.

The night before last we had the first air bombardment. I had come back home dead-tired, but could not sleep on account of the chief misery of the war—for me at least—the wireless. Izquierda Republicana has one of its militia centres round the corner from my boarding-house, and they turn on the wireless through half the night at top strength; there is no remedy against it. So I lay in bed, cursing the *Hymno de Riego*, the Spanish liberal anthem, which the wireless was just playing for the hundredth or two-hundredth time in a few days— and it is not good music. Suddenly there was a big crash very near—I was later told there had been some before, farther off, which I had not heard through the noise of the wireless— and the wireless stopped immediately. I knew at once it was a bomb, though I have not been through a war. But the one sensation I had was of relief that the maddening doodle of the wireless had disappeared. I went to a balcony looking on the Gran Via on the other side of my boarding-house, and there I found a curious scene. The street-lights in the smaller streets of our district had all been extinguished; and only the lights of the Gran Via, the Alcalá, and Cibeles were shining, unmistakably indicating the site of the telephone centre, the Central Post Office, the Bank of Spain, and, last not least, the War Ministry, which had been the object of the bombing. Was it treason, or was it simply negligence? Anyway, it was shameful. Nobody was very nervous in our boarding-house; the cool fatalism of the Spaniards showed up splendidly. But down in the street they were doing all sorts of stupid things. The militia-men fired their rifles in the air, a machine-gun, posted on the roof of the War Ministry or somewhere in the neighbourhood, started rattling and then stopped again. The bombing seemed to be over, and was so in fact, but the irregular rifle and machine-gun fire in the streets presented a real danger. I took cover behind the stone wall of the balcony. But nothing further happened, and the firing slowly quieted down.

Next morning onlookers were gathering along the gutter in the garden of the War Ministry, staring at the big hole the bomb had torn, certainly not more than ten feet distant from the building itself. The bomb was dropped more accurately than any Spanish pilot could have done it; it could only have been the work of a man who had had experience of war, either an Italian or a German. By sheer good luck the bomb had killed nobody, and only wounded two or three militia-men. But the explosion was violent enough to shatter the windows and whirl around the chairs and tables of the elegant cafés in the Alcalá, some 150 to 200 feet distant, causing a panic, not only among the customers but among the militia as well. The latter, unaware of the aeroplane, had believed that a bomb had been thrown in one of the cafés by a 'fascist', and were with difficulty restrained from firing indiscriminately at the crowd.

In the afternoon I went to visit some friends in their home in the West End, near the Manzanares River. They had a long and unpleasant tale to tell. At the corner of the street was a meadow where, every morning, a car arrived, some fifteen to twenty prisoners were rushed out, and summarily shot. The corpses were left lying there for a few hours, as a deterrent, and the inhabitants of the surrounding streets were at least not discouraged from having a look at them.

The conversation turns upon the critical situation at the front, for which most of the guests are starting as officers in a few days' time. One of the young men was just complaining bitterly about the bad quality of the *matériel*—the machine-guns are always getting stuck, the ammunition is years old—when our host excitedly called us to the balcony. There lay the Guadarrama, near by in the sunny afternoon, but thick in clouds; not clouds of rain but clouds of fire. They covered the larger part of the nearer slope of the sierra; obviously they were not rising simply from fires kindled by shells; something systematic had been done to bring about a large forest fire. Had Mangada's column, which, we knew, was operating in that direction, set the whole sierra on fire in order to stop an unexpected advance of the insurgents? We all felt the fate of Madrid terrifically near.

The Western and Southern Front

31 August.

After the customary delays, which seem endless, we do start at last, in the afternoon, towards Talavera. We are five again, driver, armed guard, two photographers from *Vue*, and myself. This countryside is already familiar to me; there are

guards and controls in all the villages; committees composed
of all the parties. But there are obvious important differences
too. The villages are much poorer than in Catalonia and
Levante, they grow wheat instead of fruit and vegetables.
Sometimes there are large granaries. We are in the zone of
large, semi-feudal estates. The dominant element on the committees are not the anarchists, but the socialists, with sometimes a communist sprinkling. But the most conspicuous
thing, totally different from the East, is the importance of the
Juventud Socialista, the joint organization of socialist and
communist youth. In most of these villages, only a short time
ago, there was no Left-wing organization whatever; certainly
there was none before the proclamation of the republic in
1931. Even now only the younger generation has been at all
deeply touched by the socialist missionaries from the town.
The lack of a political tradition of old standing makes for the
dominance of the Juventud organization and for the pre-
valence of very young men on the committees, in marked
contrast with Catalonia and Valencia, where men between
thirty and forty prevail. The administrative system is different
too. The *ayuntamientos* continue to administrate, side by side
with the political committees. Their spheres of authority
seem not to be defined in the least and their practical work
seems to overlap continually. Such a thing is striking as one
instance of the difference between socialist and anarchist
practice. Anarchist villages would hardly allow the old
municipality to continue its old authority.

In the small town of Talavera, the last point occupied by
the Government troops, the atmosphere is even gloomier
than in Madrid. Two days ago the next town, Oropesa, was
lost to the Moors, as the result of an air bombardment and an
ensuing panic among the militia. One officer explains that
about 150 bombs were dropped on the town, with two wounded (!) as the result; the bombs seem to have been no good at
all as to their material effect, but the moral impression upon
the inexperienced militia must have been tremendous. Now
Talavera is menaced, the front being a few miles beyond the
town—and it is the last town of any importance between

Franco and Madrid! Reinforcements are thrown into the town. One body of them, a fairly large anarchist column, enters in smart parade, but some of the men have not even rifles. The central staff is lodged in a small side-street, where it cannot easily be located by the enemy planes. Everybody expects and fears a bombardment to-night. The staff is very nervous indeed.

We are not allowed to proceed to the front line itself, but drive out a short distance from Talavera towards it. Shells are bursting at a distance. We are stopped at an encampment, where some hundred men are stationed as a reserve. During our stay they are mostly occupied with their food; a herd of sheep has been found masterless and now contributes to the commissariat of the militia. The militia here look very different from their comrades in Catalonia. There are more blue militia uniforms and less picturesque fancy dresses and civilian clothes. There are a few old army officers and non-commissioned officers. But there seems to be much less cohesion than at the Saragossa front. Whereas the individual columns there were politically united and all of them recruited from Barcelona, there is no unity, either political or local, in this column. There are Madrid trade unionists of different trades and political shades; a lot of politically nondescript Valencians; and a few men of the old army. There is not the slightest trace of a unified command in this motley crowd. When, suddenly, an enemy aeroplane appears on the horizon and approaches rapidly, the men, instead of scattering, crowd together and, at the approach of the plane start shooting madly with their rifles, to no purpose, but to the great danger of all of them. Fortunately the plane has no intention of bombing—if it had done so, the consequences were bound to be disastrous under the circumstances; a Government plane appears behind it and chases it away at top speed.

Returning to Talavera I found at the railway station the armoured train of the Madrid Northern Station and a personal friend of mine among its crew. He is in high spirits, and so is the whole group of them. They have just returned from bombarding Oropesa—they think they have done it with great success—and feel obviously happy to have come back safely from a dangerous enterprise. My friend, a university graduate, is particularly enthusiastic about one example of 'Roman discipline'. A few men had gone to scout from the train, but had not returned at the appointed time, because, contrary to orders, they had made prisoners and lost time doing it. Finally the train started back without them and they returned alone, courageously, through the enemy lines, and joined the train in Talavera. But there, instead of being praised for their courage, they were sentenced to death for lack of discipline, and it was only after a long discussion that this sentence was commuted into expulsion from the militia.

What is meant by the words: 'In this firm one works collectively'? These words are written on the entries of almost all shops and hotels in Talavera. They do not indicate, I learn, expropriation, but simply an agreement between the UGT and the owner that a certain share of the profits goes to the workers. The method is distinctly different from the policy of the anarchists in Catalonia, who are prone to proceed to full expropriation. But then, in Talavera, as in all the towns of New Castille, it is the socialists and not the anarchists who are predominant.

What has happened to the large, wheat-growing estates? Most of them have remained in the hands of their owners for many weeks, though these owners belonged, all of them, to the Right wing. At first only the convents and such small estates as they owned were expropriated. Now, at last, a general expropriation of the large estates has been put into effect, and the labourers are working and managing them themselves, under the leadership of the UGT. Most of the wheat is sent to the front, without payment either in money or kind; there is no desire to conceal that there is a good deal of discontent about an expropriation which has so definitely worked out to the disadvantage of the agricultural labourers.

1 September.

We drove southward towards the southern wing of the Extremadura forces. Excitement runs high everywhere. In

every village we are asked for news of the battle which is going on a few miles to the north. The villages are strongly
guarded, and occasionally we are told that there is no time to
work the fields because the whole village is on guard.

There is undoubtedly one feature in common between these
villages of Western Spain and those of the East, so entirely
different in many respects: the land-question is completely
unsolved and the greatest uncertainty prevails about the
problem of how to solve it. Where the whole land belongs to
one or two aristocrats who are with the insurgents, the problem is relatively simple. There the land is automatically
expropriated and remains in the hands of the committees and
the trade unions, who have not changed anything in the
mode of cultivation. The same hands work the same land,
the divisions between the old estates are upheld, the old
wages are paid, and the only difference is that they are no
longer paid by the landowner's estate-agent, but by the committees and unions, and that the wheat is not sold to merchants, but somehow divided between the villagers and the
troops. But in some places there are peasant farms, and some
of the peasants are rich, and sympathize with the rebels.
There has been the average number of executions, and the
land of the deceased remains in the hands of the committees.
But there are no hands to cultivate those lands of expropriated peasants formerly worked by their owners. So sometimes
the land of those expropriated remains uncultivated; sometimes agricultural labourers are called in and get their ordinary wages for the tilling. What will finally be done with
these plots remains entirely undecided. Some peasants are in
favour of distribution among the poorer members of the villages, others favour collective management; but no definite
policy is followed, either by the committees or the political
organizations.

In spite of these hesitations and shortcomings, I had not
yet seen any villages so passionately sympathizing with the
Government cause as these absolutely destitute places on the
border of Extremadura and New Castile. Probably the explanation of this enthusiasm lies partly in the fact of general

poverty itself; these villagers have nothing to lose and much to win from a revolution, and, being all poor, are not handicapped by any social antagonisms between haves and have-nots within the village itself. But an even more important fact is that, in contrast to Catalonia, the enemy in Extremadura is advancing rapidly, and hatred and horror of him spread before his approach. All the villages are full of armed peasants, many of them not belonging to the villages where they are on guard, but to other villages already occupied by the Franco troops. Hosts of peasants have fled at their approach. There is a marked shortage of rifles, and we meet groups which have first passed through the enemy lines at night, at great risk, then for a couple of days searched the neighbouring villages for arms; and finally remained in the village where they obtained arms, helping to prepare its defence. Some of these groups number not less than forty men.

We passed through Puerto San Vincente, the southern angle of the Extremadura front, and the staff told us that eleven miles ahead of the Government advance-guards is the village of Alía, which is defended by its inhabitants alone, without any help from the Government militia. This miserable village has changed hands three times, but is still holding out. Its one connection with the Government camp is a telephone call every morning from Puerto San Vincente, put through to make sure that the fascists have not yet entered. We get leave to proceed, at our own risk, to Alía. There we found a village wretched indeed, but in wild political excitement. Whoever has been able to find a rifle wears one, and numbers of peasants from villages farther west and occupied by the fascists help in the defence. At the outbreak of the civil war the *guardia civil* revolted and took possession of the village, executing those they knew as sympathizers with the Government. Then the peasants retook the village and, in their turn, massacred the guardia. Then the village was again taken and retaken. At present, there is no contact with the enemy, who is believed to have his advance-guards in Guadalupe. Nobody has any but the vaguest ideas of the actual positions of the enemy (indeed, that is so all along the front), but his coming is expected every day. In the meantime the village lives as it can. Half the land belonged to a marchioness, and her flocks are herded now as before by her former shepherds, whom the committee, for lack of money, feeds in kind. And so great is their enthusiasm that in their destitution they have sent food to the troops behind them in Puerto San Vincente without asking for pay. Still, this village, the most excited I ever saw in Spain, has not a single anarchist among its inhabitants, and the one existing political organization is a very small group of Socialist Youth. In the February elections this village, which is so undoubtedly and wholeheartedly revolutionary, voted heavily for the Right, under the pressure of the 'caziques'. When we make ready for our return one of the peasants stops us: evidently he has something upon his heart. 'Will the señores journalists who come from France, be kind and allow him to put a question?' 'With pleasure!' 'Tell me then, please, one thing! Who is the president of the French republic and is he a good republican?' In the remotest corner of Extremadura illiterate peasants, who before perhaps just vaguely knew that there was a country called France, have suddenly become aware that it might be a matter of life and death for every single one of them whether the president of the French republic is a good republican. I trust these peasants did not know the difference between the president of the republic and the *président du conseil*, and with a perfectly clear conscience I reassured them as to the reliable republicanism of M. Blum.

No greater contrast could be imagined than that between the wild excitement of the peasants at Alía and the phlegmatic mien of the troops a few miles back, in Puerto San Vincente. When we came back a car from Talavera was just arriving at the building where the staff had their quarters. 'Has the mandolin arrived repaired?' was the first question of the commander to the driver. Thus, while a few miles north the fate of Spain was at stake, here their care was for the repairing of mandolins. It was a fairly strong force, with cavalry and artillery, of the motley composition usual in this region. The commander, a young lieutenant of the old army, had his men well in hand. There was no political committee in this unit. The commander had explained to them that it was incompatible with discipline. Guns were placed upon the hills dominating the village, rudimentary trenches with a bit of barbed wire were dug. But still, it was an atmosphere of ludicrous peacefulness. The column doctor had his own tale to tell. The village doctor had left for a holiday—he seemed to be able to take a holiday as if nothing were happening—and he, the military doctor, had not a single military casualty and instead was treating gratuitously all the village children.

At night I accompanied the commander on his visit to the advance-guards. The soldiers stood to attention when he talked to them; a very uncommon sight among the Government troops. But the commander was not satisfied with this outward show of discipline. He complained bitterly about the lack of *tenue* of the militia in air bombardments. The psychological disaster worked by them, he said, was out of all proportion to the material effect, the actual losses inflicted by the bombing, which were very small indeed. And then he went on to complain, as a trained soldier among amateurs, about the incompetence of those in command. Occasional scouting had proved that the enemy in Guadalupe beyond Alía was very weak, and, according to this officer, 1,500 men of all troops would be sufficient to cut the insurgents' communications with their rear and with Portugal by a sudden thrust upon Trujillo: but the 1,500 trained men were lacking. I thought of the battle a few miles north, whose result might well be influenced by some action in the sector of Puerto San Vincente. Well, I said, you have a troop of trained cavalry, and moreover, every single member of the peasant militia in Alía has ridden horses since he was a child, and knows the district as well as he knows his own pocket. Why don't you make a sudden forced reconnaissance towards Guadalupe; it is certain to draw off enemy forces from the Talavera sector? 'Oh,' he replies, 'Guadalupe has no strategical importance.' I cannot help thinking that more activity on this amazingly quiet sector while there is a decisive battle going on not far to northward could do no harm, even if it had no 'strategical importance'. What about the famous guerilla talent of the Spaniards? But my young lieutenant, active and prone to justified criticism of the command as he is, seems to regard actions on a small scale as below his dignity.

2 September.

A long drive brought us to Toledo about noon. That is certainly at present the nastiest spot in all that part of Spain which is under the rule of the Madrid Government. The town has always been very Catholic and anti-socialist, the administration and the militia feel themselves surrounded by passive resistance and treason, and the stubborn resistance of the Alcazar against their unavailing siege maddens them. It appears that besides some twenty hostages carried by force into the Alcazar, a considerable number of civilians, men and women, joined the insurgents by their own consent in their retreat to the fortress, when the militia stormed the town. The photographs of the hostages are exhibited in the chief militia refectory, in order to protect them from the wholesale massacre which is bound to ensue should the Alcazar fall into the hands of the militia. The administrative régime in the town is truly remarkable. Nobody recognizes the orders issued in Madrid, which are accepted everywhere else. My companions and I divided the work of getting information between us, as we were short of time. They went to the Plaza de Zocodover, where the besiegers of the Alcazar are concentrated, and came back with the information that things there were exactly as they were a fortnight ago, when they last visited it, and that not the slightest attempt is being made to hasten the siege, which, it seems, consists in a simple encircling of the Alcazar, without any serious actions being planned by the militia. While they were gathering these strange impressions, I tried to get information about the fate of the works of art, notably the Grecos.

A committee for the protection of these treasures has been formed by some artists and craftsmen who were formerly occupied with work in churches, and are interested in the preservation of the beauties of their native town. They complained bitterly: the governor, for no conceivable reason, has denied them access both to the main churches and to the Greco museum, the keys of which he holds. The munition factory in Toledo has been bombed once already and is likely to be bombed again; the enemy is approaching: incalculable damage may be done to the paintings unless they are brought to a safe spot, but the stubborn resistance of the governor makes this impossible. The son of one Madrid minister, now a doctor in one of the Toledo hospitals, telephoned on my behalf to the governor, telling him on the phone that I was ready to announce in England that the Toledo paintings are untouched, provided I could see them: then I went to the governor's *palacio*—with no greater success than the art committee or any one of my journalist colleagues. The governor refused to receive me and sent a message that the works of art were untouched, but that he had no desire to show them. Should I insist, I might ask for a permit in Madrid, at the Ministry of Education. There was no time to go back to Madrid, and in any case his ill will was so obvious that I did not think it would be any use. [The story had a sequel of which I learnt during my second journey to Spain. The committee for the protection of art treasures had finally urged the governor to demand cars from Madrid in order to remove the most valuable objects. The insurgents approached Toledo rapidly, and hasty action was necessary. The request was forwarded to Madrid, and the Ministry of Education informed the governor that motor-lorries were at his disposal for the purpose of removing the art treasures. But the governor refused to accept the cars, and told the committee, without regard for truth, that Madrid had not answered the request. The committee stayed on in a heroic attempt at least to keep their eyes upon the Greco paintings till the last moment, but could do nothing to save them. Finally, when the Moors had already entered the town, two of the committee members saved their lives by swimming over the Tajo. Nothing at all was done to protect the invaluable artistic objects of Toledo, because the governor decided that nothing should be done. But no damage ensued, finally, because the militia left the town in full flight and without resistance when the Moors entered, or even before. The *objets d'art* fell into the hands of the Franco troops untouched, as there had been no fight in the town. The whole conduct of this affair was in striking contrast with the model organization displayed in the removal out of danger of the art treasures of both the Prado in Madrid and the National Catalan Museum in Barcelona].

Toledo's farewell was peculiar too. A very few miles beyond the town, at the first cross-road, we were interminably detained by an unusually talkative guard. There, a few paces farther on, we saw the corpses of two people who had apparently been executed during this delay. We were not intended to watch the execution.

3 September.

A long drive through La Mancha, until late at night, brought us to Ciudad Réal. In this region there is no enemy, but at night the villages are heavily guarded and the control of the cars which pass through is as strict as it can possibly be.

Ciudad Réal is lively at night, like all towns in Southern Spain, and picturesque, though devoid of remarkable architecture. I wandered, late at night, criss-cross through the streets, repeatedly crossing remote and empty side-streets and then returning to the main avenue. I felt that my conduct was likely to arouse suspicion, but I did not care. To be arrested would only be interesting, as I had reported to the committee immediately on my arrival. I got what I expected. Suddenly I heard a low *Ssss* behind me, and turning round I saw two men, one in militia uniform, the other in civilian clothes, their rifles pointed at my breast, at a few steps' distance. 'Manos arriba' ('Hands up'), said the militia-man very quietly. I obeyed the order; one of the men stepped sideways and continued to point at me, while the other approached and calmly and quietly started to search my body. When they realized that I was not putting up any resistance, they became less gloomy. 'Foreign Press,' I said as quietly as they had spoken to me, and laughed. The search was soon over; I showed my documents, they questioned me about my abode, and when my answer satisfied them, they released me with complete courtesy.

Socialists rule the town, which, in contrast to the surrounding countryside, voted for the Popular Front in the February elections. Only one single factory, the electricity works, has been expropriated; all the other factories are continuing under their old owners. Terrorism seems to have been out of proportion to the smallness of the economic change. The market goes on unchanged and uncontrolled; so do the cafés and the shops; but 95 per cent. of the lawyers have 'disappeared', and all the priests. From our car I see a lady in elegant mourning-dress emerge from a corner; she looks at us with an indescribable expression of splendid defiance. I imagine she must be the widow or daughter of an executed man, and her display of fashionable mourning and of contempt of the authorities needs tremendous courage.

At the provincial bureau of the Reforma Agraria I learned that although the economic life of the town is going on almost unchanged, the villages of the province are in wild social revolution. Three estates in the province were transformed into peasant collectives before the civil war, under the law of agrarian reform; since the insurrection, 256 have been expropriated and taken over by their former labourers; or, rather, 256 expropriations have been legalized by the provincial bureau of the Reforma Agraria. Actually an overwhelming majority of all the larger estates have been expropriated and collectivized by their hands, and the business of the Reforma Agraria in the whole matter has only been to give a legal *placet*; but all the same this business has been enough to take up their whole time, to the exclusion of the much more important task of giving technical advice to the newly created agricultural collectives. The legal *placet*, moreover, is a mere formality. True, the peasants have to justify the expropriation, and I saw one or two of these explanatory documents; they said, in substance, that the owner of the particular estate in question was a well-known reactionary, that he had either co-operated in the revolt, or fled to the rebels, or simply refused to give pecuniary support to the village committee, which, in consequence, had decided to lay hands on his estate. Reforma Agraria in the provincial capital, or at any rate in Ciudad Réal, does not check the substance of the concrete charges brought against the owner, but proceeds simply on the basis of his well-known political opinions. Thus, in the whole province of Ciudad Réal, only one single expropriation has been quashed by Reforma Agraria on the ground that the owner was actually not a reactionary at all, but that a political pretence was being used in order to strip him of his property.

Two members of the regional bureau of Reforma Agraria drove me out, late in the morning, to a newly organized agricultural 'collective' near Ciudad Réal. They would have preferred to show me one of the three old ones, which, probably, function splendidly; but I insisted on seeing one of the collectives started after the outbreak of the civil war, of which there are more than 200. Still, the choice they made was certainly intended to give me the best possible impression. The farm I was shown was very near the town, in direct contact with the administration of Reforma Agraria, and, last, not least, under the leadership of a socialist labourer who had belonged to the party for many years, known prison and persecution, and acquired a fairly good understanding of the task incumbent upon him. Very few villages and estates in La Mancha have at their disposal people of this type, and I am convinced that their presence or absence in the work of collectivization must make all the difference in the world. In the courtyard of this farm bits of wrecked agricultural machinery lay around. They had been destroyed by the workers during the *bienio negro*, the clerical régime from 1933 to 1935, when the landowners tried to bring down wages by dismissing hands and introducing agricultural machines in their place. The violent and unavailing reaction of the workers had been exactly the same as that against industrialization in England in the early 'twenties of the nineteenth century: to destroy the machines. Now, on the estate there was a shiningly new threshing-machine standing beside the wreckage of the old material. It had been acquired immediately after the outbreak of the civil war from the Madrid branch of a Bilbao firm, and had been paid for in money, half the price cash down from the expropriated funds of the former owner of the estate, the other half in a draft payable after the sale of the harvest. The leader of the community explained that the hands, who had been so violently opposed to the introduction of machinery as long as it put them out of work, now enthusiastically welcomed it as an enormous relief in the heavy physical burden of their labours. So far, and in this particular place, it obviously worked very satisfactorily. But my companions from Reforma Agraria told me that the same wrecking tactics had been used all over the province; but they did not pretend that usually matters were mended with so much intelligence as in this particular case. Their frankness was the more impressive as they themselves were religiously convinced of the value of collectivization, and described it as their consistent policy to discourage any attempt to divide the expropriated estates between the labourers and small tenants instead of working them collectively. Not a single estate in La Mancha had been parcelled out after expropriation. The reasons why here, in the zone of large estates, there is so little desire to parcel them, are fairly obvious. In contradistinction to Russia, there was and is no peasantry in this part of Spain which would or could fight with the large landowners for the possession of the land. In Russia the peasant farms already existed; they had only to be enlarged by the expropriation of the lands of the aristocracy. By far the larger part of the villagers in southern Spain are not peasants at all, but simply landless agricultural labourers, and the lots of the few existing tenants are so small as scarcely to support a real peasant holding. All the buildings, material implements, and social habits required for peasant households are lacking. If a landowning peasantry were wanted here, it would have to be created out of nothing: an impossible task. Thus collectivization of the larger estates, in southern Spain, goes almost automatically with expropriation. The methods of agriculture remain unchanged, but the administration is carried out by a group of newly elected leaders from the ranks of the workers, or by the local trade-union branch, instead of by the manager of the former owner; and the revenue goes directly and entirely to the labourers. This is in substance what I learned from talk with the members of the regional Reforma Agraria.

The collective farm I visited was thoroughly well managed. The cattle were kept in splendid health; the wheat had been harvested in time (it was stored in what had been the chapel of the estate); the buildings were kept clean and the machines in good order. Is it the same everywhere? There were no women on the farm. Before collectivization the labourers had lived in Ciudad Réal and come to the estate (which is very near the town) every morning. Now they had settled down in the manorial building, but had left their womenfolk behind in the town; it does not become a Castilian woman to move about among men other than those of her own family. These poor agricultural labourers, rather than infringe the strict rules of Castilian decency, preferred to do their cooking and washing themselves and to meet their families only on Sundays. I tasted the food, which was neither copious nor well cooked but certainly better than what they had had before the expropriation.

We took leave of our hospitable friends of Reforma Agraria and of Ciudad Réal itself, and through the desiccated Mancha, we drove into the picturesque Sierra Morena, and, with dusk falling, entered Andalusia.

The profound difference between Castille and Andalusia is obvious and even obtrusive, at first sight. Castille is sober, reserved, ascetic; Andalusia colourful, emotional, intrusive. People talk freely to strangers, girls wear dresses in bright colours which are a real relief after the black on black of La Mancha. The traditional mantillas, however, have completely disappeared. The men invariably wear something red, mostly red neckties; difficult to decide how far this habit, which does not date from the revolution, has now acquired the significance of a revolutionary gesture. The Andalusians have a revolutionary greeting of their own. Whereas everywhere in Spain revolutionaries greet with the raised fist, in Andalusia they greet with both arms lifted over the head and the rifle folded in clasped hands. It signifies something like 'Workers of all parties and professions, join in fight', and it looks very impressive. There are other acts, of a less demonstrative and more practical character: the miners of Valdepeñas and the surrounding districts have heavily mined many spots on the chief road through the sierra, so as to make it completely impassable in case of an attack.

Sliding down the mild slopes of the sierra, we reached the zone of olive-groves. All Eastern Andalusia consists of these olive-groves, to the exclusion of almost every other fruit or cereal. Estates are enormous, villages scarce, but the few that exist are very populous, averaging about 20,000 inhabitants, mostly wretched, landless agricultural labourers. Usually Castille and Andalusia are both described as districts of large estates. But really there is little similarity between the wheat-growing, middle-sized estates of Castille, obviously of feudal origin, whose labourers, a few generations ago, were serfs, and the enormous olive-growing *latifundia* of Andalusia, unchanged in character since Carthaginian and Roman times, whose landless proletariat derives from slaves and still retains many features of a slave population helplessly dependent on its owners. Again, the villages of Castille are of the true European type of peasant villages, whereas the Andalusian village (better described by the Spanish expression *pueblo*) clearly recalls an antique *civitas*, in which the whole population of a district crowds together, while the countryside is left uninhabited,

We were pleasantly approaching Bailén, our goal for this day, and nothing warranted the expectation of anything but a quiet evening, when suddenly we approached two motor-lorries which, to my bewilderment, did not carry lights. And then, horror of horrors, in the middle of the main road from Madrid to Cordova, there lay, in front of the first of the two motor-lorries, corpses. It was an impression unlike any I had had before. What precisely made the ghastly effect I cannot tell. Corpses in daytime are less uncanny than in the dusk, they are less horrifying in some remote corner than on a chief artery of traffic, where nobody could possibly expect to meet them. Then there were the two silent motor-lorries, which seemed to hide some appalling secret. Some of my companions believed they had heard sounds coming from them, but could not tell whether words or sobs. Impossible to find out; I wanted to stop, unaware, under the shock of the impression, of danger, and only anxious to know more; but the driver, mad with terror, drove on at top speed. How many corpses there were we could not make out in the one short moment we saw them. The body of a woman dressed in shining white clothes, with blood flowing from her breast, was clearly visible; the position of the corpse suggested that she had been put in front of the motor-lorry and shot from the driver's seat. It must have happened a few minutes before our arrival, perhaps only a few seconds before we came. There were certainly other corpses, but in the haste and dusk we did not see them clearly. My impression was that there was only one other corpse, that of an adult man. But my four companions unanimously declared they saw a dead baby in the woman's arms, and some of them had seen both a baby and a man lying dead beside the woman.

Horrors were not yet at an end. Entering Bailén, we saw huge columns of smoke on both sides of the road, at the entry of the *pueblo*. Again, close investigation was impossible, the guards at the entry ordering hysterically 'Siga, siga' ('Go on, go on'); this sharply contrasted with the usual friendly talk of the guards; and then the smoke was much too thick to allow us to interpret it as rising from the burning of refuse or anything like that. It was pitch-dark by the time of our arrival, and impossible to find out as we passed rapidly by, but the obvious interpretation was that the property of the dead we had seen on the road was being burned.

The tragedy was followed by a satirical play. With the childish impudence which one so often meets among primitive people, the committee in Bailén wanted to convince us that we had not seen what we actually had seen. The most idiotic tales were invented for the purpose. Our guards were ordered to pretend, late at night, that they had been out with some members of the committee to the macabre spot and there had found absolutely nothing but a pool of gasoline (instead of blood!). And the woman was said to be a well-known prostitute, who was making love with a man in the middle of the road. It was exasperating to listen to this silly talk, the more so as it was somewhat naïve to try to make us believe that such a thing as executions did not occur. The one conclusion emerging from these lies was that the local committee knew about the murder—one can hardly call the shooting of a baby an execution—and approved of it. Next morning the guards in the next villages excitedly questioned us, wanting to know what tragedy had happened the night before at Bailén.

4 September.

We drove on to Andujar, one of the largest *pueblos* of eastern Andalusia, where we had a long interview with the committee. This committee resembled little the institutions bearing the same name in the North of Spain. Even more than round Madrid, in Andalusia they seem to merge into the *ayuntamientos* as they existed before the civil war. The first sign of this queer process we met yesterday; as soon as we crossed the border from La Mancha into Andalusia, the control of the road was exercised *in common* by the old local police and the armed village guards. Then we saw municipal officials in their uniforms working together in the same room and on the same affairs with militia and workers in civilian clothes in the *ayuntamiento* in Bailén; and here in Andujar this co-operation is even more in evidence. The policemen of the pre-war days here simply stand at attention before the doors of the bureau of the administration, which is indifferently composed of members of the *ayuntamiento* and of the 'committee'. In practice it seems to work out in this way: the old administration continues in office, but has been strengthened by the co-option of representatives of the UGT, the socialist and communist parties, and the Socialist Youth (there are no anarchists in Andujar, any more than in any other *pueblo* of the whole province of Jaen; in this respect Jaen, the easternmost part of Andalusia, differs profoundly from its western and southern districts). True, the 'old' municipality itself is very young in Andujar, in every sense of the word; the *alcalde* is a youngster of certainly not more than twenty-five, appointed after the February elections.

Thus, there was a fairly incisive change in February 1936 from the domination of the *ayuntamiento* by the former almighty group to the administration of a few young socialists; but there was only a very slight change between February and August, between the administration of the liberal republicans and the revolutionary period. The province of Jaen seems to have stopped at the republican stage of the history of the Spanish revolution.

Equally slight is the social change which followed in the wake of the civil war. There are a couple of soap and other factories in Andujar, but none of them has been expropriated or put under control. There were no noble landowners in the *pueblo* of Andujar, but five rich bourgeois owned by far the larger part of its land. They have all been killed. But what happened to the land and what will happen to it? The committee members become even more hesitant than usual when asked this question. Nobody seems to know at all. And this is not surprising, as Andujar is really unusually backward. Not even a UGT group existed before February, and the *brazeros*, the agricultural labourers, were completely unorganized. Naturally, now, the embryonic UGT group since founded is unable to handle such a large task as the managing of enormous estates, and this business *nolens volens* rests in the hands of the *ayuntamiento*. This body, however, as a wearying cross-examination of some of its members proves, is not making any innovations; it is just carrying on the régime that prevailed before the civil war, and indeed for the past century. It has, of course, laid hands upon the stores and money of the executed landowners, expropriating not less than 2,000,000 pesetas at a stroke by this measure. Thus provided with capital, it employs the same *brazeros* that the former landowners employed, upon the same estates, for the same endless working hours, for the same starvation wages. Whether the *ayuntamiento* is good at its new job of administering olive-grove estates it is difficult to say; harvest-time is still three months ahead. As to the wheat harvest, it has been delayed considerably by the civil war, but, we are told, is now proceeding quickly. The attitude of the *brazeros* is more easily defined. As nothing has changed in their living conditions, so nothing has changed in their attitude. The actual immutability of things contrasts violently with the formal official change. Formally, the *ayuntamiento* has lost its power and has been replaced by a 'committee', which is supposed to be the direct representative of the *brazeros*. Formally, the large estates have been taken over by this committee, and to all intents and purposes the *brazeros* own the estates. Actually, and very naturally, they take no notice of this fiction. As they are ordered about as before, and for the same wages, they start fighting the new administration of the estates as they did the old one. And one member of the committee, after some hesitation, admits that the one thing the *brazeros* are really interested in at present is the paying of their arrears of wages for July and August (the first, chaotic weeks of the civil war), which have run into sums important for them. And, he explains, there is grumbling and arguing about every penny. The *brazeros* very naturally continue to treat these estates not as their own, but as land on which they are exploited, and of course they want to squeeze from the administration what they can, however little.

The facts are even more striking because it does not look as if this state of things were anybody's personal fault. The *alcalde*, for all his lack of years and maturity, is a splendid type, clear-headed, energetic, polite, and clever. Some of the members of the local administration are not Andalusians but people from the North of Spain, who have nothing of the proverbial Andalusian vagueness and unreliability about them. The town is in good order (the church not burned, but used for Government offices, as in most *pueblos* of the province of Jaen), and the administration is obviously not lacking in enthusiasm. Nor has the fighting been less passionate or shorter than in other places; far from it. The guardia revolted, and was driven out of the *pueblo*, but retreated to a castle some miles away from Andujar, where they hold out to this day. They tell us that there is another similar spot in the Sierra Morena, even more dangerous, because from their refuge the guardia occasionally raid the main road for food, killing the militia they capture with the motor-lorries. All over this district there was heavy fighting before the rebellious guardia was subdued. On the other side of the front, in the Franco camp, between Cordova and Seville, it is the reverse. There the peasants revolt, and the insurgents have to subdue the villages one by one, even on the main road, and have not yet come to an end of it.

In the afternoon we reached the front line at Villafranca. The trip was not remarkable in any respect. The troops were the same motley crowd I knew from Talavera, only this time it was the Andalusian and not the Valencian element which prevailed. The line was completely quiet. Only there was continual mention of air bombardments, from Andujar onwards; the main road was damaged in various places by bombs, and hasty repairs were proceeding. A few days before our visit a French socialist journalist, Renée Lafont, had inadvertently driven into the insurgent lines at this very spot; the car had been fired at from an ambush, she had fallen wounded, and been captured by fascist volunteers.[1]

We passed the night at Montoro, headquarters of the Cordova front. About midnight I was startled out of my sleep by four heavy detonations. Rushing downstairs, to my amazement I found the innkeeper of our *fonda* in quiet conversation with friends. When I asked him about the detonations, he smilingly and soothingly replied, 'Son solo golpes de gracia' ('It's only *coups de grace*'). It had been four volleys for a mass execution carried out just beyond the small town, and the sound seemed to be so common that nobody paid any attention to it. If the revolutionary transformation of society in this region is very slight, the civil war here is certainly more cruel than anywhere else.

[1] She has died since from her wounds, a war prisoner in Cordova.

A DIARY IN REVOLUTION

5 September.

At the Montoro headquarters we learnt that the northern wing of the Government army would attack Cordova next morning from the village of Cerro Muriano, and we went there through the mining district of Pennaroya. The mines have stopped working at various times, some of them in 1930 with the beginning of the world economic crisis, others with the revolution of 1931 or later, some in February and the subsequent months, for both economic and political reasons, and the rest (very few) after the beginning of the civil war, when, obviously, to spend money on mines certain to be expropriated soon was not profitable. About half the mines belonged to Spaniards and the other half to various foreign concerns. They produce mainly lead, bismuth, and copper, consequently a part of their produce would be very important for the munitions industry. But not the slightest attempt is made to set them working again, either by the miners themselves or under State administration. Civil war, however, has been very bitter in this district. There always was an inextinguishable blood-feud between the guardia on the one hand and the miners and *brazeros* on the other. And the civil war gave an opportunity to both sides to satiate their desire of revenge. In Pozoblanco, for instance, a *pueblo* of 20,000 to 25,000 inhabitants, the guardia revolted on the first day of the civil war, with the help of the few wealthy people living in this far corner. They had much more and much better arms than the miners and so got hold of the *pueblo*; but the miners, instead of submitting, surrounded their own *pueblo*, and, helped with arms from the Government, for four weeks laid a regular siege to it, until the guardia was starved out and surrendered; they were killed to the last man, about 170 of them. As a reprisal, the *pueblo* was air-bombarded three times during the next four days, and a couple of people were killed; Pozoblanco does not regret it; it has got rid of the guardia. The ordinary police continue to serve, as elsewhere in Andalusia. This tragedy, in all its stages, is typical of many *pueblos* in eastern Andalusia.

158

A DIARY IN REVOLUTION

At about 1 p.m. we reached the headquarters of the northern sector of the Cordova front, and were billeted in a hospital, in a very pleasant sanatorium. The staff itself was less pleasant. I have seen a number of staffs now, of various degrees of competence and pleasantness, from very good ones (by existing standards) to more unsatisfactory ones, but I never saw anything like this. The first thing we learned was that the attack had failed; that instead, since six in the morning the enemy had been attacking heavily. The coincidence of the enemies' attack preceding by just a few hours the attempt to attack from the Government side was surprising, but it did not seem to be a subject for consideration by the staff. Neither was the failure of the intended operation itself, or, for that matter, the whole war. While, a few miles ahead, a heavy attack on an important position was proceeding and (affairs were not going in favour of the Government), the staff, officers, doctors, nurses (of a more than dubious quality), were sitting down quietly to a good lunch, chatting, flirting, telling dirty stories, and not caring a bit about their duty, not even trying to establish any contact with the fighting lines for many hours; the wounded who were brought in from time to time were neglected by the nurses in the most shameless and repugnant manner. Finally, by about three o'clock, we had passed through the ordeal of standing what the staff thought was good behaviour, and proceeded to the front, to the small village of Cerro Muriano.

There, at half-past three, we found pandemonium. A little way ahead of the village there is a low wooded ridge, from which occasional rifle and machine-gun fire was sounding. The wood was burning on the right side of the village, from shelling in the morning. The fighting was obviously not very heavy at the moment of our arrival. But we witnessed a scene such as before I only knew from stories of the Thirty Years War, though probably similar things happened occasionally in the World War. The whole village was in flight; men, women, and children; on foot, by donkeys, by cars, and motorlorries. The latter had been crowded at the entrance to the village opposite the front, for troop, munition, and food transport. These cars and lorries were simply stormed by the inhabitants, a few of whom knew how to drive, and did drive the vehicles away, or if ignorant of driving, forced the drivers at the rifle point to disobey orders, leave the battlefield, and carry off the fugitives. All that naturally in a hullabaloo. Women carrying their babies in their arms, and their cattle at rope-ends; they sobbing, the babies crying; men trying to carry on their arms and backs what small portion of their movable property they could bear away in their haste. The whole village, in a few minutes, was completely derelict. Many of the fleeing men wore the CNT initials on their caps (Cerro Muriano is just in the province of Cordova, which is much more anarchist than Jaen), and carried their rifles with them, not to use them against the enemy, but against who-ever might try to stop their flight. The whole village guard, the local peasant militia, was running away, and even set the pace for the wild rush to the rear. At the moment, our war correspondents' car was the only one which did not move to-wards the rear but towards the front. We stopped, our driver and guard got down, and drew their revolvers. A few deser-ters from the Franco army, all of them old UGT and CNT members, who, by chance, found themselves in the village at the moment of the disaster, joined our guards. They stopped the flying cars and lorries, pointed their revolvers at the heads of the drivers, and, joining reproaches and imprecations to the menace of arms, ordered the cars and lorries to stop; women and children might proceed to a safer place, but all men except the drivers had to stay and defend the village. Wasn't it a shame that men armed with good rifles, and wear-ing the proud insignia of the CNT, were running away like cowards? 'Rifles are no good against bombs and shells,' the fugitives shouted back. Sometimes the menace of the drawn revolvers, closer and more immediate than that of the battle behind, succeeded for a moment; some lorries were stopped, some men descended. But as soon as the small group who tried to re-establish discipline had proceeded a few yards far-ther, to the next car or the next but one, the men mounted again and drove away in haste.

It was only hours later that I found out exactly what had happened. The village had been bombarded throughout the whole morning from the air, and occasionally with artillery fire too; then there had been the usual break in fighting during the siesta hours, from about one o'clock to half-past three, a ritual observed by both parties throughout the Spanish civil war; and just when we arrived the bombardment of the village had reopened, and the strained nerves of the inhabitants could stand it no longer. When we entered the village, it offered a sorry sight; all houses deserted; most doors locked; cats, dogs, pigs wandering helplessly in the streets and yards. But the front line, in contrast to the village guard, stood unshattered. The village, in spite of the panic, had suffered very little; nothing was either destroyed or burning.

The left flank of Cerro Muriano is protected by a railway bank, which proved to be very valuable cover. Occasionally bullets struck the streets, but on the whole we could proceed towards the lines unmolested. Directly behind the lines, at the front entry of the village, a sort of barrack, probably used in normal times for housing the railway personnel, had been transformed into a red-cross station. There we stopped. Casualties were few. The column fighting just ahead of us was the usual size of a militia column, about 300 to 400 men. There had been less than ten wounded back at the base hospital (the one where the staff were billeted), and now not more than ten men were being treated at the red-cross station. Twenty casualties, 5 to 7 per cent. of all the effectives, and these including casualties of every description from the slightest upwards, is certainly not a heavy list after more than seven hours' fighting; there were three or four dead. The panic became increasingly unintelligible. Meanwhile I watched the activity at the red-cross station. It was queer to observe that all the militia-men treated had exactly the same attitude, whether they were brought in with simple nervous shock (as was very frequently the case) or with dangerous wounds; for them, the thing was over; they considered themselves as good as dead, or rather, played dead. The two doctors, swift and efficient, started every new case with a question about what was wrong, but never once did they get an answer; they had to find out for themselves, undressing the patients and looking for wounds. Suddenly there was a big crash, as near as could possibly be. A bomb had come down a few yards from the red-cross station, which was flying the red-cross flag in a way impossible to overlook. In a second all the men were flat on the ground, and only we three journalists still stood upright (it is, of course, not the slightest use to take cover against bombs *in a building*, but training had gone already far enough to make covering an instinctive reaction with the militia-men). The wounded did not move at all, but a nurse started sobbing hysterically. The behaviour of the doctors, in great contrast to the scene we had just watched, was brilliant; they did not interrupt for a moment the fulfilment of their duties—this was not the type of doctor we had met a few hours ago at staff headquarters. The enemy bomber, after launching a few bombs farther back in the village, went away, but returned after a few minutes. In the meantime I tried to get to the front line itself, but the fire was now too heavy to pass. I decided to take cover in a tunnel under the railway bank. To my great surprise I found that the bombs the enemy were dropping were no good at all. The holes made by them were only a few fingers deep; such bombs were obviously harmless, if one was not struck by one directly. Standing at the entry of the tunnel where I had taken cover I saw a bomb explode a few yards away; the air pressure drove me back, but nothing else happened. Much more awkward was the machine-gun fire. It definitely took a nasty turn. First it had been ahead only, but it was clearly approaching from the left flank, across the railway line; a few Moorish machine-gunners had turned the flank of the Government lines, unopposed. They might enter the village any minute.

Things gradually became unpleasant. If the Moors caught us in our shelter under the railway bank, there would be very little chance to explain that we were neutrals; they would kill us at once. Thus, dangerous as it might be, we had to leave cover, go into the open, and get out of the village as quickly as possible. But this was easier said than done. At first we were lucky and got out during a break in the bombing and machine-gunning. On the main road stood a captain with a few men, who examined our papers with admirable calm and courtesy—he was the one officer who behaved firmly on this day, and that night I learned that he had restored order and confidence in the front line and thus avoided catastrophe. Very soon, however, the machine-gun fire reopened, from very near, though we could not see the Moors, who were lying on the other side of the bank; and it was cross-fire, because besides the Moors flanking us from across the bank there was the main line of the insurgents, firing at the village from the right wing. We slipped from one house to the next during occasional breaks in the firing. Meantime, the bombing continued unchanged. There were two enemy planes now, alternately fetching bombs and bombing the village; they were completely unopposed. There had been talk during lunch of Government aircraft being ordered to come and take part in the fighting, but no Government plane appeared. The bombs were ridiculously inefficient; about 50 per cent. did not explode at all, and the rest did very little damage; not a single one of the huts of which this miserable village consisted was burning when the bombardment stopped towards dusk. But the mere fact of standing in continual air bombardment for nearly three hours, unprotected and without aircraft to oppose the bombers, is nerve-shattering. Finally we got out of the village. A few hundred yards outside stood a number of cars and lorries, which, after having evacuated the village, had returned. But the scenes of flight of the afternoon were now repeated, only this time it was not the villagers but the militia from the front line, who went back, singly or in small groups, and forced the cars to drive them away. It was a scene of complete disorder. The officers, the men said, had run away first; why should they stay? One man got into our car, and when I asked him what business he had behind the lines he bluntly replied: 'To escape.'

We had to seek shelter once more, this time in a small tunnel under the road, before we could get away with our car. The bombing was too heavy and too near for us to take the risk of driving off. Our driver and guard had behaved admirably, going to fetch us in the bombarded and machine-gunned village. There was another journalists' car whose driver had ignominiously run away. There were similar differences between the various small units of militia. While the troops from Jaen and Valencia ran away before our eyes, a small group of militia from Alcoy, an old revolutionary centre in the province of Murcia, arrived. They stood the bombardment—which, I must repeat, did no real damage—with the proudest gallantry and unconcernedness; there were two girls among the group, more courageous even than the men. Discipline, however, was lacking to an almost incredible extent. The tunnel where we had taken shelter was far from being bomb-proof; at best it was a suitable hiding-place. but it became unavailing even for that, because every time the bombardment stopped for a moment the militia-men from Alcoy crawled out of cover to watch the enemy planes. Finally, we got safely back to headquarters, where they were as uninterested as at midday.

This experience of battle provided a few general observations. The enemy had not had to stand the ordeal of unopposed bombing and I have no means of judging how the Moors would behave in such circumstances. But there is no doubt that they are better soldiers than the militia; not only more courageous, but quicker in moving and seeing their advantage; this was evident in their flanking manœuvre. Still, their capacities in this respect seem to be very limited. There is no conceivable reason for their failure finally to attack and storm the village, where they would have found no resistance whatever. Such an attack would have brought them round to the rear of the Government line, and would not only have won them the day, and led to the capture of the whole column, but would have meant a shattering blow to the whole Cordova front. Instead, they, and with them the planes, stopped their action at about half-past six; they probably thought that they had done a good day's work, that dusk was approaching, and that that was enough for this time. Moreover, the bombing was utterly incompetent. I wonder where the fantastic bombing material used on this occasion can have been produced. Bombing itself consisted in the dropping of bombs from a great height, without any previous observation. In short, the whole action of the insurgents on this day was a farce, and not even a sanguinary one.

But it was worse on the Government side. It is difficult to find appropriate words to characterize the conduct of the staff. The officers in the front line lacked even ordinary courage. The village guards had run away; so had the militia, as soon as it found things really unpleasant. Some of the disastrous features of the combat witnessed were obviously due to the incompetence of the staff; and such a degree of incompetence and lack of responsibility must be exceptional. Still, there may be many staffs of inferior quality among the Government forces. And even where staff work is better than at Cerro Muriano, there remain certain disastrous peculiarities of the militia itself. It cannot stand the impact of modern arms, air-raids, and shelling, even from small guns. And it has no conception that a position must never be left without express orders from the command. When the militia runs away, the militia-men individually feel that fate has been against them; they do not feel guilty in the least. If this is not changed, the insurgents will certainly win the war. They have modern war material from abroad. It is neither copious nor good in quality, but it seems to be too much for the militia.

Thorough training would certainly help to make the militia fit for fighting, but discipline is still more important. After Cerro Muriano, I believe the stories told about Oropesa and Talavera; how the militia ran away not after heavy fighting, but at the first bombs dropped and the first shells fired. This is in direct contrast with the undeniable heroism they must have displayed in the street-fighting in Madrid and Barcelona. But then, for Spanish mentality, there seems to be all the difference in the world between fighting in one's own street and facing the enemy in the open.

A DIARY IN REVOLUTION

6 September.

We passed the night at Pozoblanco, together with some Spanish journalists, who were in no doubt about the disastrous result of the day, in spite of their eloquent and optimistic telegrams to their newspapers. One of them called my attention to the southern sector of the Cordova front, not from the military, but from the political and psychological point of view. I was well advised in following his hint. In the afternoon, after a long and trying drive, we entered Castro del Rio.

Castro, a typically populous and wretched Andalusian *pueblo*, is one of the oldest anarchist centres in Andalusia. Its CNT group looks back upon an existence of twenty-six years, and, since the defeat of the guardia in Castro, the anarchists are the one existing organization. The beginning of the revolution in Castro was very similar to that in Pozoblanco; revolt of the guardia together with the caziques and the rich against the republic, first successful, then leading to the siege of the village by its own inhabitants, the starving out of the guardia, their surrender, and finally the inevitable wholesale massacre. The insurgents, whose main lines run a few miles from the village, had attacked it twice since, but without success. All entries were heavily barricaded and watched with unusual technical competence. And so the local anarchists had had time to introduce their anarchist Eden, which, in most points, resembled closely the one introduced by the Anabaptists in Münster in 1534.

The salient point of the anarchist régime in Castro is the abolition of money. Exchange is suppressed; production has changed very little. The land of Castro belonged to three of the greatest magnates of Spain, all of them absentees, of course; it has now been expropriated. The local *ayuntamiento* has not merged with the committee, as everywhere else in Andalusia, but has been dissolved, and the committee has taken its place and introduced a sort of Soviet system. The committee took over the estates, and runs them. They have not even been merged, but are worked separately, each by

166

the hands previously employed on its lands. Money wages, of course, have been abolished. It would be incorrect to say that they have been replaced by pay in kind. There is no pay whatever; the inhabitants are fed directly from the village stores.

Under this system, the provisioning of the village is of the poorest kind; poorer, I should venture to say, than it can possibly have been before, even in the wretched conditions in which Andalusian *brazeros* are wont to live. The *pueblo* is fortunate in growing wheat, and not only olives, as many other *pueblos* of its kind; so there is at any rate bread. Moreover, the village owns large herds of sheep, expropriated with the estates, so there is some meat. And they still have a store of cigarettes. That's all. I tried in vain to get a drink, either of coffee or wine or lemonade. The village bar had been closed as nefarious commerce. I had a look at the stores. They were so low as to foretell approaching starvation. But the inhabitants seemed to be proud of this state of things. They were pleased, as they told us, that coffee-drinking had come to an end; they seemed to regard this abolition of useless things as a moral improvement. What few commodities they needed from outside, mainly clothes, they hoped to get by direct exchange of their surplus in olives (for which, however, no arrangement had yet been made). Their hatred of the upper class was far less economic than moral. They did not want to get the good living of those they had expropriated, but to get rid of their luxuries, which to them seemed to be so many vices. Their conception of the new order which was to be brought about was thoroughly ascetic.

7 September.

We passed the night at Andujar and then drove back to Madrid, hurriedly. All through the last days news from the front had been very bad, even in the optimistic distortion of the official newspapers. Yesterday it was so disquieting that we decided to drop our plans for Malaga and to return instead. Caballero has taken over the Government; maybe he will bring the radical change in war and administration which is the first condition of success for his cause.

A DIARY IN REVOLUTION

Little happened on our hasty journey.

All along the road we met fugitives; large groups of them had arrived in various places of La Mancha; they had, very naturally, spread uneasiness, but had been received with the greatest hospitality.

We took lunch in a *fonda* in La Mancha, when suddenly a man entered carrying an object which I discovered to be a bomb. It was, he explained to the excited onlookers, one of a few hundred bombs dropped the night before on the railway junction of Aranjuez without effect. He had carried it more than a hundred miles in his car, to bring it (an unexploded bomb!) back home as a souvenir; and so toy-like was the bomb that it had not exploded even under this treatment.

Madrid

8–11 September.

Most of this time was spent in getting documents for leaving Spain and establishing contacts for my next visit. The aspect of the town has changed little. There is the same unconcerned gaiety, though the difficulties of provisioning are obviously increasing and food is rather scarce in the restaurants. But at night, to be sure, the town has changed. Lights are extinguished; only a few lanterns, tramways, and cars show blue lights. Innumerable house-entries have been marked as bomb-proof shelters. Posters tell about the first measures to be taken in case of gas attacks. The population does not seem to mind. For many days there has not been an air attack, partly, it seems, because the last attempt was discovered at an early moment by the Government aircraft, and failed completely.

Well-informed circles are less unconcerned. They know, only too well, that the insurgents are approaching Madrid rapidly; that the panics of the militia are incalculable, and that Franco may attack Madrid suddenly at any moment. To stay or not to stay, that is the question which all journalists and foreign observers discuss. In the meantime, Caballero has taken his first measures, the creation of a central

168

staff being the most important. Official optimism, which was such a nuisance under the old Government, continues. Already, before having achieved anything, the Caballero Government is greeted by the whole Press as the 'Government of victory'; to help unpleasant facts to become more pleasant, it has started its career of propaganda with news of the taking of Huesca, which is obviously untrue. But at least, it seems, the new Government is willing to be more energetic than was the old one.

12 September.

Journey from Madrid to Barcelona, entirely uneventful.

13, 14 September.

Two days spent in Barcelona. Compared with August the town is empty and quiet; the revolutionary fever is withering away. Many people I knew in August have gone to the front. The dominating element in the Ramblas, at the moment, is the militia who have come back from the Mallorca expedition; the decision to drop this unhappy enterprise is one more measure of reorganization of the new cabinet. Some of the Catalan troops employed in this expedition I saw enter Madrid on the last day of my stay. They were watched by the crowd on the Alcalá, who could hardly believe that true Catalans had come to help to defend Madrid; when, from their language, their identity as Catalans became undeniable, isolated shouts of 'Viva Cataluña' were to be heard; it was so strange, compared with the earlier bitter strife between Castille and Catalonia, as to be almost incredible. These Catalans had had many weeks of heavy fighting on Mallorca, then a short rest, and then came straight to Madrid, which they entered in splendid order, looking much more impressive than any of the columns I had seen in Extremadura and Andalusia. Now, in Barcelona, I saw the remainder of the Mallorca expeditionary force, which was to go to Madrid in a few days; and their eagerness to go to fight again, after a first and thoroughly unhappy campaign, was truly admirable. There are forces in the Spanish revolution which have only just begun to make themselves felt. The greater the dangers the greater will be the stubbornness of the resistance. It may be more difficult for Franco to win than appears from the present state of things. At present, however, the position of the Government is disastrous; though no newspaper gives it, I hear unofficially of the fall of San Sebastian.

15 September.
Left Spain through Port Bou.

III

THE SECOND JOURNEY

When I came back to Spain, in mid-January 1937, the situation had changed profoundly in many respects. One of the changes concerned the facilities given to journalists. Leave to travel about freely and visit every corner of the country had become a privilege granted only to journalists with a definite party allegiance. Personally, for reasons to be explained in the following pages, I found more than the average amount of difficulty in my work. A presentation of my day-to-day observations would not be interesting, in consequence. The method of direct reproduction of my notes has had to be dropped.

On the other hand it was now easier for me to get a clear idea of general political problems, partly because I had formed more contacts, partly because I knew the situation better, and partly because the civil war, in its protracted course, now gave ampler material for generalizations. I decided, therefore, after a few days' stay in Spain, not to try again to study the regional diversity of events, but rather to concentrate upon a study of the main political problems. The following report contains the results of this study, without omitting for all that to tell of those observations on the spot which I was able to make.

The text has been written during the journey itself, and follows closely on observation and study. The part concerning Catalonia was finished a few days after my arrival at Valencia, that concerning Malaga immediately after my return thence, and the rest a few days after my return from

Spain. It is still the report of an eye-witness, written from the direct impression made by the events themselves.

That is why I feel it would be wrong to change anything in this report under the influence of weeks more recent. The period of January and February, which I was in a position to observe as an eye-witness, is only one stage in the course of the Spanish civil war, and in itself carries no more weight than any previous stage or any stage to follow. It happened to be a disastrous stage, which found its climax, politically, in a protracted Government crisis without issue, in the removal of General Kleber and the withdrawal of Mr. Rosenberg, and, in military matters, in the catastrophe of Malaga and the defeat of Jarama. My observations in this report about my second journey are occupied with this stage, and not the Spanish civil war in general, which has obviously entered a new stage since the battle of Guadalajara. This latter period I attempted to discuss in an appendix, so far as that is possible with the limited information available abroad.

But if things have eventually taken a more favourable turn for the republican camp, both in military and in political matters, since mid-March, this does not lead to the conclusion that the history of the months of disaster is without importance. Every stage of development leaves a deep imprint upon the following events. The victory of the workers in the streets of Madrid and Barcelona in the first days initiated a process of social revolution which continued to influence events deeply, even after it had come to an end; the nationalization of industry in Catalonia is only one of its more important after-effects. The defeats of September and October forced the Spanish anti-fascists to call for Russian help and, in consequence, to give in to Russian political pressure; this first period of defeat is over, but its consequences, as described in the present report, have changed and continue to change the whole trend of the civil war, both in military and in political matters. The period of political reaction, 'totalitarian' trends, and renewed military defeats which lasted throughout January and February will leave also its mark upon future developments. The military disasters have been overcome, for the time being, but the fact of the emergence of totalitarian tendencies will remain; whether it will be defeat or success for the arms of the republican Government now, will depend more on the fitness of military and administrative machinery than on the spontaneous rising of a people in arms. This, again, will determine the future fate of Spain. Nothing is lost in history, and every action, every policy, finds its adequate reward in later events, not, to be sure, in the moral, but in the political sense. Therefore it is the duty of the historian to catch, as well as he can, the concrete shape of things in concrete situations. Therefore I left my description as it stood, rather than indulge in *vaticinia ex evento*.

Barcelona Again

One point at least my second departure for Spain had in common with the first one: rumours. The crossing of the border was described by friends and acquaintances as just as awful as every one had expected it to be the first time. It was suggested that the French authorities put every possible difficulty in the way of travellers, and that the Spanish committee on the other side submitted every foreigner to a nasty and humiliating search. Nothing of the kind happened. The crossing proved to be even smoother than the first time. As to the French authorities, they merely made every passenger sign a form to say that he crossed at his own risk and renounced beforehand any claims upon the railway company in case of accident. The border tunnel between Cerbère and Port Bou had been repeatedly though not very successfully shelled by the insurgent cruiser *Canarias*. I, however, had a quiet crossing because at the moment a Government man-of-war was stationed near the frontier and hindered further attempts at a naval attack.

The train was crowded with a convoy of volunteers for the international brigade, most of them from the other side of the Atlantic: Canadians, Americans, Cubans, Mexicans, Phillipinos; a motley crowd altogether. They had been well set up with coats and boots, and, to judge from their physique, none of them can have been unemployed for long before enlistment. It was rather an adventurous type which prevailed —men seeking the excitement of a fight. Some of them were obviously splendid material for soldiers. They formed a cheerful and rather noisy crowd, and the various station buffets did fine business with them. At Perpignan they all left the train. There was a centre of the Communist Party there which subjected volunteers to a last sifting before conducting them into Spain. Two days later this same convoy entered Barcelona, amid the hearty acclamations of the crowd. The French authorities had put no difficulties in their way.

So much for the French side of the border. The Spanish side proved to be equally harmless. There was no search, only a mild investigation of the importation of foreign currencies. The political committee still existed, as in August, and still examined and passed my documents. But for the sake of greater convenience it had now officials in the station itself. In contrast to August, it now seemed to be composed mainly of anarchists, who were polite and friendly to me.

As in August the train, provided with first-class and third-class compartments and a dining-car, started and arrived in time. But the rest of the scene was entirely different. Where in August there seemed to prevail entirely normal conditions there was now a real armed camp. All along the coast-line troops were stationed and trenches built against attack from the sea. The trenches, as far as I can judge, may be quite sufficient to ward off an attack by insurgent forces, but would certainly be no good against the attack of a modern navy. The troops were entirely different from the militia I had known in August. There was a clear distinction between officers and men, the former wearing better uniforms and stripes. The pre-revolutionary police force, *asaltos* and Guardia Civil (now 'Guardia Nacional Republicana'), were very much in evidence. The *asaltos* again wore their brilliant uniforms of dark blue with peaked caps and much gold braid. The guardia had exchanged their old theatrical three-cornered black hats for modest green caps; neither guardia nor *asaltos* made the least attempt to appear proletarian. The uniform of the privates was not yet quite unified, but the multicoloured Robin Hood style of the militia-men had entirely disappeared and there was a definite attempt towards a uniformity of clothes. Very few men still wore their party initials on their caps; most of them did not wear any political insignia. And even an anarchist soldier in my compartment did not speak of the 'militia' but of the 'army'. The dining-car was full of officers and pilots; I do not think there were any privates. There were drinks, but practically no food.

Barcelona came as a shock, as in August, but in the opposite sense. Then it had overwhelmed me by the suddenness with which it revealed the real character of a workers' dictatorship. This time it struck the observer by the clean sweep of all signs of this same dictatorship. No more barricades in the streets; no more cars covered with revolutionary initials and filled with men in red neckties rushing through the town; no more workers in civilian clothes, but rifles on their shoulders; as a matter of fact, very few armed men at all, and those mostly *asaltos* and guardias in brilliant uniforms; no more seething life around the party centres and no large car-parks before their entries; and the red banners and inscriptions, so shining in August, had faded. There was still no definitely 'bourgeois' element visible in the streets. Certainly the really rich people, if there are any, did not appear in public. But the Ramblas, the chief artery of popular life in Barcelona, were far less clearly working-class now than then. In August it was dangerous to wear a hat: nobody minded doing so now, and the girls no longer hesitated to wear their prettiest clothes. A few of the more fashionable restaurants and dance-halls have reopened, and find customers. To sum it up, what one calls the petty-bourgeois element, merchants, shop-keepers, professional men, and the like, have not only made their appearance, but make a strong impress upon the general atmosphere. The Hôtel Continental, where I had stayed in August, one of a few journalists among a large crowd of bil-leted militia, had entirely resumed its pre-revolutionary aspect. The militia had been removed, the rooms were full of paying and fairly well-dressed guests, and business in this particular hotel seemed to be excellent.

Not only the revolutionary spirit had abated; even the war has receded. It was in Valencia, where I went a few days later, that a high official of the Government said to me in some bitterness, 'But the Catalans are not at war.'

This man was absolutely right. Very little recruitment is now going on in Barcelona. One meets convoys of foreign volunteers going farther south through Barcelona, but during the week of my stay I did not see a single convoy for the Aragon front. And news from this front, which had become entirely stagnant for many weeks, was awaited with little eagerness. As is natural in these conditions, few wounded and convalescents are to be seen in the streets.

On the other hand anxiety about air attack and even more about a naval attack was growing, and very efficient preparations were made against it. It was said that the recent bombardment of Valencia had spurred on preparations. Anyway, what is done is impressive and as usual the Catalans prove efficient in things they really want to do. Over-abundance of refuges have been prepared, and all over the town the windows of stores have been protected against the air-shock of falling bombs by the sticking of long strips of paper all over them. Artistic Mediterraneans that they are, the Barcelonese have transformed necessity into attraction and have arranged the paper on the windows in such pretty designs as to make the shops even more appealing than before, instead of spoiling them. One afternoon, at the Tibidado, I heard the heavy rolling of cannon shots, but it was only anti-naval batteries at practice. Two days later, at two o'clock in the morning, I was awakened by the same sound, but this time it was meant in earnest. A rebel cruiser was shelling the harbour, with little success, as we learned next morning. A few minutes after the first shots, the piercing sound of the sirens all over the town startled people out of their sleep. Then the light went out for thirty seconds as a warning, and three minutes later it went out for good. By this time everybody who wanted to had found safe shelter in one of the refuges. Mine was two floors below ground level and well provided with light and with chairs. It was only a few minutes after the beginning of the alarm that a night-guard arrived to see whether everything was according to regulations. I felt thoroughly well protected under such an efficient organization.

But the big problem of Barcelona is not bombs; the problem is food. And the food problem is inextricably involved in political antagonisms. To understand it a few words must first be said about the political situation.

Since August the political system of Catalonia has undergone a thorough process of simplification and unification. All the old political organizations still exist, but most of them have lost influence and significance. On the Left side the POUM, the party of the Trotskyists and the semi-Trotskyists, is in obvious decline. On the Right wing the smaller Catalan republican groups have lost what little significance they had. The Esquerra, the traditional party of radical Catalan nationalism and the one important non-working-class force in present-day Catalonia, is formally still on the top; Companys, the president of Catalonia, and Tarradellas, its Prime Minister, both belong to the Esquerra. But the process of decline of the Esquerra, obvious already in August, has continued, and it has very little power at all now. It is in circles linked with the Esquerra that one may still hear complaints about the oppressive and increasing domination of the CNT. But the Esquerra deceives itself. The time when the bourgeois republicans lost ground to the anarchists is over. The Esquerra is gradually being eliminated, but not in favour of the anarchists; in favour rather of the PSUC, the Unified Socialist-Communist Party. In reality there remain only two protagonists on the Catalan political scene, the anarchists and the PSUC. And it is the PSUC which is now obviously gaining ground.

It must be remembered that before the proclamation of the republic in 1931 there was no labour movement in Barcelona outside the CNT, though the CNT itself harboured many different political opinions. Señor Comorera, the one socialist of old standing in Barcelona, was then not a leader but an individual of hardly any political influence. Moscow communists there were practically none, but a number of Marxist elements had set out to create what later became the POUM. Since 1931 the UGT, the socialist trade-union centre, had repeatedly tried to get a foothold in Barcelona with the help of the Madrid Government, in which the socialists then held an important position. They had not been entirely unsuccessful, and the unwarrantable policy of non-participation in the 1934 insurrection did considerable damage to the anarchists. But then the anarchists had changed their policy, had taken a leading part in the July days, and *en fin de compte* had won over almost all the manual workers. Among clerks, railwaymen, and similar groups the positions of the UGT and CNT were fairly closely balanced, and hence sharply contrasted. But in the balance of forces in Catalonia as a whole the anarchists were overwhelmingly the stronger party.

Since July this balance has been upset, first slowly and then rapidly, by two concomitant factors. The first of these is the terror spread by the anarchist régime. Mass expropriations and mass executions have frightened to death the small owners, who are a very important element in Barcelona. This element had always been with the Esquerra, but since July the Esquerra has proved powerless against the anarchists. The Catalan petty bourgeoisie is more passionately Catalanist than any other group and for that reason alone, if for no other, it could never bestow its sympathies upon the fascists, who are grim Castilian centralists. But since July they were on the lookout for some protection against the CNT which would be more efficient than the Esquerra.

The attitude of the peasants, the second strong element in the social texture of Catalonia, is more problematic. In the first days of the civil war the anarchists had dealt the village bourgeoisie a terrible blow, and the process of extermination continued roughly until November. The peasant was none the worse off for it when the anarchist executed the landlord. But then terrorism sometimes did not only hit the village bourgeoisie but genuine peasant elements too. The advantages won by the extermination of the higher layer of the village proved in the end less tangible than at first appeared. The socialists and communists objected to wholesale expropriation of rents and large estates on principle. The anarchists objected to sweeping legislation on the matter for the dogmatic reason that they are opposed to centralized legislation of any kind. The outcome was that the peasant did not get an established legal status for his newly acquired property rights. On the other hand requisitions for the militia and the towns grew more burdensome as time went on. The result is that the peasants seem to be falling away from the anarchists in large numbers, and that the villages as a whole are withdrawing again from the political movement of the towns. These molecular movements weakened the position of the anarchists.

Then came the crisis of the beginning of November, when the insurgents, after having taken Toledo, rapidly approached Madrid, and everything seemed lost. At this moment Russian help came as a salvation. But Russian help did not only change the military position; it definitely upset the political balance in favour of the communists.

The Russian help was by no means extensive. They sent a certain number of specialists, instruction officers, artillery officers, pilots, and the like, whom they keep in monastic seclusion and absolute separation from the rest of the Government troops, though the fact of their existence is not kept secret. They sent, moreover, a considerable amount of material, not only once, but all through the critical time. This sending of Russian material is the more important on account of the slow development of the native Spanish armaments industry, in spite of all efforts. This slowness is mainly due, besides the traditional Spanish inefficiency in industrial matters, to the antagonism between anarchists and communists in Barcelona. The material sent by the Russians is paid for, of course. But perhaps the most important element of Russian help was neither Russian officers nor Russian bombs but the 'international brigades', the foreign volunteer forces recruited by the communists all over the world, which have played a decisive role in the defence of Madrid. These international brigades have men of almost every country of the world in their ranks, with the one exception of Russians. No volunteers except the specialists just mentioned have been recruited in Russia. But even this limited help was salvation at the moment of supreme crisis.

The arms, of course, went mostly to the Valencia Government. What remained in Catalonia went to the PSUC, to the exclusion of all other political forces, with the result that all the traditional political mechanisms in Catalonia were upset. In August the PSUC had been afraid of the overwhelming superiority of the anarchist arms, which might be used for a *coup de main* after the fall of Saragossa, then naïvely expected by everybody. Now at a stroke the PSUC grew superior in arms to the anarchists. At the same time it was put into the position of carrying on a large propaganda with considerable means; in this respect too the anarchists became inferior, and with all that all the molecular processes which had been going on since July suddenly found a point of concentration. All the elements dissatisfied with anarchist preponderance at once ranged themselves behind the PSUC.

An old rule about revolutions was once more confirmed: a revolution must either be carried through to the end, or had better not start at all. The anarchists had frightened large layers of the population without finally being able to take power into their own hands and crush all resistance. The inevitable result was the reaction against them which to-day is so evident in Barcelona. They still dominate the smaller and less important factories, especially the textile mills (whether expropriated or still managed by their former owners), because they have still the support of the majority of the manual workers. But in the much more important war industries, though still holding the allegiance of the majority of the workers, they have become dependent on the indispensable help of technical advisers who are almost invariably communists, Catalan or foreign. And among the population at large their influence is declining.

As to the PSUC its forces are increasing steadily, to a small extent from the ranks of the manual workers, to a larger one from black-coated workers and small owners. At the same time it is changing in character; at the time of the unification of socialists and communists, a few days after the July battle, the communists were a very small group indeed. Now, with the overwhelming importance of Russian material help, Russian ideological influence, and Comintern advice, and with the very strong influx of foreign communists (the great majority of them not Russians), the PSUC has become a party directed for all practical purposes by the Comintern.

And now the PSUC is attacking, attacking. The anarchists had joined the Catalan Government a few weeks before the crisis of the war in November, and before their comrades in Madrid had joined the central Spanish Government. As far as I can make out, it then was an act dictated by realistic insight into the necessity of co-operation of all anti-fascist forces in an emergency. The Catalan Government, which until then had consisted only of members of the Esquerra and smaller similar groups, was completely transformed. Together with the anarchists the PSUC joined, and Nin from the POUM got a seat as Minister of Justice. It seemed to be a move away from anarchist anti-political dogmatism, but at the same time a big move to the Left in Catalan politics. After the November crisis, however, the significance of these transformations changed completely.

Together with material and ideological help the Russians, through the intermediary of the PSUC, introduced political pressure. As a first step they obtained the dissolution of the 'central militia committee', which had been a second and more powerful government besides the official Government of the Generalitat, and had been under predominant anarchist influence. Now that the forces of the labour movement were represented in the Government, such a separate body with an authority of its own had to disappear in the interest of unified action, the PSUC argued. It is almost incredible how easily the PSUC went through with it. The Comité Central de Milicias had been the most advanced outpost of a Soviet system in Spain. It had been the intention of the anarchists to extend its powers to the limit of silent extinction of the Generalitat. Now, instead, the militia committee was extinguished, and the anarchists, instead of a powerful independent position of their own, kept nothing but a few ministerial seats. Miravitlles, the president of the Comité and the unofficial contact between the anarchists and the Esquerra, was removed to the Propaganda Ministry. The Comité de Investigaciones, a sub-section of the militia committee, which had been terrible in repressing all enemies of the revolution, was dissolved, and instead a Comité de Vigilancia was created, working under the regular administration. The Soviet phase of the Catalan revolution was at an end.

The second blow was dealt to the POUM. It is difficult to say whether it was more hateful to the PSUC on account of its anti-Stalinism in Russian affairs or its extreme Leftist tendencies in Spanish questions. Strangely enough the PSUC this second time did not pull it off so easily. As a matter of fact the POUM was liked by nobody, being overbearing and claiming with its small forces leadership over the old established mass organizations, both anarchist and socialist. All through the time of their supremacy the anarchists had handled the POUM rather rudely, but this time they felt that they were themselves concerned in the attack. The PSUC claimed the exclusion of the POUM from the Catalan Government on the ground of their alleged 'counter-revolutionary activities', meaning by that the pretended collaboration of Trotsky with the Gestapo. The anarchists resisted, and a ministerial crisis of four days ensued. But the Russians withheld important arms they had promised, and finally the anarchists had to give in.

There was no holding back the PSUC after that. They launched a campaign for the dissolution of all sorts of committees and for the full re-establishment of administrative authority of the Generalitat. At the same time, about New Year's Day, they enforced a new reconstruction of the Catalan Government, putting into the Food Ministry the man most to the Right in present Catalan politics, Comorera. The anarchist attitude to these moves was hesitant and equivocal, as the policy of revolutionary parties on the decline always is. They have lost orientation. They had to give up their old anti-authoritarian and anti-political panaceas, and now they obviously do not see a way of combining the role of a revolutionary advance-guard with co-operation in a centralized and disciplined organization of front and hinterland. The POUM is in open and obvious disintegration, some of its elements tending towards a striking of the flag; the anarchists are not in open disintegration but in a slow process of decline. They are managed in every way by the PSUC, who obviously hope either to swallow them at one moment of their evolution away from their starting-point, or to deal them a blow at a moment of still greater weakness.

With the arrival of Comorera at the Food Ministry, open conflict broke out between communists and anarchists in Catalonia. Comorera personally was heartily disliked by the anarchists, because he represented a political attitude which can best be compared with that of the extreme right wing of the German social-democracy. He had always regarded the fight against anarchism as the chief aim of socialist policy in Spain. He had disliked, from the first, the policy of nationalization of the anarchists. To his surprise, he had found unexpected allies for his dislike in the communists, who, as early as September, launched the slogan: 'Protect the property of the small industrialist.' But it was impossible to put this policy through in Catalonia. Expropriation of factories had gone much farther in Catalonia than in the rest of Spain, and had mostly started with the killing of the owners and of their heirs, unless they had managed to escape abroad or to the Franco camp. In consequence the nationalized factories under CNT control could not be denationalized. But Comorera found an opportunity to deal the policy of nationalization a big blow in his own department. It was easier to abolish State interference in the sphere of commerce than in the sphere of industry: Comorera abolished State intervention in the provisioning of Barcelona.

This provisioning had been carried out, until then, by

'bread committees' in the villages, which acted as sections of the political committees, which, in their turn, were mostly under the influence of the CNT. These bread committees co-operated with the CNT in delivering flour to the towns; the PSUC, naturally, claim that they did not co-operate but obstruct. The villages certainly were not happy about the necessity to send bread to Barcelona without adequate reward. Things certainly could not remain in such a chaotic state in this any more than in other respects. But Comorera, starting from those principles of abstract liberalism which no administration has followed during the war, but of which right-wing socialists are the last and most religious admirers, did not substitute for the chaotic bread committees a centralized administration. He restored private commerce in bread, simply and completely. There was, in January, not even a system of rationing in Barcelona. Workers were simply left to get their bread, with wages which had hardly changed since May, at increased prices, as well as they could. In practice it meant that the women had to form queues from four o'clock in the morning onwards. The resentment in the working-class districts was naturally acute, the more so as the scarcity of bread rapidly increased after Comorera had taken office. It is doubtful whether Comorera is personally responsible for this scarcity; it might have arisen anyway, in pace with the consumption of the harvest. But now the anarchists saw their opportunity to charge Comorera with the bread shortage. He had attempted to break the economic policy of the anarchists; he had, they alleged, created a major crisis in consequence. And both parties began to attack one another publicly with the utmost acerbity. 'Stickybacks' of the anarchist youth organization (which could hardly have been issued without the consent of CNT headquarters) clamoured for the resignation of Comorera, a man 'inept and of bad faith'. The PSUC replied by posters, some of them anonymous, reading 'Less talk; less committees; more bread; all power to the Generalitat!'

The food problem, thus, must be envisaged under at least three aspects. In one sense, it is an object of contention between the anarchist ideal of collective management of supplies and the republican and communist policy of protecting private trade all along the line. In another respect, it serves as a weapon in the general fight between anarchists on the one hand and republicans and PSUC on the other hand; the PSUC utilizing it to discredit the committees and the anarchists trying to discredit, with the food shortage, the PSUC Food Minister. But finally the problem of supplies, inevitably, however much politicians of all shades would like not to think of that, is the problem of feeding the population with food, rather than with mutual recriminations. And in this last respect the consequences are disastrous. There is, of course, nothing as yet comparable to the sufferings of the civil population of the Central Powers in the last years of the World War; there is, however, considerable shortage. This shortage undermines the morale, the enthusiasm, the pride, and the sense of power of precisely that class which, in July, seemed to own complete power, while small shopkeepers and merchants are much better off in this respect. And this, in its turn, leads to incidents. One Sunday afternoon I watched a particularly unpleasant scene. In the street I was passing through were two bakeries and queues waiting at their doors, of together perhaps 300 or 400 people. They were watched by nine *asaltos*, seven on foot and two on horse, all in their pre-revolutionary uniforms, rifles shouldered and loaded with live cartridges. As it was Sunday the queues were composed of men and women in about equal numbers. Both shops were closed, and the people were vainly waiting for bread. At one moment one of the two bakers put a poster at his door, to the effect that no bread would be distributed on this day. Murmurs, outcries, a certain amount of unrest, but no attempt at any sort of action, among the waiting crowd. But the *asaltos* are used to certain methods from pre-revolutionary times and they do not hesitate to use them now. The two horsemen drove their horses up the pavement, and made them turn round and round on the pavement among the exasperated crowd in such a way that the men and women in the queue came again and again in contact with the hind

185

hoofs of the horses. It is not a cruel, but a particularly unpleasant procedure, the more unpleasant as there had been
no sort of disorder. The crowd, after all, was small, and what
was needed, what, I believe, every police officer in London
would have done in a similar situation, was not to make the
people acquainted with the hind hoofs of horses, but to talk to
them quietly and ask them to go home. But the *asaltos* judged
it expedient to intimate to the crowd the advisability of going
home, not with words but with hind hoofs. The reason is obvious. The Spanish police of the old régime has no democratic
training whatever; the guardia was accustomed to killing and
handcuffing and to nothing else. The *asaltos*, to be true, have
been created under the republic, but have served, for most of
their existence, under an anti-democratic government and
differ little in their mentality from the guardia. And these
police forces, trained under the autocracy, are now put in
contact with revolutionary workers trained by the CNT,
standing hungrily in queues. I told some friends of the incident, only to learn that what I had observed by chance was
far from being the worst case. There had been, I was told,
two very bad bread riots, and the police had dispersed the
crowd, mostly women, by beating them with the butt-ends of
their rifles.

There are other matters of contention between the parties,
less distressing to the masses, but not less important. One
of them is the army question. At present Catalonia has practically two armies. The one is the Ejército Popular, based on
recruitment, composed of non-party units commanded by old
police and army officers, practically in the hands of the
PSUC; this army is guarding the coast-line. They were the
troops I saw on my journey from Port Bou to Barcelona. The
other is the Huesca-Saragossa army, which continues, I am
told, on the old lines of the militia of the early days, with very
little change, is under dominating anarchist influence, and
still has its political commanders, with military officers in an
advisory capacity only. The antagonism between these two
armies is doubtless one important factor in the complete
standstill of operations at the Aragon front. In principle the

anarchists admit the necessity of reorganizing the militia. But in practice every item is contentious. The PSUC aim at the complete abolition of all features of a revolutionary army. Not only shall the officers be appointed from above, but there shall be no soldiers' councils, no soldiers' meetings. The privates shall salute the officers in a military manner. The old ranks and distinctions shall be re-established. In one word, they want a regular army, under a military commander, who, inevitably, would be either an officer of the old army or a foreign specialist, and in either case a man under their influence. The anarchists are in a bad dilemma. The whole reorganization goes against their principles. The militia of the type created in the first days is their pet achievement. Still, the military inadequacy of this type of armed force is beyond doubt. But if they reorganize the force, it will slip out of their hands. Deadlock, then, indecision, wavering, with the probable result that for months to come Catalonia will be severely handicapped in its participation in the war. On the other hand, the anarchists, if armed power slips completely out of their hands, cannot expect to find mercy at the hands of the PSUC. In every revolution armed power decides, in the last resort; the anarchists can hardly be reproached for knowing it. Sooner or later they will be destroyed unless they keep an army of their own. No middle way, then, between remaining inefficient in the field and making a big step back from the revolutionary starting-point in politics. This is the dilemma, the blank wall against which the Spanish revolution has been constantly and painfully butting since November 1936.

To sum up, one must realize that the swing of the pendulum has been wider in Catalonia than in other parts of Spain. Catalonia was always the centre of revolutionary movements in Spain, and after 19 July had far outdistanced the rest of the country in the drive towards social revolution. Before the rest of Spain could follow, the war became a matter of such overwhelming importance as to swallow up all other considerations; and with the defeats came communist preponderance in the rest of Spain, and Catalonia, with its advanced tendencies, was isolated. It is this isolation of a re-volutionary vanguard which advanced too far in the first days that gives an acute and cruel note to the antagonisms in Barcelona. All the moderate groups have lived in greater fear in Barcelona than anywhere else, and are more eager now to take their revenge, the more so because the CNT is still the strongest and a very menacing power on the spot, and the forces brought into action against it are mostly non-Catalan and partly non-Spanish. The deadlock at the Aragon front is one more important factor in the present tension. A serious defeat there might, however, bring about a sudden concilia-tion between the contending parties.

Valencia: The Central Government

The journey from Barcelona to Valencia this time was very different from that in August. Then it was like peace. Now it reminded me very much of trains during the World War. On the way the train, first as well as third class, got crowded with troops, who were being rushed from the North to the Anda-lusian front, where the issue of the fighting lies in the balance. We arrived in Valencia three hours late, at two o'clock in the morning. The town was pitch-dark, all the hotels over-crowded, and I spent the second half of the night uncomfort-ably in an armchair. Next day I found myself a room in an hotel, not without difficulty. But if the lodgings problem in Valencia is naturally very acute, the food situation was a very easy one. Only meat and potatoes were somewhat scarce; in the hotels there are so-called 'war meals' of 'only' four dishes, which may seem a restriction to Spaniards, who are spoiled as to cooking; for me anyway it was more than I could con-sume.

Barcelona was obviously restless, Valencia was not at all. It has kept its gay and easy-going ways unchanged. There seems to have been considerable excitement during the naval bom-bardment of the harbour in mid-January, but it was already forgotten. The complete extinction of lights in the streets at ten at night was thus the one measure involving a real change in the habits of life. Moreover, Valencia has reason to be gay. The arrival of the Government with so many people has brought a boom to shops and hotels, while the construction of refuges is keeping the building trade busy. There was a bit more recruiting in Valencia than in Barcelona. There were numbers of military parades and similar displays just suited to the Valencian temperament.

On the whole, things in Valencia had not so definitely moved away from the July days as in Barcelona. As in Barcelona, there are fortunately many less executions now than then. As in Barcelona, there is a certain reassertion of centralism. The days when Valencia was governed by its Comité Ejecutivo Popular in practical independence of the central Government were over. Once the Comité Ejecutivo has even been officially dissolved, but it continues to exist and to co-operate with the Government with not more than the usual amount of friction. The November crisis was a turning-point in Valencia as elsewhere. It brought the Government, and an armed clash between communists and anarchists, ending with the defeat of the latter. But the trend of local political opinion is rather towards the Left compared not only with Barcelona to-day but even compared with Valencia itself in August. Then Valencia had what almost amounted to a Soviet system, but behind the screen of a revolutionary régime it remained thoroughly 'petty bourgeois' and non-revolutionary. Now, with the headquarters of the whole socialist and communist organization within its walls, it is much more genuinely tinged with socialism. Expropriation has continued. Most of the hotels, restaurants, and cinemas are now either under the control of workers, or under direct workers' management. The orange trade is controlled by the two trade unions. There are still armed workers in civilian clothes acting as street- and night-guards.

When we turn from local to national conditions, the picture is somewhat different. National conditions to-day must be studied chiefly in Valencia because here is the seat of the Government. And the outcome of such a study is again to

emphasize the rapidly increasing importance of the Communist Party.

The formation of the Caballero Government, after the
complete failure of the republicans to organize the defence
against Franco and to secure foreign help, had marked the
high tide of the tendency to the Left. But then Caballero was
not more successful in defending Toledo and San Sebastian
than the republicans had been in defending Extremadura. Under the blows dealt to the republican cause by
Franco the intrinsic weakness of the Left-wing socialists even
within their own party became apparent. Only a very few of
the old socialist leaders had really moved to the Left. Of
them, Araquistain had gone as Ambassador to Paris. Caballero is not a young man, and thus Alvarez del Vayo remained
as the one strong personality of the Left wing. But one man is
an individual and not a tendency. The hold of the UGT and
the Socialist Party on the masses is weak as compared with
the roots of the CNT. And the one region really deeply influenced by the UGT, Asturias, is· with the right wing of the
party, at least as far as the leader of this region, Gonzalez
Peña, is concerned. Caballero owed his position not to his
own force but to the defeat of the republicans, and to the un-
willingness or incapacity of the CNT to assume political
power.

November came, and with it the Moors of Franco approached the suburbs of Madrid. Caballero had to hand over
the reality of power to the first claimant who could offer
genuine help. The Communist Party, with Russia behind it,
was this claimant. And, in consequence, the communists became the predominant power in the camp of the anti-Franco
forces. This predominance they derive mainly from the armed
help they have given, in forms explained above, and from the
organizing achievements they have to their credit. But how
are these achievements transformed into political power?
Not, in the first place, by increased influence among the
masses of the workers. It is true that the membership of the
Communist Party has increased very considerably. They
went into the civil war with some 3,000 members at the ut-

most. At the end of January they claimed a membership of 220,000. As a matter of fact, all or almost all Left parties have increased their membership, but such an increase as that claimed by the communists is out of proportion to the average. Spanish figures are not precisely the most reliable thing in the world of statistics, but general observation indicates that at least the general trend is correctly reflected in the official membership figures of the Communist Party. Moreover, there is no doubt that the military recruitment of the communist Fifth Regiment has been much more successful, both in quantity and quality, than that of any other army unit. But this is only one side of the picture. The real influence of a party in the working-class movement is measured more correctly by the control it is able to exert over definite sections of the movement than by membership figures. In this respect the balance is less favourable for the communists than the increase of their membership and military influence might suggest. Since July the communists have not won over, either from the anarchists or from the socialists, a single trade-union branch of manual workers, a single large factory, a single industrial region. They have won over branches of State and private employee trade unions, and villages and country districts in considerable number. The communists claim that if and when there are free elections in the UGT—which are suspended during the civil war—they would win over a considerable number of the UGT branches. The fact is, however, that where the communist influence became really overwhelming, it had to be taken into account, even without elections. Again, in factories, the change of political leadership can be effected by means other than elections, notably by the change of political allegiance of the most influential workers. There seems to be very little of that. The explanation of the contrast between membership figures and influence among the workers seems to lie in the fact that the Communist Party has changed its social character. This is most obvious in the case of the Catalan PSUC, practically a section of the Spanish communists. Not many industrial workers are members of the PSUC, but it claims, nevertheless, 46,000 members, the majority of whom are State and private employees, shopkeepers, merchants, officers, members of the police forces, intellectuals both in town and country, and a certain number of peasants. The percentage of workers in the Communist Party must be somewhat larger in the rest of Spain than in Catalonia, but still it is certainly not a very high one; and, on the other hand, the communists have undoubtedly stronger peasant support in some parts of Spain, particularly in the *huerta de Valencia*, than in Catalonia. The Communist Party, to a large extent, is to-day the party of the military and administrative personnel, in the second place the party of the petty bourgeoisie and certain well-to-do peasant groups, in the third place the party of the employees, and only in the fourth place the party of the industrial workers. Having entered the movement with almost no organization, it has attracted, in the course of the civil war, those elements with whose views and interests its policy agreed. It is an evolution of wide significance, not only for the present and future political situation in Spain, but for international politics in general.

But communist influence does not work to-day through its party organization only, or even in the first place. It mainly works through a policy of merging organizations formerly independent, under predominant communist influence. The PSUC in Catalonia is one classical example, and the Unified Socialist Youth, which in September was overwhelmingly under the influence of the Caballero group and is now practically a communist organization, is another. The process, of course, finds its limits where anarchist influence of old standing exists.

Two years ago the Communist International could not even conceive of political advance by any other means than by fighting every other organization to a knock-out. Now, on the contrary, there is very little open fighting, but a truly Fabian policy of permeation which, as far as the influence of the Comintern is concerned, is proving much more successful. The basic original communist conception of a fight to the finish with all other working-class organizations has been abandoned.

The remarkable thing in Spain, however, is that this process of permeation does not proceed by personal influence. The two strong personalities the communists had in Spain, Nin and Maurin, have both left the Comintern long ago and founded the POUM (Maurin, it seems, has fallen into the hands of the insurgents and been executed). The present leaders of the Communist Party, Diaz, Mije, Jesus Hernandez, Uribe, and others, are hardly known to the masses, and certainly do not owe their influence to their personal prestige. And La Passionaria, who has an enormous amount of personal influence, is not a political leader. A certain amount of political leadership is provided by the Russian ambassador, Rosenberg, and the Russian consul in Barcelona, Antonov-Ovseenko, the latter being the military leader of the Bolshevist insurrection in Petrograd in November 1917. But these are foreigners, who can give advice but who cannot stand before the eyes of the masses.

Communist influence, after all, works neither through a dominating organization nor through dominating personalities, but through a policy which is welcome to the republicans and the Right-wing socialists and which has the backing of such supremely important factors as the international brigades, the command of General Kleber in Madrid, and Russian help in general. Neither the republicans nor the Right-wing socialists are strong political forces in themselves. In fine, increasing communist influence to-day is a symptom of the shifting of the movement from the political to the military and from the social to the organizational factor. It is military and organizing, not political, influence which gives the communists their strength, and indirectly makes them the politically dominant factor.

How is this domination expressed? In the policy followed. And that policy is one of strict limitation of the movement to the fight against Franco. This is expressed in the slogan, 'the defence of the democratic republic', but if democratic republic means freedom of organization, of the Press, and of movement for political forces, then there is no such thing and there can be no such thing in Spain at present. The Spanish revolution in its bitter straits could not allow itself the luxury which has proved too much for revolutions in an easier situation: the luxury of free political movement. 'Democratic republic' then is not a present state of things to be defended, but a former state of things which it is hoped will be reinstated after the victory over Franco. In reality it is impossible to predict what conditions will then obtain. The slogan of the democratic republic in Spain is a serious departure from the original ideas of Lenin and his organization. It is on the whole apt to create for the communists more new allies than new enemies. Such revolutionary trends as take offence at the new turn, anarchists and Trotskyists are declining. On the other hand the new political attitude allows the communists to move swiftly towards a union with the socialists, at least with those of the Right wing, with whom their principles have become practically identical. It is common knowledge that attempts are being made to bring about the complete merging of socialists and communists in Spain. At present they have a common newspaper in Valencia, *Verdad* (the title being a literal translation of the Russian *Pravda*). And behind the chance of merging with the socialists lurks the bigger chance of closer alliance with the democratic countries.

A policy ought not to be interpreted in terms of its general ideology but more in terms of its concrete acts. What are the communists driving at in Spain at present? Besides unification with the socialists the communists aim, and quite successfully, at the closest possible collaboration with the republicans. This collaboration is not made too public as far as Señor Martinez Barrios's Union Republicana is concerned. But it is known that such a close collaboration exists, and at one time Martinez Barrios was even mentioned as a future Prime Minister who would be agreeable to the communists.

But if communist collaboration with Union Republicana is going on behind the scenes, this is not the case with Izquierda Republicana, the party of Azaña, the president of the republic. One day, not long ago, Azaña made a speech in which he expressly deprecated any attempt at revolution, and limited the aims of the struggle to the defence of the parliamentary

THE SECOND JOURNEY

democracy within the framework of the existing social system. This speech, which was almost a declaration of war on the anarchists and a formal repeal of the revolutionary declarations made at the accession of the Caballero Government, has found emphatic and unlimited approval in the communist Press, and is known to have been based on a previous agreement between Azaña and the communists. The anarchists, as usual, were wavering. *Fragua Social*, their Valencia newspaper, attacked Azaña, and got a scolding for it from *Solidaridad Obrera*, the Barcelona anarchist paper and central organ of the CNT-FAI. There is no difference whatever, at present, nor has been since the beginning of the civil war, between Izquierda Republicana, the party of the non-socialist republicans, and the communists. And this agreement of views is not limited to the present phase of the civil war but, for reasons soon to be explained, seems to be an understanding for good, even in the field of the social régime. To-day a unification of the communists with Izquierda Republicana might find fewer obstacles than even one with the socialists. Members of both parties speak with the highest respect of their respective organizations. As one young republican editor, now political commissar of a militia column in Malaga, put it to me, 'The communists have been best in organizing work: and moreover they are by far the most conservative section of the movement. I do not see any reason why I should not be a communist, and probably I will join the party one day.' The saying about the communists as the most conservative section has become almost proverbial among all sorts of people, from stiffly anti-socialist foreign observers to anarchists.

Summing up, and taking into account the disintegration of the POUM on the one hand, of the Left wing of the socialists on the other, the close collaboration of the communists with the Right-wing socialists on the one hand and the two republican groups on the other, one is faced with a definite tendency towards a complete political unification of the movement, with the anarchists as the one serious obstacle to it. But this *is* a serious obstacle, in spite of the undeniable

195

decline of the anarchists. And anarchist opposition proves of considerable weight in the crucial question of the moment, which is the transformation of the Government.

The communists are decided that Caballero must go. They find it awkward, and at critical moments almost intolerable, that the group which really directs affairs should not be formally and publicly at the helm. If a dramatic turn to the Right, away from social revolution is intended—as no doubt it is—it cannot possibly be done while Caballero is in the supreme office. Various names have been mentioned as candidates for the premiership, among them Martinez Barrios, Prieto, and Negrin, the socialist Minister of Finance. Since at least the last week of January well-informed people have been talking about the cabinet crisis. But so far nothing has come of it. And that mainly on account of anarchist resistance. A cabinet with Prieto as premier or in a dominating position, as War Minister, would make their participation either impossible or transform it into a formal renunciation of their revolutionary faith.

Many attempts have been made to subdue anarchist resistance. In this matter, as in so many others, November was the decisive moment. When the Government evacuated Madrid complete chaos automatically ensued for a short while in many parts of the country, and the anarchists, as the one remaining revolutionary force, saw themselves automatically in command. In Madrid, while all the rest of the cabinet had gone, two anarchist ministers remained. They did not, however, make a bid for power and after a few days, the Junta de Defensa was formed, under predominantly communist influence. Two roads were open from Madrid to Valencia, the one through Tarancon, the other one through Cuenca. Both places, at this moment of general disintegration, fell into the hands of the anarchists. An anarchist picket at Tarancon made it its business to stop all male fugitives from Madrid, among them the Government. Only through the personal energy of del Vayo was the Government allowed to pass. Still, the incident was sufficiently significant. The anarchists made themselves a great nuisance on the road, but they did not seriously attempt to arrest the Government, and after having been scolded by one single energetic man, allowed the Government to continue on its way. The chief officials of the UGT made their way through Cuenca. There they found themselves seriously menaced and in danger of their lives for a few hours, but were later released finally and unconditionally. Half-hearted and aimless anarchist risings called for violent repression from the other side. In Valencia the anarchists organized a big demonstration on the occasion of a funeral, and showed some intention of turning it into a *coup de main*. But the intention was not definite, they got their cortège into a trap, incidents produced a row, and the anarchists, surprised in a narrow square by communist machine-guns from three sides, suffered heavy losses. The *élan* of the anarchist offensive in Valencia was broken. Tarancon, I was told, from a source which had otherwise proved reliable, one day found itself bombed by planes which did not seem to belong to Franco. In Cuenca the process seems to have been long drawn out. There, the local communists managed to get police work into the hands of the Unified Socialist Youth, which made short work of the anarchist 'uncontrollables'. It seems that in Cuenca, earlier than in other places, one chief element of communist policy found application; a skilful distinction between 'good' and 'bad' anarchists. In the meantime the Junta de Defensa had been created in Madrid, the first international brigades and the first Russian air squadrons had appeared and scored the first successes for the Government. Even the anarchists had to admit that discipline and organization had been some use. Under these circumstances the distinction between official anarchists and the so-called 'uncontrollables' got hold.

What are the 'uncontrollables'? The meaning varies with the political purpose for which the term is employed. Sometimes one calls 'uncontrollables' simply those criminal elements which, in decreasing numbers, commit 'expropriations' and 'executions' on their own account, without any sort of authorization, but under the guise of anarchist opinions. But at other times all elements which display some sort

THE SECOND JOURNEY

of activity escaping centralized control are called 'uncontrollables'; then many dozens of village committees whose views on the agrarian question differ from those of the Minister of Agriculture (the communist Uribe) may find themselves, to their surprise, qualified as 'uncontrollables' and put in the same rank with simple criminals. After the November crisis the anarchist leadership decided to collaborate in the fight against the 'uncontrollables'. And it seems that in Cuenca earlier than in other places a wedge was driven, by this fight, between the anarchist leadership and its 'uncontrollable' supporters. Anyway, Cuenca, which had been a centre of anarchism, became soon a model UGT town. Dozens and dozens of similar processes must have evolved in these weeks all over republican Spain. First a half-hearted and aimless anarchist attack, then serious reprisals of one sort or another by the communists, the UGT, and the Government, backed by the new material force and moral authority of the international brigades, the Russian command and help, and the Russian pilots. The invariable result was that the communists got the superiority in material strength, and the allegiance of the whole non-proletarian element, and that the anarchist advance was stopped. The anarchists kept control over those elements which had followed them before 19 July, and not much more.

But these initial successes against anarchist violence were only the prelude to a more important subsequent fight about important social matters. None of these is more characteristic than the one raging around the CLUEA. Its description may stand for many other similar instances. The CLUEA is an official organization for the marketing of the orange crop, which is supremely important for the acquisition of foreign exchange. It is a joint organization of CNT and UGT, representing all trades concerned in handling the orange crop, packers, transport workers, shippers; but, characteristically enough, not the orange-growing peasants themselves. These latter, on the average, are one of the wealthiest elements among the Spanish peasantry, and before the civil war were the backbone of the Derecha Valenciana, a Catholic conservative regionalistic group. To-day, one of the best observers of the problem tells me, they are mostly with the Communist Party. Technically, the CLUEA works fairly well. Oranges are sold and transported, partly by ship, but not, of course, in such quantities as in normal times. But the CLUEA is able to fulfil its contracts as to the delivery of oranges and is able to pay for its own buyings abroad cash down. There are only a few complaints as to the quality of the oranges. But the main trouble lies in the furious antagonism between the CLUEA as a representative of the trade unions on the one hand and the communists and the peasants on the other. The Ministry of Agriculture, under the Communist Uribe as minister, is fighting the CLUEA, and as a reply *Fragua Social*, the anarchist newspaper, attacks Uribe bitterly. The contest, as is natural, is about the prices the peasant gets for his oranges. In abstract, these prices are fixed by the prices obtainable on the international market. But these prices never directly touched the peasant, who, before the civil war, sold his oranges, not to a public organization, but to local merchants. These merchants, now, have been excluded from the local market and only a few of the more important ones are still active in helping the CLUEA on the markets abroad. Instead, the Ministry of Agriculture pays to the CLUEA 50 per cent. of the international prices in advance on the delivery of their crop, the remaining 50 per cent., after deduction of the expenses, to be paid after the sale of the oranges has become effective. This latter half of the revenue is not tangible at present; the orange harvest is just proceeding. And the first half is not paid directly to the peasants, but to the CLUEA, which has not only to pay for the oranges, but its own staff and the wages of the transport workers and seamen as well. The communists contend that as a result of the mediation of the CLUEA very little of the money paid out by the Ministry of Agriculture reaches the peasants. There is no reason to doubt the substantial truth of this contention. On the other hand, the trade unions represented in the CLUEA and the anarchists charge the communists with the intention of breaking up trade-union control altogether and wanting to hand back the orange trade to private merchants, who, as a matter of fact, still hold the trade in agricultural products in most parts of Spain. Again there is no reason to doubt the substantial truth of this contention of the partisans of the CLUEA. The CLUEA further contend that private merchants, when delivering the oranges abroad, would be paid with drafts upon foreign places; that there are no means to control their dealings abroad; and that they certainly would not care to get their accounts in foreign exchange into republican Spain, but would prefer either to let them stay abroad or, still worse, bring them into insurgent territory. And foreign exchange is the crucial matter. The peasant may be badly provided for in the CLUEA organization, but as to foreign exchange the CLUEA, being virtually a State monopoly in foreign trade of the most important Spanish export commodity, is as efficient as it can reasonably be expected to be.

Who is right and who is wrong in this debate? It seems to me that, as is so often the case, every party is right in its criticism of its adversaries. Not one side seems to be wrong, but rather the whole position seems to be untenable. The root of the evil is the profound antagonism between the wealthy peasants of the *huerta de Valencia* and the trade unions. Only a joint organization of both elements could smooth out differences and establish rules which would satisfy all parties concerned. An organization of the peasants alone, which would be bound to be dominated by the wealthy element, would naturally be out of sympathy with the present régime. An exclusively trade unionist organization under anarchist predominance, as the CLUEA, can hardly be expected to take account even of the most elementary needs of the peasants. Were the peasantry of the *huerta* poor and starving, as that of Andalusia or La Mancha, no such antagonism would exist. But, unfortunately for the republican Government, the olivegroves of Andalusia are mostly in the hands of the insurgents. The Valencia Government must treat about the valorization of its most important crop with a disaffected element. In the matter of the CLUEA the Spanish revolution meets, on a reduced scale, the problem which was paramount in the

Russian revolution, the 'kulak', the wealthy, conservative, disaffected peasant. One cannot pretend that its methods of dealing with the problem are very happily chosen. It seems, that, *en fin de compte*, the orange crop is collected by the peasants under the impression that they will get an advance of 50 per cent. of its value, a promise which is not kept; and that 'soft' violence is helping where promises fail. One or two serious incidents have already arisen. The village of Cullera revolted, declared its independence (!), burned flashlights at the coast, and turned a few cannons dramatically against Valencia, more than fifteen miles away. It was a childish attempt, which, besides swift repression by the Government, brought on them a bombardment by insurgent planes attracted by the flashlights. But it is symptomatic. The basic element of the whole situation is that the communists, in contrast with past practice in Russia, are not here and now with the workers ruthlessly against the 'kulak', but with the 'kulak' against the trade unions. Some people go so far as to contend that they try to work directly through the old Catholic organizations.

I do not know whether this is true. Anyway the communists please the rich peasants by opposing the anti-religious movement. They have expressed their disapproval at the recent conference of the Unified Socialist Youth. I do not think many people will approve of the church-burning which occurred in many parts of Spain in July; it was a barbarism and a political mistake. Where Catholicism was on the decline the measure was useless; where it was vigorous it must have created increased antagonism to the republican cause. The present situation, however, is that there are surprisingly few difficulties about religion in republican Spain. There is hardly any instance of a movement similar to the passionate defence of Catholicism in the French Revolution. No secret masses said, no priests going to give the blessings of religion to the faithful at the danger of their lives. Catholic convictions, or at least Catholic habits, have been deeply ingrained in the lower classes of the Spanish people, and penetrate deeply into the revolutionary ranks. If they have failed to produce any effect whatsoever in the present crisis of Spanish Catholicism, that is mainly due to the attitude of the Spanish clergy. It is not only, and not in the first place, a problem of their behaviour before the civil war. Undoubtedly many members of the Spanish hierarchy have not led the sort of life they might reasonably be expected to lead. They have sinned through lack of care, lack of knowledge, through greediness and vice; but all this might be readily forgotten if the Spanish Church, in compensation for a past not altogether creditable, had proved able to win the glory of martyrdom. It has demonstrated its deep decay by its complete incapacity to do so. Many priests have been surprised by the July events and been killed because they were unable to flee in time. But very few cases are known where a priest has gone back to his parish in order secretly to dispense to his flock the blessings of the sacrament under persecution. French Catholicism survived the crisis of the revolution successfully, in spite of many misdeeds under the *ancien régime*, because, when called to martyrdom, it gave martyrs in large numbers for the Catholic faith. Nothing like this is happening to-day in Spain. And the flocks, abandoned by their natural leaders, the priests, lose interest. In a time of wholesale self-sacrifice of hundreds and thousands of revolutionaries for their convictions, the fact that the Catholic Church cannot put forward a dozen cases of heroic self-sacrifice is naturally disastrous for its cause. Hence there is certainly no immediate difficulty for the Government in the religious problem. (And no more priests are killed, no more churches burnt now. On the other hand, the Catholic clergy in the Basque country readily sacrifice everything for the cause of their flocks in the struggle against Franco.)

Other problems too turn upon this inextricable muddle, the agrarian question. It is a question to which many journalists and foreign observers pay very little attention, but it seems to me to be in reality almost the crucial point of the whole movement. In practice very little seems to have changed in the conditions of landed property since August. But instead a major political conflict has arisen about the conditions created in the countryside during the first months of the movement.

Investigation has become much more difficult since. Neutral journalists simply do not get permits now to go and investigate on the spot. Still, from newspapers, travellers' tales, and occasional observations during my own trip to Malaga, I found I could get a fair amount of information. Rents to the large landowners have been paid nowhere. The effect of this abolition of rents ought to be enormous because the usual arrangement is that 50 per cent. of the total crop is paid as rent in kind. In practice the effect is diminished by requisitioning, direct and indirect, such as has been described in the case of the CLUEA. The large expropriated estates remain on the hands of the committees, or rather, with the decline of the committees (to which further reference will be made), in the hands of the municipalities, which run them by the labour of their old workers under the old conditions. But sometimes, as on some wheat farms in La Mancha, or on the sugar-cane farms of Malaga, they have been collectivized by the labourers and are worked by them under their own management. Peasant property, on the whole, has not been touched, with the exception of the land of friends of the insurgents. The crops of the peasant go still largely to the local merchants, who make splendid profits from them. But in a certain not altogether insignificant number of cases peasant lands have been 'collectivized' by the anarchists. Sometimes such collectivized farms seem to work fairly well; one famous case is the collectivization of a couple of orange-groves in the province of Murcia. Very often they do not work well at all. (I described one such utterly unsatisfactory collectivization, in Castro del Rio, in the diary of my first journey; this particular village has since been occupied by the rebels.) The communists have started a big campaign against these collectivizations, which, they contend, are mostly forced upon the peasants by the anarchists, against their will. And what insufficient attention is given to the agrarian problem is centred, in all parties, upon this question of the peasant 'collectivities'.

The communists have undoubtedly a very strong case. Collectivization, without introduction of modern agricultural engines for large-scale production, such as tractors, cannot appeal to the peasant, must remain inefficient, and is likely to muddle up things in the villages, where the situation is already difficult enough. It is difficult to decide how far, in individual cases, these collectivizations are voluntary and how far enforced. What really matters is how far these new economic units have a chance to succeed, and in consequence to appeal to the peasant in a reasonably near future. I think the scepticism of the communists in this respect is well justified. Capital is needed to make large collectivized estates practicable, and, in addition, competent advice and leadership. Neither is available under the conditions of civil war. As things stand premature agricultural collectivizations are rather the last remnants of the old anarchist faith, which attempted to base a new society on moral enthusiasm and force only, irrespective of immediate practical conditions. The Ministry of Agriculture tries an alternative policy: it has at its disposal a certain amount of foreign exchange and uses it to acquire agricultural implements, mostly fertilizers, which it puts into the hands of individual landowners. It did so first at prices considerably lower than its own costs, and does so now at cost prices, i.e. still at prices considerably lower than ordinary market prices. Still, fertilizers are not within the reach of the average Spanish peasant (who would be more apt, in his destitution, to welcome collectivization than the small stratum of wealthy peasants). Again, in the problem of collectivization and agricultural implements, the communists play the wealthy peasants against the poor and against the anarchists. The attempts of the anarchists are childish.

But the worst thing about the whole matter of collectivization is the attention it gets at all. Collectivization is a pet idea of the anarchists and consequently makes a fit bone of contention between them and their adversaries. But that does not mean that it is the most important aspect of the agrarian problem. Busy with their wild antagonism, both communists and anarchists forget that the peasant is completely in the dark about the official policy concerning the expropriated land, both of the large landowners and of those smaller peasants who have fled or been executed as enemies of the régime. Sometimes this oblivion of the central problem is almost grotesque. The province of Jaen (which I described in the diary of my first journey) is one where at least 90 per cent. of the land not only belongs to grandees, but is managed as large estates. At the congress of the Unified Socialist Youth a young peasant from this province got up and at some length discussed the matter of the collectivization of the miserable lots which the peasants of his district prefer to hold in private ownership rather than to have collectively managed. But he forgot to mention the enormous estates which had remained in the hands of such municipalities as Andujar and Bailén, and which, if dealt with either by collectivization or popular division, would make the peasants forget altogether the argument about their miserable holdings, from which they draw starvation crops. The Spanish revolution set out to give the peasant the land of the grandee, individually or collectively. Instead of doing so it has landed itself in the *impasse* of discussing whether the peasants' *own* land ought to be owned individually or collectively. And the blindness as to this central problem is the same among communists, socialists, and anarchists, not to mention the POUM, which prefers to remain in the lofty realm of Marxist abstractions.

Still worse, the peasant is not sure, at present, about the fate of the crops of his own land. Requisitions are an inevitable necessity of war, whether done openly or under the screen of currency inflation. The peasant does not know clearly, however, what he is expected to give; and does not know in what way he will later be rewarded. He is left in uncertainty and growing restlessness. The wealthy peasants of the *huerta de Valencia* and similar districts may be at least indifferent to a success of the insurgents. But this is not the case in the larger part of Spain. Wherever the insurgents advance, thousands and thousands of peasants leave their homes. They do so not only to avoid bombs and shells; else they would hide in the mountains and come back after a few days. They flee because they are dead-scared of the rebels. They have listened to the tales of peasants from villages occupied by the Franco troops; those peasants tell of executions and of ruthless oppression.

The large majority of the Spanish peasants are poor, and they are used to regard the landowner, the police, the troops, and even the priests as their natural enemies, against whom they now seek shelter behind the lines of the republican army. But at the same time these peasants have given very few volunteers indeed to the Government troops, and even the spontaneous defence of their own villages has now, in contrast to the first months, become rather the exception than the rule. They know from what to flee, but they hardly know for what to fight. The insurgents would take much from them, but the republic has given them nothing substantial. Their attitude is in accordance with this situation.

Still, if there is practically no volunteering for the army in the villages, there is no resistance against conscription either. In a general way, all men between twenty and thirty should be conscripted. But as there are not sufficient registers, those who want to do so can easily hide. It is the more significant that the majority of the young men of the villages present themselves at the conscription offices and regard it as a shame if they are rejected for some physical defect. Still, there is a long way between being accepted and getting to the front. If boys dislike the training—and many do—it is not difficult for them to find their way back to their native village, and there they are beyond any efficient control. One must keep in mind, in judging this state of things, that anyway there would not be enough rifles to arm all the men available for the Government, which, in consequence, has little interest in forcing unwilling elements into the army. Compulsory military service is the chief slogan of the Communist Party (together with the demand for a unified command), but its realization is not only dependent on the willingness of the authorities to accept it, but upon a satisfactory solution of the armament problem. Those young men who finally get into the war are distributed among the so-called 'mixed brigades', an institution similar to the famous *amalgame* of the French Revolution. They consist partly of old militia volunteers and partly of new conscripts. The militia organization, of course, has disappeared; commanders are named, discipline is introduced. But these mixed brigades are not yet organized all over Spain. In some parts, Malaga, for instance, the old system, based exclusively on volunteers, still prevails, for no particular reason except the slowness with which reorganization is put into effect. All over Spain there exist anarchist columns which now are unified as *milicias confederales*, but which, owing to their exclusive political character, do not willingly accept politically nondescript recruits.

After all, the formation of one unified republican army is a thing easier to demand than to put into effect. The communists too, though they are the chief promoters of army reorganization, have their own troops, the so-called Fifth Regiment, which, to-day, is anything but a 'regiment'. It has between 60,000 and 70,000 men, and is by far the strongest military unit of the republic. Among its thirty-two brigades are the international brigades which have played such an important part in saving Madrid. The membership of the Fifth Regiment is not exclusively communist; one brigade even consists in the main of foreign anarchists. But the leadership and the general political spirit is definitely communist. There is talk about the dissolution of the Fifth Regiment and its merging in the regular army of the republic, but so far none of its brigades has been dissolved and it is not easy to see how it could be done as long as other political groups keep their own troops. It is perhaps no exaggeration to say that in a revolution a unified army is dependent on complete unification of political leadership. The latter everybody desires, but very naturally everybody desires it to be his own leadership. Unified political leadership would mean agreement about immediate policy; and this is lacking. In the meantime nobody doubts that the communists have given the republic its best troops. It is obviously their chief service to the republican cause.

But they try to introduce the methods of military discipline into civil politics too. I have already mentioned their drive towards a unified political party. Another aspect of the same tendency is their hostility to the committees. It does not take such violent forms in Spain proper as in Catalonia. Still,

there is a definite and well-planned drive towards the dissolution of the political committees, those embryos of a Spanish
Soviet system. Generally speaking, the communists, in this
respect, have not yet obtained everything they want, but
they are well on the way to obtain it. Their chief means is
communal reform. A ministerial order has outlined the reform of the *ayuntamientos*, the municipalities. In future they
will be composed of representatives of the trade unions and
other mass organizations, but with the alcalde, the mayor, at
their head. The alcalde is nominated by the civil governor of
the province, who, in his turn, is nominated by the Government. The members of the *ayuntamiento*, for their part, are
appointed by their respective political and trade-union organizations. Technically there is not so very much difference
between the committees and these reformed *ayuntamientos*.
The committees too were formed of representatives of the
various political parties and trade unions, designated by their
respective organizations. It may seem the only difference
that the committees did not act under the chairmanship of
the alcalde. But, in actual practice, the difference is more
considerable. The alcalde, if he is any good at all, is likely to
have the most influence in this corporation, and he is a
Government employee. Moreover, the *ayuntamiento*, as against
the committee, is an official institution, bound to proceed,
not by the 'inborn free right of revolution' but by the rule of
law. If it fails to do so its acts are void, and the alcalde is there
to watch that it does not depart from legality.

One consideration cannot be omitted in this context. Officially, the Valencia Government fights for a 'parliamentary
democratic republic'. Now this, at present, is and inevitably
must be a programme and not a reality in *national* politics.
Anarchists and Trotskyists are not represented in the Cortes,
the first because they refused to put up candidates, the latter
because they were too weak. So, there is no opposition in the
Cortes, and their activities are limited, at present, to the
holding of sessions with the maximum legal interval between
them, sessions which adjourn after the unanimous passing of
a few resolutions; lately by an emergency law the Cortes has

even been relieved of the duty of sitting at regular intervals. But in the sphere of *municipal* administration, republican and parliamentary democracy could be and, in the policy of republican parties, ought to be, a reality. There must be restrictions, of course, in civil war. But the municipal reform just described does not introduce restrictions as an emergency measure. It is not intended so at all. It abolishes elections entirely, and instead puts the *nomination* of representatives of the various parties, not even on the basis of proportional representation according to the following of the different parties, but on the basis of parity. In practice, it works out in such a way that the municipal council is formed after the local secretary of the UGT, the secretary of the communists, the president of the local republican group, and the representatives of the anarchists—if there are any in that particular spot—have come to an agreement.

Thus municipal democracy is abolished. I do not think that this is incidental. It is not due to neglect, because the law was carefully considered; and it is not due to any special features of the Spanish municipalities. For a correct interpretation one must remember that usually socialists, communists, and republicans are not politically divided, though their personal rivalries are frequently important. The law hands over municipal administration to the party bureaucracies, which are guaranteed equal rights as to their different groups, whereas no heed is taken of the wishes of the population. If elections took place—even with the strictest banning of all elements sympathizing with Franco—the vital issues of the day would become planks in electioneering platforms and the various party bureaucracies would be forced to take some account of the wishes of the electorate if they wanted to get their candidates elected. It is this that all the parties want to avoid. The need for absolute unity in civil war provides a plausible argument, but it is no argument for a reform which is not intended as an emergency measure. This municipal reform marks an important stage in the development towards the dictatorship of party bureaucracies, not, as is pretended, towards parliamentary republican democracy. And the only difference from the present state of things in Russia is this: in Russia the ruling bureaucracy belongs to one party, whereas in Spain it is still divided between three or four parties; but these parties are rapidly moving away from their historical antagonisms and towards absolute political unity, notwithstanding clan rivalries. As the rule of the committees marked the anarchist and Soviet stage of the revolution, so the new municipal legislation marks its bureaucratic stage. The profound decay of the anarchists can be measured by the fact that they accepted, though with some hesitation, the introduction into the municipalities of the political régime most violently opposed to their ideals.

At present, things are still in a state of transition and disorganization in this respect, as they are in so many others. The old civil service exists, but in most places it lost authority in July and has recovered very little since. The political committees, on the other hand, are in a state of disintegration, partly because they now lack official recognition, partly because they are disabled from within by the communists, partly because the fervour of the mass movement which brought them into the forefront has abated. The new *ayuntamientos* are far from working as yet in a regular manner. Moreover, in every town and village there exist a multitude of committees for special tasks of all sorts, recruiting, provisioning, policing, controlling cars, controlling arms, controlling lodgings, etc., usually formed on an all-party basis. These committees originally derived their authority from the local political committee, of which they were sections. Now they continue to work because they are indispensable, but without any clear authority whatever. It is no longer, as in August, a double régime, here the bureaucracy, there the Soviets, but instead it is a multiple administration. The revolutionary trends have been stopped; but central organization has not yet come in its stead. The most serious consequence of this plurality of independent political and administrative forces is the failure to transform the Government.

Malaga

While I was staying in Valencia the insurgents' offensive against Malaga, which had started the very day I arrived in Spain, got stuck, after a few initial successes. But as everybody expected important developments from this corner, I decided to visit it. It took me three days, from the morning of 29 January till the morning of 1 February, to get there.

I had not seen the revolution before in most of this particular part of Spain. But how different it was from the countryside in general, as I knew it in August and September! In the villages there existed committees; one could learn that during conversations at meals. But these committees no longer had a place in the consciousness of the villagers. In September a simple question about 'the committee' would always bring information about the 'political committee', which, as the prime source of authority, was clearly differentiated, in the mind of the population, from all the sub-committees which might work under its auspices. Now it would happen that people, when asked about the seat of 'the committee', did not even understand what was meant. Sometimes they enumerated various committees. 'Do you want the committee of the CNT? Or of the UGT? Or the transport committee, in order to get gasoline?' 'No, the political committee,' I answer. There is no such thing. But finally it appears that a committee of the Popular Front exists, a so-called *comité de enlace*, a joint body for the establishment of contact between the various parties. Still, in the particular place where this happened to me, this committee had kept certain of its old attributes, notably police functions. We were stopped in the streets and ordered to show our papers by agents under the orders of this committee. The same place, Lorca, was the one spot on our whole journey with road guards organized by the villagers themselves. 'Stop or fire,' large posters declared at both entries of the village.

In August and September the guarding of the roads by

the peasants and the stopping and searching of the car at every village had been rather a nuisance, and certainly, after the first days, had been of little value in fighting the counter-revolution. But this guard-keeping had expressed the passionate desire of the villages to do whatever they could in fighting the insurgents, and at the same time it symbolized one aspect of the Soviet system. The peasants and the workers of the smaller places had pushed the guardia civil and the other police forces aside and had themselves assumed the job of policing the roads. Now it was the opposite. The nuisance of hundreds of independent village police bodies had disappeared, but with it the passionate interest of the village in the civil war. And with the slackening of the interest of the masses themselves the old police had reappeared. Certain points of the road were still guarded, but not by armed civilians nor by militia. They were guarded by the old police forces, guardia civil and *asaltos*. The short interlude of the Spanish Soviet system was at an end.

It was different with the political parties. Their activities were obvious: many banners, more, as a matter of fact, than farther north; lots of posters, some of them printed on the spot, others sent from the north, especially CNT ones, some of which had come directly from Barcelona and bore Catalan inscriptions. In the province of Alicante the CNT was preponderant. Farther south, from Murcia to Malaga, CNT and UGT seemed to be in about equal strength. Here, as elsewhere, the UGT must have gained considerably in membership; before, this region was known as exclusively anarchist.

Generally the impression was that the war weighed less heavily here than in the large towns farther north. Food conditions were still very good. Gasoline seemed to be available, not, as a matter of fact, for people from abroad, but for local people. Anyway, many more cars were circulating than in the north. (A few days before, stringent regulations about gasoline had been introduced in Valencia which made it almost impossible for journalists to get cars.) With the exception of Cartagena (which we did not pass through) this part of the country had suffered very little from bombing. Alicante, as a matter of fact, had been bombed in November for seven hours at a time, but with little effect, and not since. In Almeria, near the front, the situation was quite different, in this and other respects.

Apart from Catalonia, the country between Valencia and Almeria was perhaps the most peaceful part of republican Spain when I passed there; and it was obviously less torn by political dissensions than Catalonia. Still one could hardly forget war for one moment. In Alicante and Murcia, as well as in Almeria, the finest avenues and squares were disfigured by the hasty building of subterranean refuges against air attacks; a precaution of cruel necessity in Southern Spain, where the walls even of large houses are like paper. And troops were everywhere. The German contingent of the international brigades lay in Murcia, as I went through, and the town was full of both very 'Nordic' German proletarian refugees and Polish Jews, all in the same uniforms and serving in the same unit. The considerable number of Polish Jews serving with the Government forces had been incorporated with the German contingent because they all understood German and because there was no material for the formation of a command in Yiddish. Moreover, Murcia was full of wounded. And every small town we passed through had either an aviation camp or an artillery school, or a soldiers' training camp, or a military car park; there was no place untouched by the war.

Things became much more difficult in Almeria. The town had been bombed repeatedly and a large part of the population preferred to sleep in the fields in January! (Winter, in these mountainous regions of Southern Spain, is not nearly so mild as one would be inclined to think.) Food was scarce. There was a considerable number of refugees in the town, even from as far as Madrid; our hotel hall was at one time full of them. And no car, absolutely no car to be got, not even the regular bus between Almeria and Malaga. The civil governor had a transport of troops and armaments to Malaga on his hands, and no carriages to send them in. Being an exceptionally energetic man (at least for a Spanish civil governor) he had simply requisitioned the cars in Almeria at the moment, without exception and irrespective of their origin and destination. In order to make the measure efficient, guards were put at the entries of the town to stop and requisition every car. There I was, and did not know what to do. After a day of uneasy waiting and unavailing search for a car I tried a forlorn hope and succeeded. I knew that journalists were not allowed to go with troop transports, but, trusting in good documents I carried with me, I tried, and was accepted.

Thus, at about half-past six in the evening, when it got dark, I set off in the car of the commander of the reinforcements going to Malaga. He was, I believe, a characteristic specimen of the new officer corps. He had been for five years a sergeant in Morocco and served there in Primo de Rivera's campaign against Abd-el-Krim. Then he retired, learned locomotive engineering, and got a job at the Madrid Northern Station, one of the strongholds of the UGT. There he became a trade unionist and a socialist. He enlisted again in the republican forces when the civil war broke out, as a lieutenant, and soon advanced to the rank of captain. He had commanded the force he now brought to Malaga for three months in Madrid, in the Casa del Campo. His men obviously liked him, but not in the deferential manner one is used to in continental armies. They treated him absolutely as their equal.

From a military point of view the road from Almeria to Malaga is dangerous. Most of the time it runs along the shore, and the rebels dominate the sea. At various points it passes for many miles between an abyss above the sea on one hand and rocks many hundred feet high on the other. Shelling from the sea or bombing from the air on such a spot would inevitably produce ghastly disaster. Yet our convoy proceeded without precautions. Lights were not extinguished; not even blinded with blue paper. Nobody attempted even to make the single cars and motor-lorries keep a distance from each other. A few shells could have destroyed the whole convoy, which was clearly visible from the sea on this moonlit night. Half-way between Almeria and Malaga there lies the small town of Motril. The insurgents, in their first offensive against Malaga, had come down from Granada and, in an unavailing attempt to cut the road, had approached to eight miles from Motril. At this point of the road our convoy got stuck for about an hour from sheer congestion of the road. Behind Motril the main road had been broken by inundation, it was explained. The road had been repeatedly bombed between Almeria and Malaga, and quickly repaired. Whether the damage at this point was really due to inundation or to bombing, I do not know. Anyway, the broken bridge had not been repaired for more than a week and we had to make a long détour. At first we drove along miserable paths, but finally had to use the river-bed itself, which was full of water. It was too much for our car, which suddenly stuck and would not move again. We had to change into one of the large motor-lorries which carried the men. A convoy of cannons, badly needed in Malaga, had been unable to pass for many days. As the sea was closed by the insurgents, the slowness in repairing the bridge at Motril kept Malaga unprovided with artillery. Only in the very last days was the defect partly mended and a few cannons got in.

In the motor-lorry I met a typical troop such as had fought in Madrid. They were totally different from the old militia. They were all very young, most of them conscripts, and had an entirely military attitude. 'Military' not in the sense of military smartness (though they were quite decently disciplined), but in their outlook. Not once in the course of the night's conversation were politics mentioned. There was talk about food, about arms, about fights, about lodgings. A suspect sound made us all, at one moment, expect the sudden arrival of enemy planes. They were used to that and not particularly excited, though the situation, on this particular spot, would have been pretty bad. At five o'clock we arrived at Nerja, fifteen miles from Malaga, where our transport stopped. The men in my camion, together with my captain, went to a theatre-hall where they were billeted. In a few minutes the hall had been emptied of seats and prepared as a dormitory, without disorder and without any damage to the furniture. It contrasted favourably with the militia lodgings in August. Altogether it was obvious that this was not a mass of political crusaders, but an army of regular soldiers.

I slept for two hours, and then went on to Malaga in a regular overland bus. Clouds gathered and it started to rain heavily. At first I regretted this, but as soon as I had entered the town, about nine o'clock in the morning, I gave a big sigh of relief because of the rain. For a few hours at least, it would give safety from bombing. The impression Malaga made upon me was ghastly.

It is difficult to say which side displayed the greater destructive fury in Malaga. I entered through working-class suburbs. A few houses are destroyed by shells from the sea. My first idea was that this was much less terrible than what I had expected. I soon changed my mind. Next comes the fashionable Caleta district. It has been destroyed wholesale, burnt down in the first days by the crowd. A few hotels are standing, the largest, the Miramar, requisitioned as a hospital; all the rich villas have only their walls left. It is impossible to describe the impression made by such a city of the dead. The bus follows the coast-line to the harbour. Along the harbour runs a beautiful esplanade and behind it, a few hundred yards from the shore, is the centre of the town. Here fewer houses had been burned. Instead, there were the indescribable effects of bombing and shelling. Ruins, ruins, ruins, some of them still smoking in the dreary rain. The actual amount of destruction is somewhat smaller than one thinks at first. After the first impression one is inclined to say, 'The whole centre of the town is in ruins.' But this is not true. Even in the centre something like two-thirds of the buildings are untouched, and the percentage is considerably greater in the suburbs. Taking the whole town and suburbs together, I think that it would be an exaggeration to say that even 5 per cent. of the houses have been destroyed. Still, the impression is one of absolute disaster, partly because most of the destruction is concentrated in the two richest districts, the Caleta and the centre. But more important is the feeling of helplessness conveyed by the ruins. How could I protect myself in an air-raid, one is tempted to ask. There is absolutely no protection. Four and five-story houses have been cut through by the bombs. There are no cellars. There are no refuges, with the exception of caves in the rocks at the edge of the town, and there can be none, because the sea-water is in Malaga directly under the land-level. And there was an air-raid every day except on days of bad weather, which, in Malaga, are exceptional. The worst of these raids happened when Quiepo de Llano's first offensive got stuck at Marbella. The population had believed it was used to the worst and did not mind hearing about one or two dozen dead as the result of one raid. But this time, at half-past one in the afternoon, just at the closing hour of shops and offices, when large crowds were in the streets, nine bombers swept down over the centre of the town; in a few minutes there were, I was told, 260 dead and over 1,000 wounded, men, women, and children. At that time the military command in Malaga had not a single scout plane at its disposal. It was a massacre without resistance. The military command moved to a place somewhat out of town. The population never after rid itself of the terror inspired by that slaughter. There was no more laughter, hardly a smile in this southern town. Even a squadron of scouts, which arrived the day before I came to Malaga and, after months of helplessness, had brought protection, did not relieve the tension.

The whole first day of my stay it rained. The rain gave me an opportunity to inquire quietly. I went to the civil governor, who sat alone in his office; nobody seemed to bother about him. He obviously carried little authority. But he was capable of lying with the utmost effrontery, telling me, within sight of the ruins, that nothing had happened, that complete normality prevailed, that no air-raid had taken place for many days, and that the worst raid had cost them two dead and seven wounded. He ended by recommending me an hotel in the zone most hit by bombs, probably in order to display confidence. (To make the point clear I must add that his attitude was peculiar to himself. The next day a cable of mine indicating the true extent of the disaster passed the military censorship without the slightest difficulty.) From the governor I went to the political committee, transformed into a *comité de enlace*. They did not tell me lies, and they were kind in helping me in technicalities; but they, too, obviously sat aimlessly about. There was no working civil administration in Malaga, except that represented by special committees for provisioning and similar matters. The old administration, represented by the civil governor, had lost authority in July; the new one, represented by the committee, had slowly lost authority in the communist fight against the committees. (The communists are very important in Malaga; it was already their first stronghold, before July.) And now there was no authority except the military command. But this was unable and unwilling to take account of matters not purely military. Strangely enough, this absence of authority did not create a state of chaos. The town lacked bread, but was fairly well provided in many other respects. It was not under the terror of gangs; far from it. It had had an evil reputation in this respect in the first days of the movement, but it was common knowledge that these gangs had been cleared out in Malaga with more thoroughness than anywhere else; I know not how. Other matters were less well arranged. To my surprise the cathedral was open. It was full of refugees from those parts of the province which the insurgents had occupied; they slept on the stone floor, in complete destitution, practically without food and without any provision for sanitation.

Nights were uncanny in Valencia streets, dark after ten o'clock at night. In Malaga, lights were never put on. In Valencia, even after ten o'clock, there are people in the street. In Malaga, a town which usually lives more by night than by day, the streets were empty even at eight o'clock. Very few people hurried, and they spoke in subdued voices, in a meaningless reaction of fear from some disaster to come. Occasionally a flashlight from the tramway, which was running all night through, lighted for a moment the sombre scene.

During the three days of my stay my colleagues and I were spared the experience of shelling from the sea, but we did not escape the experience of being bombed from the air. The second morning was fine, and immediately the bombers

arrived. The harbour and the centre of the town were
bombed, but after fifteen minutes the newly arrived Government scouts interfered and brought the bombardment to an
end, not, we later learnt, without losing two of their planes.
The insurgents bombed the centre of the town again next
morning at about six o'clock, and again at about eight
o'clock; but then I slept quietly. We had taken lodgings some-.
what out of town.

The most surprising aspect of the whole situation was the
relation between the population of the town and the front.
There was very little contact at all. The troops at the front
consisted almost exclusively of Andalusians, and by far the
greater part of them were men from the province of Malaga.
Still, the town did not seem eager to help them. The enemy
was approaching and large posters asked for new voluntary
recruits, but very few seemed to come in. The town, after too
much suffering, had become passive. On the other hand, the
comandancia militar had very little contact with the town, in its
quarters almost two miles distant from the centre, and did
not seem to trouble about the creation of a mass movement
of defence. At the head of the *comandancia* and of the whole
southern front was now Lieutenant-Colonel Villalba, newly
appointed and arrived a few days ago. He had scored a conspicuous success in Barcelona on 10 July, had at least not
proved a failure before Huesca since, and been appointed to
the command in Malaga as one of the few capable officers
who had remained faithful to the republic. I saw him repeatedly, though I had only very few words with him. He
was the type of officer turned out by a military training
corps; very formal in his manners, which must have ap-
pealed little to the democratic spirit of his subordinates; obviously not caring for any contact with the popular movement, uneasy and even nervous in the political and military
situation he was sent to master. Friends who knew him well
described him as a complete officer, who in the secrecy of his
heart hated the spirit of the militia. Such a man was certainly the type least adapted to the task of holding Malaga.
He interpreted this task as a purely military one, whereas in

reality he had no military means at his disposal but only the forces of a popular movement.

I visited various points on the Malaga front, together with colleagues who knew Madrid well. They were emphatic about the difference between the two fronts. Madrid had been militarized, here in Malaga it was still the old militia, slightly transformed. The troops consisted exclusively of volunteers. They were still, to a certain degree, formed out of old columns of a political character. The political commissars were appointed by the *comandancia*, but put forward by the *comité de enlace*, and all political parties were represented among the commissars. This militia had undergone a certain amount of military training and had had some experience in fighting; its spirit was not bad at all; it was definitely better than that of the town. There had been one moment of panic at Estepona, but then the militia had stood firm, held the insurgents back, and even gained ground. They felt satisfied with the situation. And our whole group of journalists, with one notable exception, were misled by their self-confidence. The decisive point was that they had never had any experience in fighting against modern arms of high efficiency. And they had none.

But they had learnt to construct some kind of fortifications. The roads were barred with barbed wire and covered trenches. Still there were large undefended gaps between the separate positions. And machine-guns and cannons, rather than being put into the front line, were held back, together with the majority of the troops, in the villages behind, 'for an emergency'.

We stopped for an hour at one of the villages behind the front line in the sierra. We met the alcalde there. He had been the president of the socialist group of the village, which was founded in 1930 and now dominated the place. A communist group had been founded later, in 1933. The alcalde was a hairdresser by profession; most of his adherents naturally were peasants. In this poor part of the sierra there were no large landowners and, in consequence, practically no expropriations. 'Have the peasants had any material advantage from the revolution?' we asked; and they agreed, that they had not. The wheat harvest was now dealt with by the *ayuntamiento* (the political committee had been abolished 'in accordance with the policy of the Government'), which was hardly an improvement for the peasants, who had to contribute to the feeding of the local militia. Still, we have more wheat than we want, the peasants explained. One must take into account the extremely low standard of living to understand their attitude. But they were genuinely devoted to the Government. The many refugees from the other camp brought detailed stories of horror with them, executions, tortures. So the peasants of this village had voluntarily contributed a great deal of unpaid labour for the construction of fortifications. (All along the Malaga front this work was done by unpaid volunteers.) We asked one of the peasants: 'For what are you fighting?' 'For liberty,' was the answer. It did not occur to him that his fight might have any economic implications. Though the enemy was only a few miles away all these peasants obviously did not scent any imminent danger. At this particular spot the front had been stable for many months.

But the danger came, a few days later, and before it the front broke. I had no opportunity to watch this disaster on the spot, but having known the situation less than a week before the fall, and with the help of information from people who had remained almost till the end, I formed an idea about what had happened. The front had broken, in panic, under a tank attack directed at many points, but mainly from due north and from north-east. The latter attack, directed against the pass of Venta de Zefaraya (a position dominating the small town of Velez-Malaga), was particularly dangerous. Once the heights of the Venta were taken there was no other practicable line of resistance for the republicans in this sector; the main road from Malaga to Almeria, the one artery linking Malaga with the rest of republican Spain, could no longer be defended. Malaga was menaced with being cut off in the rear. This decided the command to give the order of evacuation at what it believed to be the last moment; in fact, the insurgents never cut the menaced road. They repeated the tactics they had applied repeatedly before, at Toledo, for instance, and left the road open, building golden bridges to their enemies and thus avoiding a desperate resistance.

Other attacks were made along the coast-line and were supported by heavy shelling from three insurgent cruisers. All reports agree that a German cruiser, the *Graf Spee*, followed the Spanish men-of-war closely in their movements, but the observers were not certain whether she had actually participated in the shelling. The cannonade proved a hard trial for the nerves of the militia, but it did not bring tactical decision. Long before the insurgents reached Fuengirola, the defence centre of the republicans on the coast-line, it had been completely evacuated by the militia on account of the menace in the rear, from Venta de Zefaraya.

The same happened with the tank attack from due north. It was very efficient and proceeded rapidly, but before it had attained its aim the republicans evacuated their positions in order to escape encirclement from the rear.

The tank itself, both from due north and from the rear, and at most of the other sectors of the front, presents a difficult problem to the student of the Spanish civil war. How many tanks were there and of what origin? The republicans, in a natural desire to explain their defeat by overwhelming forces of the adversary, spoke of about one hundred tanks. No means are available to check the figure, but I am not inclined to trust such figures on such occasions. Anyway, there were numerous tanks, but not concentrated on one sector, rather acting all along the front. One point seems to be well ascertained: they were all, or almost all of them, tanks of the smallest type, with only one machine-gun and two men. Reports agree that the manning was German.

Other reports concerning foreign intervention at the Malaga front merit less confidence. Naturally, there were the usual German and Italian planes and pilots. But the Press, both Spanish and foreign, was full of news about the intervention of Italian infantry units since the beginning of the offensive; actually no such units participated. My companions and I, visiting all the important sectors of the Malaga front in the first days of February, invariably inquired about the enemy troops holding the positions opposite the republican lines. Invariably the answer was that there were Moors (by far the larger part of the Moorish contingent seems to have been concentrated before Malaga during the winter), foreign legion, and Falange. We consistently inquired about Italians; every commander of a subsector replied that in his sector there were no Italians; there might be in other subsectors. Prisoners had been taken; there were no Italians among them. No similar systematic checking has been done for the last days before the fall. But then even rumour did not talk of Italians but of Germans. Had German infantry units participated in the taking of Malaga they would probably have continued to appear in the following fights at Motril. They did not, however. Probably rumour increased the German tank units, which in fact participated, into German mixed divisions. It is, moreover, a fact that no German and Italian prisoners had been made for many months (with the exception of pilots) either at Malaga or elsewhere; this changed soon after Malaga.

One of the chief responsibilities of the Malaga command was to prepare to meet the tank attack. It was entirely unprepared. One of our group of journalists, the one who distinguished himself from the rest of us by his clear-sighted pessimism, inquired at every subsector what preparations had been made against tank attacks. There were none. Still, the quality of the German small tanks is notoriously far from being perfect; ditches a few feet deep and wide are sufficient to stop them. But there were no such ditches. There was a battalion occupied in construction of fortifications in Malaga, and in the villages the peasants volunteered for fortification work in order to defend their homes. But nothing was done. Even less care was given to the question of artillery. The terrain of the sierra offers a multitude of brilliant opportunities for mounting guns on positions dominating the road and almost unassailable. Newspaper reports, both Spanish and foreign, spoke about camouflaged guns; but the existence of the newspaper reports did not give existence to the guns.

This cannot be blamed on the local commands in the first place. What few guns and machine-guns they had they did not know how to handle adequately. But the main defect was the lack of adequate supplies, both of men and material. Quiepo's offensive started on 13 January. The first scout planes arrived at Malaga on 31 January, the first artillery reinforcements (a very few small guns) on 1 February, the first six small tanks on 3 February. Small reinforcements of infantry began dropping in from the last days of January onwards. Still, contingents of the international brigades were lying in Murcia for weeks, awaiting orders to march. They were thrown into battle at Motril, some days after the fall of Malaga. The transport of the heavier material was gravely handicapped by the broken and unrepaired section of the road behind Motril. But the chief reason of the disaster was that adequate reinforcements were not ordered to Malaga in time by the central staff at the War Ministry.

The most inexplicable aspect of the Malaga disaster is the inactivity of the fleet. After the defeat the Government circulated an official explanation to the effect that Italian cruisers, camouflaged as insurgent men-of-war, had appeared on the horizon and made it impossible for the republican units to proceed on their way to Malaga; Italian attack was alleged. What can one think about the commander of a man-of-war who for twenty-four hours does not manage to discover whether the units lying ahead of him are or are not those he has been fighting for months? But the republican fleet has perhaps been treated unfairly by its own Government in this official declaration. The officers on the largest republican cruisers revolted in the first days and were killed by the crews; there was no way to replace them. Then two modern cruisers, the *Canarias* and the *Balearez*, happened to be under construction in insurgent shipyards at the moment of the rising, were made ready in haste, and now out-distance with their guns the older types of the republican navy. It is not surprising that the latter were not able to do much. But what about submarines? Not a single submarine went over to the insurgents. The insurgents are supposed to have since got *one* submarine from a foreign power. The mutinous and un-reliable submarine officers on the republican fleet could easily be exchanged for foreign volunteers. And with one or two submarine actions Malaga might have been freed from shelling from the sea; more, the blockade of the whole Government camp might have been broken. But the submarines, for no conceivable reason, did not appear.

Considering the limitations of the type of tanks brought into action by the insurgents, probably the balance of arguments leads to the conclusion that Malaga need not have fallen. At the moment of the catastrophe the impression in the republican camp was that it had been taken by over-whelming forces. But later developments, notably the speedy stopping of the insurgents' advance at Motril, proved that had only one of many factors functioned a little better the disaster might have been avoided. Let us have a look at these different factors and the reasons of their failure!

The militia had lost the habit of running before bombs, light shells, and machine-gun fire. It had stood firm, as long as there were no tanks; it ran before this new unexpected arm, which it had not learnt how to oppose. It was a test from which they came out badly. The weakness was not of the militia in general as compared with the new mixed brigades—there is no evidence that the contingent sent from Madrid in the last days held out better than the slightly centralized local militia—but it was a sign of the inefficiency of the commands and of Spanish troops in general as compared with foreigners. Where the Spaniards had been unable to avert an utter rout, one small international contingent, a few days later, at Motril, stopped the advance of the Franco troops swiftly and without much difficulty.

As to the local command, it has certainly not proved up to its task. The root of its inefficiency, in my opinion, lay in its incomprehension of the type of war it was directing. The failure to make adequate preparations against a tank attack was in itself enough to decide the issue; but what followed turned defeat into disaster. Once the point supposed to be the key position, La Venta de Zefaraya, had been taken by the enemy, Villalba ordered a general retreat; no attempt at a counter-attack was made. Worse, no attempt was made to organize a desperate resistance near the town itself. In a military sense, Villalba's judgement of the situation may have been sound. Malaga would be encircled and taken from land and sea; better to evacuate it at top speed. But he had left out the political factor. The insurgents, who were little afraid of his troops, were afraid of one thing only: of a fight of desperation. That's why they left the main road open. The assumption on which was based Villalba's whole appreciation of the situation did not take effect. On the other hand, the order to retreat had disastrous effects in the republican camp. The troops got out of hand immediately. The retreat of those sectors near the point of escape (*i.e.* nearer to the main road to Almeria) was so hasty that considerable contingents in the sierra were cut off and captured without resistance. In the town itself chaos ensued. There are unverifiable reports that the cathedral was burnt at the last moment. Other reports that for as much as three days before the fall of Malaga there was wild and aimless rifle-fire in the streets are more reliable. The wild excitement was present which might have been made the basis of a fight of despair. But the disintegration of the political forces was too deep to make use of it. In July and August the anarchists might have led such a fight and still later the political committee. Now the anarchists had been pushed back, and had been compromised by the memory of their sanguinary excesses; the political committee had been weakened from without and within. The civil administration carried no authority whatsoever. And the military command, far from being able to compensate for these shortcomings, did not only not understand what such a fight would mean, it disliked heartily the popular elements on which it needed to rely at such a moment. The case of the Basque country in mid-September, the case of Madrid on 8 November, both show that in situations apparently hopeless in a military sense, a fight to the finish, backed by popular enthusiasm, has always a chance in this civil war, where popular forces are at least as important as military ones. The intrinsic weakness of the insurgents on this front became apparent soon afterwards. A command determined to stay and die on the spot rather than leave it, and prepared to call the people to its assistance, had still a chance. But in order to launch such a desperate defence the various sections of the political movement must co-operate; and the education of a popular officers' corps capable of understanding the necessities of a civil war depends on the existence of a political régime strong and attractive enough to make them not merely obey formally, but participate in the movement with all their heart. Malaga demonstrated the failure to achieve this, within the Spanish forces of the republicans (the foreign brigades are another matter). And finally, even the military object of the evacuation was not obtained. Thousands and thousands of people sympathizing with the republicans were caught in Malaga; and worse, in many cases, was the fate of those who managed to leave. They had to walk, most of them, the hundred miles from Malaga to Almeria and farther north; the German tanks followed, and with them Moorish advance-guards. They stopped the fugitives, let the women go free (they would only increase the food difficulties in the republican camp), but shot the men, sometimes under the eyes of their womenfolk. Those who escaped went on and went on; many of them finally lay down at the roadside, starved and exhausted, the children dying. No fight in the encircled town could have been worse than this disaster.

The very necessity of a fight of despair would never have arisen had Valencia sent adequate reinforcements in time. But Valencia had forgotten Malaga in practice, though it was continually talking about it. At this point the disintegration of the régime which took effect at Malaga is linked with its crisis at the centre at Valencia. These were the days when republicans and communists were considering a change of the Government; when the anarchists decided to resist such a change—which would formally and factually make an end of the period of social revolution—with all the means available. During the two weeks preceding the fall of Malaga, in Valencia everybody who had only a slight contact with political events wondered whether they would awake one morning to the noise of a street-fight. One day before the fall of Malaga the anarchists marched their following through the town—under the pretext of a demonstration in favour of the hospitals. On this occasion the situation was tense to breaking-point. Both sides notoriously kept large numbers of armed men back in Valencia—not on account of the local situation, but because it was supposed that here the issue would be fought out for the republican camp as a whole. They did not keep back armed men only, they kept modern war material of all sorts. The Government offices and the military staffs, busy with the preparation for a supreme political crisis and its possible military implications, paid little attention to what was happening in a remote corner. The Spanish republic paid with the fall of Malaga for the decision of the Right wing of its camp to make an end of social revolution and of its Left wing not to allow that. On the very same day and for reasons very similar, which will be discussed in later pages, ensued the catastrophe of the southern wing of the Madrid front, at Jarama. The price once paid, it appeared that it had been no use. Both sides had to renounce their aims, the Government was not transformed. For the time being, the political crisis ended in a stalemate.

Fight in the Air

I left Malaga, with two colleagues, in a car, on the afternoon of 3 February. We did not expect the town to fall soon. It was quiet. We had had bombings while we were there, but they had not been very awkward for us. We felt perfectly safe now; we were mistaken.

Some fifteen miles east of Malaga lies the village of Nerja. There, on the beach, lay the *Delphin*, a cargo-boat torpedoed four days ago and now stranded on the shore. Most of its cargo had been removed, but that the insurgents seemed not to know. We drove near the ship, when our car stopped suddenly and my companions got out in haste. I did not realize at once what was happening, but when I got out to follow them (believing they intended to investigate the stranded wreck) they were already lying under the rocks which lined the road, and a hydroplane was over our heads. I had just time to join them, when the first bomb fell, in the direction of the ship. Peasant women were running away crazy with fear and seeking shelter. Our position was neither comfortable nor safe, but fortunately the bombing of a definite object is not such a swift affair as one might be inclined to think. The hydroplane had to circle over its objective, and at least two or three minutes passed between each bomb it threw. In the meantime, it went out of sight behind a hill and we took the opportunity it gave us to seek better cover, getting up whenever it went away and throwing ourselves to the ground when the plane came back. We repeated this procedure three times, until we had found a fairly well-protected spot, somewhat outside its range, in the shadow behind some rocks. We were nearly out of danger now. The bombs fell on the road (one very near our car) and in the water near the ship. We heard the deep sound of the explosions, much less loud than one would expect; yet it was dropping heavy bombs of perhaps 400 lb. each. Suddenly a cloud of smoke went up to heaven from the wreck; it had been struck by an incendiary bomb. The hydroplane, satisfied with its success, went farther away and started bombing the road towards Nerja. It was accompanied by two scout planes. We felt safe now. At first I had felt very uneasy at the approach of the plane. Its first circles were somewhat indefinite. The plane was not yet quite sure of its objective; nor were the observers on the ground. But as soon as I knew what it was aiming at I found the situation much more pleasant.

Suddenly there was a terrific noise, and the next moment Russian scouts, which had arrived at incredible speed, were over our heads. There was first one of them, who immediately attacked the Italians, then a second one, and then two more. There was a wild scene of rising, falling and looping under incessant machine-gun fire. The noise was terrific, but at the same time of an indescribable musical beauty. Both the Italians and the Russians have seven to nine machine-guns on their scouts, which are worked automatically from one lever, so as to make the sound almost as strong as from cannon-shells, but the fire as swift as that of single machine-guns. The special note of an air-fight is conditioned by the fact that both sides cannot fire at the same time. If one plane is in a good position to attack, his adversary has to move away and must try to escape. Then it is his turn, he attacks and the other one backs out. The machine-gun fire, in the somewhat different types of planes, sounds like challenge and reply, like the cursing of two giants who, in frenzy, try to shout down one another. The situation had become much more unpleasant for us now. The fight was going on directly over our heads. Somewhere the shots must come down; as likely as not they would come down upon us. But we almost forgot ourselves. One of my colleagues, who had clearly felt the bombardment on his nerves (as, in fact, we all had), said to himself: 'How grand.' It was the feeling of us all. And I envied the pilots who were not passive and helpless objects of the bombing but could fight. It lasted for between five and ten minutes. The decision was not in doubt. The Russians were quicker, and they were in superior numbers. The Italians went out to sea, pursued by the Russians. Then the latter came back, and triumphantly flew a last time over the battlefield. We returned to our car. Peasants with their women and children had taken shelter under a bridge and now came out, the women and children crying. We tried to comfort them. Nobody had been hurt. But a peasant cart had fallen over on the road and been crushed, not by a bomb but by the restiveness of the oxen who stood there, shaking in their bones. It was wrecked and the peasant was distressed: it was an important piece of his property. The bomb which had fallen near our car apparently had not done it any damage. But as we drove on we could see for miles the smoke from the bombed ship. And at night our car suddenly broke down, for no obvious reason, and we had to stop. It seems that the bombing had wrecked the whole machinery through the air pressure. We borrowed a car from the committee at Lorca and thus went back to Valencia.

Crisis

In the meantime the situation in Valencia had become more unpleasant and became increasingly so every day. Food shortage was more acute now, especially after the fall of Malaga. Official proclamations asked the population to renounce completely the use of bread for three days, in order to feed the refugees in Almeria. But even at more regular times it was a problem to get bread. So it was to get sugar, meat, and many other foodstuffs. Housing conditions had become intolerable and I was not able to secure a room at an hotel. I lived with friends, where I felt the difficulties of providing food more directly. The reaction of the women in the long queues to these troubles became as unpleasant as in Barcelona. For all I know they started to curse the whole war. There was nothing in Valencia of the heroism related from Madrid by all observers. And the allegation that people in office had backstairs methods of procuring food for themselves, not untrue by any means, gave an especially bitter note to the complaints.

News from the front was continually bad. On one and the same day spread the news about the fall of Malaga and about the break-through of the insurgents on the southern wing of the Madrid front. The first report was officially recognized after three days, the second was never openly and explicitly admitted but everybody knew it. These reports produced depression and distrust, but, in spite of many newspaper articles, there was no rush to the recruiting offices, no spontaneous display of political passion. Some days after the fall of Malaga a demonstration in favour of increased activity and unified command was organized by the Popular Front; it was a happy gathering of flags and of many, many people singing and listening to military music, but without the slightest sign of an increased decision to fight. Valencia reacted passively to the defeats. In the meantime, new menaces appeared.

Valencia had once been shelled from the sea, with a couple of casualties in the harbour, but never since. But during the week after the fall of Malaga we were shelled twice by an insurgent cruiser, with very heavy shells, once at half-past two in the morning, once after ten o'clock in the evening. Neither of these shellings had a military object. The enemy cruiser shelled the town while passing by, strewing its shells at random. The second time our house, one of the biggest in Valencia, shook to its very foundations, and the inhabitants were frightened accordingly, though nothing happened to us. But in the town as a whole there were a number of casualties each time, and the anxious question 'Will they come back to-night?' remained and racked the nerves of the Valencians. One particular trouble was the complete lack of refuges. They had been under construction for a long time, but were still far from completion. And the alarm both times was sounded only after half a dozen shells had fallen into the town.

In exchange, the night-guards developed a very unpleasant habit. All lights had to be covered at the moment of an attack, with good reason, of course; and the militia had the right to shoot at lights which had remained visible. They made a habit out of this right, and every bombing was accompanied by incessant revolver shots from the street. But the nights without raids were not much more quiet. From time to time a shot was to be heard in the streets. It became positively dangerous to leave after about nine o'clock. People spoke about certain anarchist columns terrorizing and killing socialists and communists.

It was learned from many and various quarters that the insurgents were preparing a landing from Majorca. The probable place of the landing would be Sagunto, sixteen miles north of Valencia, near the railway-line between Valencia and Barcelona. The landing column would try to join hands with another column coming down from Teruel, and both together would march upon Valencia. A surprising number of people found strange and unexpected reasons for leaving Valencia and making for the North.

But it was not so easy to leave. In the meantime transport

had entered on a process of acute disintegration. All had gone well till the beginning, and to some extent till the middle of January. Trains had run lustily, including the trains for the Sunday trips of the Barcelonese. Nobody seemed to think coal could run short. But one day it was short, and so short that sometimes the train took eighteen hours between Port Bou and Barcelona (a route of something like 110 miles), because the engine-driver had to look after coal from station to station. It was much the same with gasoline. It had been wasted without restrictions. Then, in mid-January, suddenly, a serious shortage became apparent and stern measures had to be taken. This shortage of gasoline made it very difficult for journalists to get cars; but, more important, it made it impossible to evacuate Madrid, and even troop movements were seriously hampered. As a result, the commands resorted to troop transport by railway, thus increasing the crisis of the latter, and, to make disaster complete, the insurgents started to bomb the main railway arteries systematically, first at short intervals, and finally night by night. The railway line from Valencia to Barcelona from time to time became practically unworkable. The railway service from Barcelona to France, though somewhat better protected, was still repeatedly interrupted. And, worst of all, the bombings not only aimed at the line, but at the trains themselves. Valencia itself felt cut off from the rest of Spain.

The political crisis had been allowed to drift without a decision. The communists, who had first launched the candidature of Martinez Barrios, then of Prieto, then of the socialist Negrin, with Prieto as war minister, and had almost provoked civil war in the republican camp by these attempts, had renounced these intentions for the moment after the fall of Malaga. But everybody knew that sooner or later the political issue between the adversaries and the partisans of a social revolution must be fought out. Deep unrest lay upon the town.

One small incident will give an idea of the political atmosphere at this juncture. A young Englishman who was acting as correspondent for the Hearst Press, though himself of Leftist opinions, a few days after his arrival in Valencia got an interview with Prieto. And Prieto opened his heart to him. 'I do not understand', he said, 'the attitude of the public in the democratic countries of the West. Why do they back the policy of non-intervention? Don't they realize that this government must be helped, because it is the last government to stand between Spain and Bolshevism?' This, if not the actual words, was certainly the general drift of Prieto's statement. I saw the text, revised by Prieto, with my own eyes. When I saw it the censor's red pencil had marked all the essential parts of it as inadmissible, and the correspondent had been given to understand that should he try to send the interview out unofficially, his life would not be safe. This incident reflects a state of affairs completely paradoxical. Prieto, the Communists' candidate for the Premiership and one of the leading members of the Cabinet, in which the Communists are the predominant element (not in numbers, but in influence), explains to the correspondent of one of the most 'reactionary' news agencies of the world that he and the communists are the one remaining bulwark against 'Bolshevism' in Spain. Then this account of an interview with one of the leading members of the Cabinet is banned by the censor appointed by this same Cabinet, and banned not for reasons of military or administrative secrecy (which, after all, would be intelligible) but precisely on account of declarations which explain, correctly though paradoxically, the Government's policy to the democratic public of the West. The censor himself, probably sympathizing not with Prieto, but with the Caballero-group, the Left wing of the Socialist Party, seemed more concerned about the possible effect of the interview in Spain than abroad.

Prieto is not the man responsible for the muddle which this incident illustrates. *He* has never been in favour of 'Bolshevism', or, in other words, of social revolution. He has always been the head of that section of the Socialist Party which opposed revolutionary politics. He is fully justified in appealing for the help of the democratic West in the attempt to carry through his policy. The irony begins when the mantle of Prieto is thrown over the whole Cabinet and so extends to cover the Communist ministers. For thus it happens that the 'Bolshevik' ministers in Spain together with Prieto are described as Spain's last bulwark against 'Bolshevism', and that the censor does not allow the public, either Spanish or foreign, to know it. The communists, less candid than Prieto, do not admit what is the notorious truth, namely that there is all the difference in the world between their policy in 1917 in Russia and their policy in 1937 in Spain; that they have ceased to be a revolutionary party and become one of the mainstays of the anti-revolutionary forces. They could bring forward many and weighty arguments in favour of this change, but unfortunately they prefer not to bring forward any argument at all but to deny that there has been a change. The result is that it is at present impossible in Spain to discuss openly even the basic facts of the political situation. The fight between the revolutionary and the non-revolutionary principle, as embodied in anarchists and communists respectively, is inevitable, because fire and water cannot merge. This fight, unhappy as it is, may have a healthy effect, if it is a clear fight between opposing principles. But as the Press is not even allowed to mention it, nobody is fully aware of the position, and the political antagonism breaks through, not in open fight to win over public opinion, but in backstairs intrigues, assassinations by anarchist bravoes, legal assassinations by communist police, subdued allusions, rumours; in one word all those forms of political activity which may be inevitable in a revolution, but which certainly must, if unchecked, affect most disastrously both the present morale of the country and the creative power of its political parties in the future. The concealment of the main political facts from the public and the maintenance of this deception by means of censorship and terrorism carries with it far-reaching detrimental effects, which will be felt in the future even more than at present. Unfortunately this was better understood in the nineteenth century than it is in the twentieth. It is better understood by a man of thorough non-revolutionary convictions, such as Prieto, than by the communists, who will not admit, either to themselves or to others, what things really are.

It was at this moment that my work in Valencia, which I had intended to continue as long as there was a chance of observing things, came suddenly to an end by police interference. But this cutting short of my work was not an exceptional affair. It was only one incident in a large campaign of arrests conducted by a maddened police. Mass arrests were one feature, and one of the most unpleasant, of those days. If they made me miss the chance of seeing Madrid and its defence, they gave me in exchange an opportunity to get a first-hand impression of Spanish prisons during the civil war, an opportunity which, it is true, I shared with many people; but few of them are likely to speak in public about their experiences. In itself, this experience was short, not very dramatic, and not more unpleasant than one would expect such an accident to be in most countries of the world. But it opened my eyes to certain specific features of the régime.

In Jail. The Police Régime

Much in contrast with my first journey, I was, during the second one, continually molested and hampered in my work by being shadowed and repeatedly denounced. This went on almost from the first days. There was no doubt that the difference was due to the greater influence of the communists now than in the summer of 1936. I had not been reticent of criticism during the first journey. I had talked little with communists then, but a great deal with republicans, socialists, anarchists, and Trotskyists, and had found them all equally devoid of heresy-hunting. I had openly expressed my doubts, sometimes my disgust, about many aspects of the movement to many people. I had emphatically stated, repeatedly, that I did not identify myself with any particular section of it. I had even gone so far as to insist, at various occasions, on my character as a neutral in the whole civil war as such. It created no difficulties, or almost none. My interlocutors understood that my reserve was not prompted by any particular sympathy for the cause of Franco, that, on the contrary, I wished the movement well, and that my reserve was only due to the specific task I had set myself, that of making a descriptive scientific field-study of events. In fact, this observing and critical attitude proved to be an advantage. It put me in a position to be sincerely friendly with various people of very different shades of opinion, and to voice my impressions, both favourable and unfavourable, with a certain amount of freedom. This would have been impossible had I taken sides for one of the existing organizations. I was very careful never to do that, and, I believe, as a result, voiced my criticisms more freely even than my sympathies. The first was non-committal, the second would have put me in the dubious position of a partisan of one tendency as against others, a position incompatible with my field-work and inconsistent with my real views. I did not think any of the parties participating in the fight had a panacea for winning it.

I started by behaving just in the same way on my second journey, but with very different results. True, the situation had become much more involved since, the antagonism between tendencies, which had always been great, had become of a menacing acuteness, and criticism was bound to be much sharper now than before. Still, it was not difficult at all, no more than in August, to talk with members of most groups about their weak points; but I committed a great mistake in using the same frankness with the communists. The first time I told a few communists in Barcelona of my doubts about the policy of their party I got only a few angry replies, and soon none at all. These people were obviously convinced, as nobody else was, that they knew all about everything and were infallible. It was an unpleasant and sterile talk but not particularly harmful.

The second time it was worse. I met with an attitude which I had little expected, because I had never met it before during my travels all over republican Spain: the attitude of the amateur spy. This communist was an American working in Barcelona. Right at the beginning of our conversation he declared that he shared my doubts; he pretended to be very critical of the policy of the party; he said he could not understand it at all. Could I explain it to him? I said I could not. It was not a very enlightening, but it seemed a pleasant conversation.

It had, however, an unexpected sequel. Two or three days after my arrival in Valencia, another communist asked me to have a chat with him. After a few minutes of light talk, he began to explain what he called the real aim of his invitation. He wanted to warn me. I should be careful. The man with whom I had had the talk just referred to in Barcelona had denounced me. I was rather worried about the unpleasant event, but for a short time intensely pleased as well. After all, this amateur spying seemed to be exceptional. Communists in positions of confidence seemed to be so keen to repudiate it as to warn the unhappy object of this misdemeanour. But my pleasure subsided quickly.

The good man continued exactly where his predecessor in Barcelona had started. He too was deeply worried about the political evolution. He too sympathized with the Trotskyists, as I seemed to do. I protested at once against the inference that I was a Trotskyist, which was untrue. But he went on, imperturbably. He was happy to find, after a long time, an intelligent man to whom he could open his heart. It would be too dangerous to do so with anybody working in the administration in Valencia. I cooled down considerably; I was surprised that a man who felt himself surrounded by so many dangers should open his heart to a stranger, about whom he knew nothing but the fact that he had been denounced as an anti-communist. 'How is it possible', I asked, 'that, with your opinions, you got the job you are holding at present?' 'But nobody knows about my opinions,' he replied. And he mentioned the name of one of the leaders of the Government who had put him in his present job. I said no more. It was impossible to decide whether the man was naïve or whether again he was acting as an amateur spy. But I decided to take the safer side and to treat him as if he were spying, which, after all, was much more likely. Had he been really sincere but as careless as he was with me, he must probably long ago have fallen into one of many pits lurking for critical people in these days. He finally showed me the letter of denunciation of his comrade in Barcelona. The key sentence ran: 'he is a bastard who is not all he ought to be', or something very like that. I was struck by the peculiarities of this denunciator: he had not said a word about *what* was really wrong with me in his opinion and from his expression one could at least as well infer that I was a spy of Franco as that I was critical of communist policy. True, being critical of the communists is not officially a crime in Spain, and it was more effective to throw a vague shadow over my character than to specify an accusation where there was none. I thanked my interlocutor for his frankness, but did not allow myself to be induced to be more frank myself. For a few weeks I heard nothing about this particular affair. There were other troubles, however.

I had hardly settled down in my hotel room in Valencia (a few days before the conversation just related, and perhaps one hour after my arrival at the hotel) before two members of the secret police presented themselves and took my passport away with them. No such practice had been followed in August, nor had it been followed in January in Barcelona. But in itself it seemed quite intelligible and defensible on many grounds. I soon learned, however, that the department which had got hold of my passport was not a regular body at all. It was an institution calling itself 'Informacion de la Seguridad General' (Information Department of the General Police), but had been formally dissolved by this same 'Seguridad General'. It was still active nevertheless. I had to go next day to its offices, 15 Plaza Tetuan, in order to fetch my passport. I did not get it at once, however, but was subjected to an interrogatory about my political past centring round the question whether I had ever in my life been a Trotskyist. The denunciation from Barcelona had not arrived then, so I suppose that many other people were subjected to similar interrogatories. When I had proved to their satisfaction that I had never been one, no further interest was taken in my past and I got my passport back next day. Number 15 Plaza Tetuan was directed by foreign communists. Later I heard bitter complaints about its actions in arresting people and keeping them in prison for a long time without due investigation and occasionally shooting the wrong man (for this unofficial police body performed executions). Enmity between them and the ordinary police was patent in the personal relations of the staffs, as far as I could observe them.

It must be explained, in order to make intelligible the attitude of the communist police, that Trotskyism is an obsession with the communists in Spain. As to real Trotskyism, as embodied in one section of the POUM, it definitely does not deserve the attention it gets, being quite a minor element of Spanish political life. Were it only for the real forces of the Trotskyists, the best thing for the communists to do would certainly be not to talk about them, as nobody else would pay any attention to this small and congenitally sectarian group. But the communists have to take account not only of the Spanish situation but of what is the official view about Trotskyism in Russia. Still, this is only one of the aspects of Trotskyism in Spain which has been artificially worked up by the communists. The peculiar atmosphere which to-day exists about Trotskyism in Spain is created, not by the importance of the Trotskyists themselves, nor even by the reflex of Russian events upon Spain; it derives from the fact that the communists have got into the habit of denouncing as a Trotskyist everybody who disagrees with them about anything. For in communist mentality, every disagreement in political matters is a major crime, and every political criminal is a Trotskyist. A Trotskyist, in communist vocabulary, is synonymous with a man who deserves to be killed. But as usually happens in such cases, people get caught themselves by their own demagogic propaganda. The communists, in Spain at least, are getting into the habit of believing that people whom they decided to call Trotskyists, for the sake of insulting them, are Trotskyists in the sense of co-operating with the Trotskyist political party. In this respect the Spanish communists do not differ in any way from the German Nazis. The Nazis call everybody who dislikes their political régime a 'communist' and finish by actually believing that all their adversaries *are* communists; the same happens with the communist propaganda against the Trotskyists. It is an atmosphere of suspicion and denunciation, whose unpleasantness it is difficult to convey to those who have not lived through it. Thus, in my case, I have no doubt that all the communists who took care to make things unpleasant for me in Spain were genuinely convinced that I actually *was* a Trotskyist. The inferences from which they drew this conclusion were twofold: first, I had been highly critical of the type of bureaucratic tyranny towards which the communists are driving in Spain, and have achieved in Russia, as others have achieved it in Germany and Italy. Second, among many friends and acquaintances, I had some who were Trotskyist. What else but a Trotskyist could a man be, if he is opposed to the totalitarian state and talks to Trotskyists? I repeatedly tried, indirectly, to convey to various communists that they were mistaken, that after all I had published a good many things which proved that I was anything but a Trotskyist; that I did not even take the Trotskyists seriously. It was in vain. I was critical of bureaucratic totalitarianism, hence I was a Trotskyist. I had talked with Trotskyists, hence I was a Trotskyist. The fact that a few fairly important countries in the world are not living under bureaucratic dictatorship, and yet, for all that, are not Trotskyist, has passed out of the ken of the ordinary communist.

Fortunately, 15 Plaza Tetuan did not know that I was critical of bureaucratic dictatorships, nor did they know that I had known Trotskyists in Barcelona. Had I fallen into their hands under the charge of being a Trotskyist, things probably would have been even more unpleasant for me than they were soon to become. For the communists know no mercy where pretended Trotskyists are concerned, and it is impossible to disprove the charge unless one approves of every single item of communist policy. Still, in spite of the ignorance of 15 Plaza Tetuan as to my objectionable political opinions, I was to have more trouble with them.

A few days after my return from Malaga I sat chatting with a lady colleague of our Malaga party in a small café when we both were summoned, by two agents of this institution, to follow them. On the way they called for two militiamen, who followed close behind us, probably with revolvers in their pockets. At one moment, by inadvertency, I put my hand into my pocket to get out my handkerchief. One of the agents hysterically summoned me to show immediately what I was holding in my hand and was visibly disappointed when he saw that he had been frightened by a handkerchief. He ordered me severely not to put my hands in my pockets again. On arrival at 15 Plaza Tetuan we were both searched for arms. Obviously we were regarded as dangerous criminals. After some delay I was called, alone, before a committee whose character I did not understand. It was not a court, but might have been a jury. At least ten people were sitting in the room, some of them civilians, but most in either police or army uniform. I had not the slightest idea what it could all mean. I was offered a seat, and, after a few introductory questions, was interrogated about my former visits to Catalonia. I told them I had been there for the first time in 1928, for a short visit of a few days, and had not had any personal contacts whatever in Barcelona at that time. I was asked in menacing tone how it was, then, that I knew Catalan and had been in touch with the Radical Party of Alejandro Lerroux. I could not but reply that I did not know Catalan beyond the ability to read it a little, and that I had never in my life seen a member of the Radical Party. At that a young man upbraided me sharply: I was lying, for it was proved that I knew Catalan. The situation became at the same time humorous and unpleasant. Their firm conviction that they had caught a dangerous bird contrasted comically with my complete ignorance of what they were aiming at; but the situation might become very awkward. I repeated three or four times, rather peremptorily, that I did not know Catalan, that it was certainly difficult to prove the fact, but that they must be mistaken about my identity. At that they said the agents who had arrested us had heard us talk in Catalan. I grew rather angry at this nonsense; in fact we had been talking German. Finally, I was sent to another room and the lady was submitted to a similar interrogatory. As she told me afterwards, she had some difficulty in convincing them that she was not my wife in any possible interpretation of this term, and that there was no connection between us beyond an acquaintance begun in Malaga. Then they searched carefully through the letters she was carrying on her, and after something like fifteen minutes I was called back, we were both declared released, and it was explained, with many excuses, that it had all been a matter of mistaken identity. I never learnt with whom I had been wrongly identified. But I told the chief of the strange court, as politely as I could, that his spies ought either to know the difference between Catalan and German or be more careful in their denunciations. We parted in peace and friendship.

There was one more funny coincidence in the story. The very moment we were arrested we had been talking about the fate of another man arrested by 15 Plaza Tetuan, a German socialist, who had just arrived and had been put in jail immediately because something seemed dubious—to 15 Plaza Tetuan—about his documents. He was well known to all the German refugees, there was not the slightest doubt about his genuine fervour for the republican cause, and the arrest was a stupidity, made unpleasant by the fact that he had to stay in jail through the night instead of being interrogated and released immediately. We were just talking about the steps to be taken in order to speed up the inevitable release of the man when we were arrested. I met him next day; he was silent about his little accident.

Things were now settled with 15 Plaza Tetuan, as far as I was concerned; I continued to hear, from time to time, about trouble emanating from this quarter for others, all genuine partisans of the republican cause, some of them lifelong active members of the socialist movement, but generally people whose communist orthodoxy was justly doubted. But I myself felt pretty safe now, without reason, as later events proved, and hoped for a successful continuation of my work. Trouble, however, came from another quarter.

One afternoon I was again stopped by secret agents, this

243

time belonging to the foreigners' department of the 'Seguridad General'. 'You are not arrested,' they told me; 'we only want you to give a few explanations.' At first things looked not particularly unpleasant. They were men of the old police force, less hysterical, in consequence, than the amateurs of 15 Plaza Tetuan. I expected to be set free after a few questions, I did not know about what. But I had to wait instead for hours, all my documents, including my passport, being taken from me. In the meantime, an air alarm was sounded in the town. If the building were struck everybody would certainly run away and my documents would be lost. But no actual air-attack ensued. After about three hours of waiting ('Paciencia, paciencia,' is the Spanish advice for such situations) I was led to another department. It was nine o'clock now, and all the officials were leaving. I realized that I had to stay for the night, and when I protested against such treatment I learnt that my case was in the hands of the director of the Seguridad himself and could not be taken before to-morrow. So it seemed that something serious must have happened.

I was led to the jail. I did not think, then, that I ought to blame its peculiarities upon the people now in the service. I believed it to be a jail of the old régime. Next morning, however, I saw that a good deal of the jail was still under construction, and learned that it had been started after the transference of the Government to Valencia. I was put into a cell about eight feet long and four feet broad, with a single bench long enough for three people to sit on; it was horribly humid and cold. When I entered there were already two others, and during the succeeding hours two more joined us; there was not even room to sit. Still, all the other cells were more crowded than ours. There was no mattress, no blanket of any kind, and no food provided by the administration. I was soon to learn that this was much more an advantage than a drawback for the prisoners. Those who happened to have money with them at the moment of their arrest—by no means the majority—could buy food from a woman who made a round of the cells. I did so, but it was so repugnant that I could not swallow it. I asked the militia-men on guard for a

blanket. It was not their fault that I did not get one. Very
kindly they tried to find a blanket for me and finally found
one. But at this moment an *asalto* officer interfered. 'What?'
I heard him say from my cell, 'you would give blankets to
such people? For the wounded, yes; not for them!' And I did
not get it. It was characteristic that this one police officer of
the old régime was the one man in the jail who tried to make
life unpleasant for the prisoners and identified himself entirely with the arresting forces; whereas the militia-men on
guard were as helpful as they could possibly be to these re-
puted fascists, who, they knew very well, were mostly not
fascists at all but simply people who, for one reason or another, had had the bad luck to attract the displeasure of the
Seguridad.

One of the men in my cell was very reluctant to give information about who he was, but seemed to be a merchant. One
was a militia-man who had fought in the Guadarrama, and
declared he did not know on what charge he was arrested.
(As a matter of fact, most of the prisoners were absolutely
unaware of the reason of their imprisonment, as I was myself, and some of those who believed they knew proved to be
mistaken.) Both these prisoners were called for an interrogatory about midnight, and did not come back. I do not
think the Seguridad would execute a man after one single
interrogatory late at night; the cars for the model prison, on
the other hand, left the Seguridad only at six and seven
o'clock in the evening. Thus I hope they were released after
a short interrogatory, though other prisoners, told about it in
the morning, were less optimistic. The third man in the cell
was an unskilled labourer, a peasant type, the only one of us
who did not mind the conditions of the prison but squatted
on the earth and started snoring almost immediately. He had
had some trouble with his trade-union documents, and been
arrested at home, was called to an interrogatory after the
two who went out first, came back after a short time, and said
he had been told that his assertions would be checked and
that he would be released in the morning if they proved to be
correct. The fourth man in the cell was an active anarchist of

foreign nationality, but closely related to one of the most famous names of the Spanish progressive movement. By chance he had had a look at his arrestation warrant and there had read the words 'at the disposition of the international brigade'. The international brigade has a reputation of being quick in shooting people, and he himself believed he knew what they had against him. He was editing a small anarchist paper intended for distribution among communists, and particularly among members of the international brigade. He was deeply concerned, and the more he told me the more I understood his anxiety. But it was all a mistake. In the morning he was called for an interrogatory and came back from it only to tell me that he had been released and that his arrest had been a case of mistaken identity.

In the morning the militia-men showed all their kindness. Many of them, and especially the sergeants, were old members of the trade-union movement, who, in contrast with the *asaltos* and civil guards, must have been in prison themselves and treated the prisoners as well as they could. Under one pretext or another all the cells were opened and the inmates allowed to stay in the courtyard, in pleasant sunshine, all the day through. There all the prisoners stood or sat, chatting among themselves and with the guards, the prisoners and the guards calling one another 'comrade', the guards not even refusing to talk politics. Only at the change of the guards, when officers were present, were we hurried back to our cells, to be released again immediately afterwards. And all this the guards did without the slightest advantage to themselves. Nobody tried to offer them money, and they even refused the cigarettes which, in Spain more than anywhere else, are offered and accepted as a matter of common courtesy. Whether they were under the eyes of their officers or alone, they refused to accept anything looking like a bribe. It was regrettable to have nothing but thanks to offer for their friendliness. I cannot generalize from one personal experience, but friends who had passed through other prisons told me that the watching of the prisoners was sometimes more exact but the behaviour invariably correct. In this particular prison anyway, the very idea of tortures (of which a certain section of the Press does not cease to speak) looked funny. Under these conditions it was easy to get an idea of the other prisoners. None of them were 'bourgeois' or aristocratic. One or two were small merchants. Most of them clearly belonged to the lowest stratum of the lower middle classes and to the working classes. On the ground floor there were three more cells beyond mine. The inmates of one of them were difficult to place, but to judge from their clothes they were poor. Among them was an old woman accompanied by a younger one, the latter blind and half lame. In the next cell two complete families were crowded, three generations together. They seemed a bit better off, and tried to look on the whole thing from a humorous point of view. In the last cell sat eight men, obviously unskilled workers of peasant origin. It would have been useless to question all those people about the reasons of their imprisonment. Most of them would not have known, and all would have pretended not to know. I learnt that as a rule nobody was kept in these cells for more than three days; then, if not released, he would be transferred to a regular prison. But some of the prisoners had been there for forty-eight hours already without having been subjected to an interrogatory.

The kindness of the guards combined with the laziness of the higher officials to make the preparation of one's defence very easy. Disorganization did the rest. As no food was provided, it was impossible to refuse prisoners the right to inform their families about their arrest and to have food brought them. The food was controlled, but the relatives were allowed to bring it to the prisoners direct. It was very easy to send news out by this way. At seven o'clock in the morning arrived the wife of the labourer who was in the same cell with me. She was in tears, expecting her husband to be dead by the time she came; she embraced him passionately. I comforted her by telling her that her husband would certainly be released after a few hours, as indeed he was, and then asked her to inform friends of mine of my arrest. Would they bring me a blanket and my coat? I put my message on a scrap of paper, it was duly read, and allowed to pass by the sergeant. Soon I had my blanket, and all my friends knew that I had been arrested and where I was. I was satisfied, for I was convinced they would help me efficiently.

I told them to go to the place where I lived and to destroy immediately the part of my manuscript which I had written in Valencia, which was lying there. The existence of this manuscript, which would fall into the hands of the police as soon as they went to search my room, upset me seriously. I did not know then what charge had been brought against me—did not know, in consequence, that the charge bore directly on the contents of the manuscript—but felt certain that I should be kept in jail for an unpleasantly long time if the police got hold of it. From day to day I had wanted to remove it from my home; but I did not want to remove it in small sections, and so had decided to keep it until one large section had been completed. This had been done the very day of my arrest, and I had decided to remove it next morning, when I was unexpectedly arrested. Though I was upset about this matter, still I was not deeply disturbed by it. I knew the Spaniards too well already. I was more or less confident they would not act in time. Had they brought me before the head of the department in the afternoon the situation might have been awkward. But they did not, and so they did not learn my address until late at night. They had not known that I had moved from my hotel after my return from Malaga, and had looked for me, in vain, at my former residence, and only by chance finally met and arrested me near this hotel, in the street. So they could not search my room immediately after my arrest; or rather, they could only have done so had they inquired immediately for my address. This, however, they did not do until nine o'clock at night. And by then I knew that the worst danger was over. For the head of the department had gone home by then, and I knew only too well that no Spanish official attempts to tackle any business he can possibly avoid dealing with. The head of the department would certainly not come back before ten o'clock in the morning, or nine o'clock at the worst. He would—I felt ab-

solutely certain about that—be in no hurry to take up the
business of the preceding day (as a matter of fact I was called
for my interrogatory at four o'clock in the afternoon). And by
eight o'clock in the morning one of my friends knew what he
had to do; he would have performed it half an hour later.
Actually things turned out even better than I had hoped. I
had ordered the manuscript to be destroyed but my friend
decided that it would be a pity to lose or seriously damage
the fruits of my journey by destroying that part of the manuscript which was written under the fresh impressions gathered on the spot. On his own responsibility he decided to
hide it in a safe place. It was a feat of considerable courage.
If things went wrong an order to search might have been
given in the meantime, the house might have been watched,
and the bearer of the manuscript might have been arrested
when entering or leaving the house. This would have been
more disastrous for him even than for me. In the light of later
information, when I learnt that the whole trouble was about
the manuscript, the danger seemed even greater than at the
time when the manuscript was removed. But, in fact, strange
as it may seem, no such measure was taken by the police, and
the manuscript was brought to a safe place without accident.
Police work in republican Spain is obviously not very efficient.

A few hours later I knew the manuscript was safe; I knew,
moreover, that friends had taken interest in my case. Everything was O.K. now so far. When I was finally brought up in
the afternoon for interrogation—an armed guard sitting behind me, three officials of the pre-revolutionary police force
in front of me—I learned that the one person who had seen
my manuscript, my English secretary, a communist who,
however, had known of my critical opinion towards her party
before taking on the job and had been informed that her
work was to be confidential—had denounced me. I saw the
written protocol of the denunciation. It described the whole
manuscript as highly dangerous stuff—not omitting the fact
that the part of it which dealt with the first journey was already in England. The Valencia Seguridad was given to un-

derstand that an important part of the dangerous thing was no longer available for destruction, but in exchange they had at least got the wicked man who had written it. But what she could tell about the part of the manuscript I had dictated to her—I had stopped working with her weeks before—seemed strange as a basis of a serious charge. At least one of the items she mentioned had never been in the manuscript; a second one was a remark about the slogan, 'All arms to the front,' and its role in the fight between the parties, which she had misunderstood. One charge remained; I had described in detail the political pressure the Russians had brought to bear upon Spain in exchange for the help they had given it. If it was a crime to mention this fact, then I was guilty. The Seguridad people certainly seemed to regard it as a crime. They showed the protocol of denunciation to one another with important faces and I heard the man who was directing the investigation say to his companions, with a serious shaking of the head: 'Es mucho' (that's a lot).

But it was no matter whether it was a lot or a trifle. They had to face the fact that they could not prove anything, unless I wanted to confess it freely. I made them understand that, politely but distinctly; the manuscript was no longer available, I told them. It had been destroyed, I told them, and they understood perfectly that this was only diplomatic language to convey that it was well hidden. They might have kept me in prison for a few days, but they could hardly keep me there indefinitely without the slightest proof. After all, I was writing the incriminating book for a British firm. They decided not to insist. From the moment I had told them about the disappearance of the manuscript the interrogatory ceased being serious. I knew after a few minutes that it had become a purely formal affair. If I was still a bit upset it was because I had no desire to spend a second night in my unpleasant jail. A British friend, to whom I here express my profound gratitude, pledged himself for my good behaviour, and I was set free immediately.

Such cases as mine were by no means exceptional. In the few days I still stayed in Valencia I had one humorous experience which aptly illustrates how common at this time was the accident which had happened to me. I told the story of my arrest to a company of six people of various nationalities, some of them foreign journalists working in the republican interests and others direct employees of Government services. Only two of them had never been in jail during their stay in Spain, and of those two one expected to be arrested any minute for a matter very far from being anti-republican. They at once began to talk about numbers of other people who had been arrested on the slightest charges, at least one of them a leader of the labour movement, well known in his own country. They took the matter humorously, but I felt profound disappointment behind their smiles. As to me, it was clear by now that the communists would do what they could to make further work in Spain impossible. Thus, the one thing to do was to leave; and all my friends insisted that I had been lucky this time and ought not to try my luck again. So I secured a berth on a British cargo-boat sailing for Sète in France. It was only immediately before I went on board that I made the discovery that it had delayed its departure and that, in consequence, I had to lie in harbour for at least three days. I did not like it then, but it happened to prove lucky; I had more than one interesting experience during my stay on board. But before relating them I want to add a few general conclusions concerning the police régime, just as they occurred to me at the moment of my departure.

When, in August, I had come to Spain I had intended not to make terrorism a special subject of investigation. Two days' stay in Barcelona convinced me of the profound incorrectness of my intention from the field-work point of view. Everybody talked about terrorism, anarchist terrorism in particular; some exalted, others loathed, it. Social groups took their position in the movement, chose their party allegiances, according to their views about terrorism. Later I learnt that terrorism in town and village was by far the most important lever of social revolution. Executions preceded expropriations, and fear of executions bullied the remaining rich into submission to the revolutionary régime. The suggestion that the anarchists in Catalonia owed their preponderance exclusively to their terrorist methods was wrong; they would have commanded the allegiance of a large majority of the working class without terrorism. But the other allegation that only terrorism made it possible for them to take the first steps in the direction of social revolution was true. Anarchist terrorism, in these first days, was only the most ruthless type of that terrorism which all labour class organizations exerted against the enemies of the régime all over Spain. This terrorism of the first days, the massacres and mass executions by political groups, without rule of law and orderly court, have entirely or almost entirely disappeared since. The obvious conclusion seems to be that the terroristic phase of the Spanish revolution is over. I am, however, inclined to think that it is an incorrect conclusion.

It depends, of course, on the definition one gives the word 'terrorism'. If it means executions without trial, then terrorism is rapidly disappearing in Spain. If 'terrorism' means mass executions as against separate consideration of individual cases, then again there is no more terrorism now. He who is thinking in terms of legality and morality only, who is exclusively interested in the keeping of the rule of law on the one hand and the amount of human suffering on the other, will not ask further questions. But for the sociologist as for the politician neither the legal nor the moral viewpoint, important as they are, ought to exhaust his interest. Beyond the simple question whether there is 'terrorism' or no 'terrorism' in a particular country and at a particular moment, he ought to study the transformation of the police régime and its social and political implications. A comparison of the repression of the enemies of the régime in August and in February is illuminating.

The revolutionary terrorism of July, August, and September in Spain was the thing called 'mass terrorism'; the word carrying the double signification of terrorism exerted by the masses themselves, not by an organized police force, and against a very great number, a 'mass' of victims. It has its close analogies in the Paris massacres of September 1792, and in the massacres of the year 1918 in Russia. Let us remember 1792 in Paris and compare it with 1936 in Barcelona. In Paris the volunteers massacred the prisoners before going to the front; so they did in Barcelona. They performed the massacres at a moment of supreme danger for the cause of the revolution, while the enemy approached Paris, and in the conviction that the massacre was the best means of avoiding a rising or counter-revolution in the city while they were away at the front. It was exactly the same in Barcelona. The massacre was performed without any real rule of law, with extreme ruthlessness and cruelty, but without any of the more refined tortures so characteristic of certain police régimes. Terrorism in Paris in 1792, exactly as in Barcelona in 1936, was by no means organized by a body specially created for the purpose, or, for that matter, by any organization at all. True, political groups have always backed the thing: in 1792 Danton and his group, in Russia in 1918 the Bolsheviks, in Barcelona the anarchists. But it was not performed by the party organizations but by the masses in action themselves. From this one might be inclined to conclude that it was aimless, that it struck by chance. How could nondescript masses know whom to strike? But this is not quite true. The mass only strikes, not so much at people who have perpetrated or tried to perpetrate any definite *act* against the régime, but at people who, by their station in life, are supposed to be the natural enemies of the régime which these masses defend. In Russia as in Spain and as in France the aristocrats were killed as aristocrats, the priests as priests, and in Russia and Spain the bourgeois as bourgeois; in all these cases, moreover, those individuals who were known to belong to organizations inimical to the régime. Guilt, in these outbreaks of mass terrorism, was not constituted by criminal actions but by opinions publicly displayed and by certain stations in life in general. There were certainly a great number of mistakes, even in the sense of the aims of the terrorist movement itself. But in general it was not difficult to strike precisely at those people who were aimed at. In strict contrast to a regular police régime mass terrorism obtains its aims the better the more it is decentralized. Local people are more likely to know about the political attitude and the social standing of people than any improvised central organization could possibly be.

The ruthlessness in the killing, the wild exultation of the killers over the destruction of their enemies, the irregularity of the procedure, or rather the complete lack of anything like a procedure, the execution of people not guilty of any offence, have made mass terrorism an object of horror not only for those who have lived through it but even more for later generations. But precisely on account of its characteristics mass terrorism can hardly become an efficient instrument of feud inside the revolutionary camp itself.

Not the *septembriseurs* but the revolutionary tribunal sent the Girondins and so many other French revolutionaries to the guillotine. Not the sailors of Kronstadt and the exasperated peasants but the G.P.U. have exterminated dissident socialists and communists. These persecutions have been put into effect by a centralized police machinery at the disposal of a small circle of rulers. Every revolution seems to undergo, in its course, this transformation from mass terrorism to police terrorism. The transformation was cut short in France by the fall of Robespierre, not before having made considerable progress. It came to full strength in Russia in the years after the end of the civil war. In Spain, where the properly revolutionary processes have been so quickly superseded by something entirely different, it has made great strides in the few months since the beginning of the civil war.

What are the characteristics of the second form of terrorism compared with its first form? There is contrast at every point. Instead of the revolutionary masses themselves the agents of the new terrorism are police forces. Sometimes the revolutionary police have arisen mainly out of the revolutionary ranks; in other cases, and especially to-day in Spain, it is simply the old police force, purged, as much as possible, from openly counter-revolutionary elements, and replenished with elements from the governing parties. But, in Spain at least, the bulk of the new personnel is identical with the bulk of the old, and so is their attitude; they are simply serving the new legal Government. The notion of guilt is reintroduced accordingly. The procedure is not the old procedure, rather an emergency procedure including the right of the police to execute without trial; but, apart from a few exceptions, even the police, and even the irregular police forces like 15 Plaza Tetuan, will not execute unless they are satisfied that the accused did not only dislike the Government but has committed some act against it; even committed something sufficient to justify execution, however vaguely the limits of the accused man's responsibility may be defined. Accordingly, there is a tremendous number of arrests, but the number of executions, though still considerable, bears no proportion to them. With the increasing crisis the police had gone half crazy and arrested people at random, for the silliest reasons or by mistake. But, after all, it was not proceeding in such an irresponsible manner with executions. There was an enormous improvement in this respect, mainly due to republican and communist influence, and people who had lived through the mass terrorism of the first months were particularly appreciative of the change.

But there are other aspects of the matter. Terrorism had ceased to be exercised by the masses and had ceased to be directed against definite classes. With that repression became an instrument of the ruling group against all dissentients. Repression was not limited to the Trotskyists. One day I learnt that a personal friend I had known for many years, of whose genuine socialist convictions there was not the slightest doubt, and who was very far indeed from being a Trotskyist, was in serious danger simply because he had been, in the past (!) a dissident communist. The anarchist with whom I shared my cell was in deadly fear because he had edited a paper for propaganda among communists—and I do not think he was in the least unjustified in his general ideas about what might happen to him, though in this concrete case he proved to be mistaken. One day I was introduced to a man who had been simply critical of certain technical aspects of the work of the international brigades—and, as far as I could judge, was right in his criticisms, which were obviously prompted by a deep concern for the republican cause—and who had to use all sorts of tricks in order to escape persecution and get out of Spain. In general the political commissars of the international brigades are in the habit of supposing that every man who leaves the brigade in order to take up work in another capacity—not under direct communist control—is a deserter, and treat him accordingly.

The police already acts as a G.P.U., whose chief business it is to hunt dissidents. The man who was trembling every hour to see himself arrested, tried, possibly executed, was in August the aristocrat, the priest, the industrialist, the rich merchant, the wealthy peasant. To-day, besides direct agents in the pay of Franco, he is the man who disagrees with communist policy, even on minor items. In August it was the man who, through his social status, was an adversary of the lower classes. In February it was the man who, through his opinions, was not even an adversary but a critic of the official policy of the Communist Party.

Other historical comparisons apt to throw light upon the problem may be discovered. The régime enforcing political conformity in Russia, Italy, Germany, and lastly in 'republican' Spain is often likened to the Inquisition; with very little foundation. The Catholic Church, in the Middle Ages, declared a few out of its many teachings as 'dogma' and persecuted every disbelief in these dogmas as 'heresy'. Heresy was a thing well and narrowly defined. Doctrines not completely orthodox but not heresy could be thought and written. The whole history of medieval Catholicism is full of theological dissensions of the widest and deepest implications, most of them discussed and fought without any intervention of the Inquisition; it is full of tendencies opposed to the asceticism of the Church, both in life and art. Man, in medieval Catholicism, was free to live and to think as he liked except for certain items. The intention of the totalitarian States is, on the contrary, to enforce complete unity of life and thought in every matter concerning the State, and to make every matter concern the State. Mass terrorism, far apart from the Catholic Inquisition as it is in many other respects, is nearer to it in this one aspect than to the totalitarian régime. The masses too want to terrorize in the first place the decided and active enemies of the régime as a whole; they are less concerned with dissensions inside the revolutionary camp. Revolutionary periods under mass terrorism have been, accordingly, times of intense dissension and freedom of thought—within the limits of the fight against the *ancien régime*. But wherever the totalitarian police appears every class of individuality, of intellectual, artistic, or, in a general sense, creative effort, is certain to be strangled. One must certainly feel relief in seeing the number of the victims decrease—Mussolini and Hitler have both boasted of the small number of victims of their revolutions—and those classes which have been the object of mass terrorism will be particularly grateful. But civilization is bound to perish, not simply by the existence of *certain* restrictions on the expression of freedom of thought, for which there can be ample justification—but by the whole-sale submission of thinking to orders from a party centre.

Moreover, in a civil war like that of Spain, no organization, efficient as it may be otherwise—and the Spanish Seguridad is not even efficient—can work without the free support of the people. And it remains to be seen whether the police methods applied by the Seguridad will not, in the end, prove a serious drawback for the Spanish republicans, because they strangle that popular enthusiasm which can only evolve in an atmosphere of freedom—if not for everybody, then at least for those various shades of opinion that prevail among the adversaries of Franco themselves.

Leaving Spain

Over the week-end our boat stayed out of port, in the neutral zone. It was the first day of the operation of the ban on volunteers, and everybody expected the insurgents to fête it with a bombardment. They did not, however, so on Monday the boat went back into port, not expecting any more danger. But at half-past two in the morning I was awakened

THE SECOND JOURNEY

by the thunder of five bombs dropped almost at the same time, and by the violent shaking of the windows of my cabin. Rushing out I saw that it was not one of the usual naval bombardments, but an air-raid, the first Valencia had had. Preparations for it were anything but brilliant. There were no flashlights, only light rockets. Three anti-aircraft guns were attempting to defend the port, but had no effect upon the action of the bomber, which alone, unprotected by scouts, proceeded to seek its objective imperturbably. A huge flame rose from a building in the port, some 500 or 600 feet from our boat. It had been struck by an incendiary bomb. The enemy plane went away, I drew out my watch. It took the fire-brigades twenty-two minutes to arrive. The 'all clear' signal was sounded almost as they reached the fire; it had hardly ceased sounding when the enemy bomber came back —or was it another one? Anyway, the same scene of inefficient anti-aircraft work and untroubled bombing operations was repeated. This time the bombs went into the water, farther away from our boat, and we believed the bomber had completely missed his objective. He had indeed missed it, but by a much narrower margin than we at first believed. In the morning we learned that his object had been to hit an oil-tanker, which he had just failed to do by a few yards. Had he succeeded the whole port would have been in flames. The anti-aircraft guns, however, had hit the *Royal Oak*, the largest of the British men-of-war in the neutral zone, and wounded four officers, including the commander, and one sailor.

I went to bed again and was fast asleep when, at a quarter-past seven, I was again awakened by the crash of bombs. It was bright daylight now, the enemy bomber was clearly visible, was again unprotected by scouts, arrived again without unnecessary speed, and dropped his bombs where he wanted to, on some object somewhat removed from us in the harbour district. It was an act of the utmost daring. And it was repeated half an hour later! This time, besides the anti-aircraft guns, the guns from two destroyers lying in port participated in warding off the attack. The combined sound of the anti-aircraft artillery, the destroyer's guns with their deep thundering note, and the falling bombs with their sullen crash was pandemonium. But the bomber got away, after having unloaded all his bombs.

In the morning satire followed tragedy. The port workers went on board the ships at half-past ten instead of nine o'clock, because, quite intelligibly, they were afraid of a repetition of the bombing. But they sniffed at the neutrals who, in their opinion, had shown little courage by removing certain of their ships out of the danger zone during the night. As if it were the business of onlookers to get themselves bombed for the mere sake of showing themselves 'valiant'! I talked with one anarchist transport worker who had fought long before Teruel. His judgement of foreigners was still more sweeping. He related the alleged cowardice of the neutrals to the case of a German commander who had been shot for treason at his front in Teruel, and wound up the conversation with the friendly remark: 'Once the war is over we will kick all these foreigners out.' The remark was almost incredible in the mouth of an active anarchist. In fact it would have been unthinkable in August. But as an expression of xenophobia it was far from standing alone. A very cultured Spaniard in whose company I had seen the German refugee brigade at Murcia, remarked afterwards: 'I do not like these Germans,' and when asked why, he replied: 'Because to-day they are with us and to-morrow will be with Franco,' a reply so meaningless in the circumstances as to make me really angry. I repressed my anger, but could not help thinking that every single insurgent offensive had been successful until one of the international brigades had been called to the menaced sector.

A curse on foreigners was about the last thing I heard in the Spanish tongue. It was not the last thing I saw of the Spanish civil war. I got an impression of the efficiency of the blockade of the Government camp from the sea. We had left port for a little more than two hours, and, proceeding slowly, were still not far from Valencia, when we were sighted by a large modern battleship, either the *Canarias* or the *Baleares*. She changed her course in order to follow us, caught up with us in a very short time, put her enormous searchlight on us, saw that we were English, and did not formally stop us, but came alongside and then, with her smaller guns trained upon us, asked questions as to whence we came, where we were going, what cargo we carried, and so on. Then she went back. The night before a Spanish steamer bound for Bilbao from Alicante, with a large cargo and many passengers, was stopped and brought into Melilla. I was horrified at the idea of what may have happened to some of the passengers. Obviously the port of Valencia was so well guarded that hardly any ship could leave without the silent permission of the insurgent fleet. If a good deal of commerce was permitted, it was because the insurgents were afraid of showing lack of respect for certain foreign flags, notably the British, Scandinavian, and Dutch. But this respect was relative, as I was soon to realize. Next afternoon we were caught up, in our course, by an insurgent plane, which first flew over us very low, a proceeding not in itself objectionable, but proving that we were being closely watched. Then he suddenly turned and began to circle over our heads, and put himself into an inclined position as if preparing to bomb us. At the last moment he returned to the horizontal position, flying closely over our stern. The threat was hardly to be mistaken.

That night, I saw, for the first time for many weeks, an unaccustomed sight: two lights on the coast, where for a long time all lights, including those of the lighthouses, have been extinguished. The one was the light of Port Bou, indicating the entry into Spanish waters, the other the lighthouse of the French port of Port Vendres. We were leaving the territory of Spain and of the war. I saw the lights with deep emotion. I regretted that I had had to leave Spain. Like so many other foreigners I was magnetically attracted by the struggle. It was no longer the political issue that counted, but the country itself, the people, who, apart from a few politicians, I had learnt deeply to love, as so many, almost all who have watched them in these tragical months, have learnt to love them. Already this country had become the grave of more than one friend. What would become of the others? Would I ever meet them again, and if so, how would I meet them? I had to look on now from a distance. It would be more exasperating even than watching at close quarters. My heart shrank. But next morning, 25 February, at Sète, there was peace in the people's faces, as if there was not and had never been, a few miles south, a terrible civil war.

IV

THE BATTLE OF GUADALAJARA

How far have the impressions I gathered during my second journey been confirmed and contradicted by later events? What new trends have appeared in the Spanish revolution since the combined catastrophes of Malaga and of the southern wing of the Madrid front? I am not able to discuss these questions on the basis of observations on the spot. I can only submit the conclusions I tried to draw from sources which, I believe, are reliable. Some of the facts to be taken into consideration are overt in so far as they have been reported by the Press; but, having become sceptical from many experiences, and being convinced that under the censorship regulations prevailing in both camps in Spain and under the present conditions of international tension Press reports are much more unreliable than one would expect them to be, I was careful not to accept a single fact only on the strength of Press reports.

Two facts are obvious: the insurgents have allowed the republicans to gather troops west of Almeria in time to stop the fascist advance after the fall of Malaga in the south; similarly, the offensive on the southern wing of the Madrid front, which, after the break-through at Jarama had begun with such good auspices for Franco, has been stopped at an early stage. Thus, the offensives started in February have had no definite success. Secondly, the landing at Sagunto in February, which was expected to cut Valencia from Barcelona and thus bring a decisive end to the war, has not taken place. Information about the preparations for this

262

offensive on the islands was too definite to allow of any doubt; if the offensive did not take place, it must be due to a change in the strategic plans of Franco.

It is difficult to see why the insurgents have dropped, for the present moment, their original intention to land. The coastal defences were infinitely weaker than any other part of the Government positions, for the simple reason that no good troops were allotted for this task, because none could be spared from the decisive battlefields for a front which was not actually existing but only potential. Before one of the international brigades could be thrown into battle at the coast-line something between twenty-four and forty-eight hours, at the minimum, must pass; this delay must mean a considerable advantage for the insurgents. Moreover, the point they intended to attack was obviously much more sensitive than any other region of the Government camp.

I see no military explanation for the change of plans in the Franco camp. But there is perhaps a political one. The landing at Sagunto ought to start from Majorca. Very few Spanish troops are stationed in Majorca. None could easily be thrown on this island as reinforcements. The contingents at Malaga, Cordova, and Madrid were implied in heavy fighting. Those at Teruel were supposed to participate in the landing by a subsidiary attack from the west. Only the Saragossa front might have been able to spare troops, but there the transport difficulties were considerable. Thus the landing would be an almost exclusively Italian affair. Starting from Majorca, it would demonstrate to the world that the islands had become Italian for all practical purposes. But both Britain and France have much stronger strategical interests in Majorca than the rest of Spain. The landing from Majorca might involve international complications of a serious character.

Up to this moment the intervention of the great fascist powers had remained in the stage of hesitating experiments. The preparations in Majorca were one of these experiments. But the violent reaction of both France and Britain against the first serious attempt at a German occupation of Spanish

THE BATTLE OF GUADALAJARA

Morocco in January had demonstrated that it was impossible for Mussolini to go too far in this direction. The preparations in Majorca were procrastinated, an object not only easy to achieve in all Spanish matters, but producing itself almost automatically unless the natural trend of the Spanish national character is overcome by very heavy pressure.

I do not pretend that I have definite facts to back this interpretation. It only seems to me the most likely one. Another fact, however, is undeniable. By the end of February, after the deadlock in Motril and on the Madrid-Valencia road, foreign help became an urgent necessity for Franco. It was given, not in Sagunto, but in Guadalajara, at the northern angle of the Madrid front. In order to understand the importance of this new attempt, one must realize to its full extent the gap between the current ideas about foreign intervention in Spain and reality. Public opinion believed thousands of Germans and Italians were fighting in the trenches. In reality only special units, such as aviation, anti-aircraft artillery, field artillery, and tanks had co-operated in the Franco camp until then. There was an assumption, probably justified, that thousands of Italians, and possibly of Germans, lay behind the lines in garrison, waiting for possible orders to participate in the fighting. Since the beginning of January every single success of the insurgents had been attributed to German and Italian troops. But in every single case, whether it were the first offensive against Malaga, the attack on the Escorial, or the Jarama catastrophe, the republicans had counter-attacked, not without success. Invariably these counter-attacks had brought Spanish prisoners to the republican headquarters, but not a single German or Italian prisoner; only the second, decisive offensive against Malaga had proceeded without counter-attacks and thus remained the one case where the theory of actual participation of German and Italian infantry units could not be disproved. But it is not proved either. On the whole it seems true, though maybe unlikely, that there was little intervention with infantry units of any importance before March. Occasionally, a few German and Italian units seem to have been brought up to the front line to participate in an attack for one or two days, but withdrawn as soon as they began to take part in the activities. Such behaviour is incomprehensible from the military point of view, but one must not forget that there are divergences of opinion between the fascist parties and the military, both in Germany and Italy, as to the advisability of intervention in Spain; that, moreover, there is distrust and rivalry between Germans and Italians; that, last, not least, the Franco commands, Spanish nationalists as they are, profoundly dislike the interference of the foreigner. (The situation in the republican camp is somewhat different. There are the international brigades, but no Russian volunteers. The brigades correspond to the foreign legion in the Franco camp.)

But Guadalajara was a different matter; this time the participation of Italian infantry was thorough. In consequence, Italian prisoners existed, not only in Press telegrams, but in the streets of Madrid, which is very different. They were there in considerable numbers, owing to the extent of the defeat of the Italian units. Had the republican success been as small as at Motril, at the Escorial, at Arganda, the number of the prisoners would have been smaller, but they would have been there. But in these other cases there were no foreign prisoners because there were very few foreign troops.

Two facts, then, emerge out of misleading and contradicting reports: for the first time Italian units have seriously fought in Spain, and immediately they have been heavily beaten. They have even been defeated more heavily than any Spanish or Moorish section of the Franco troops ever before. It is important to understand the real bearing of this event.

To start with, what units were they? They were, according to reliable information, which does not fully agree with Spanish official reports, neither regular army units nor fascist militia, at least the greater part of them were not. This statement, like all the scepticism here displayed concerning foreign intervention in Spain, undoubtedly clashes with the formal and emphatic declarations of Signor Mussolini, who has emphasized again and again the glory of the Italian arms in

THE BATTLE OF GUADALAJARA

Spain. But Signor Mussolini has a reputation for being a clever propagandist. As a lot of Italian pilots, tank officers, and others were actually participating in the civil war, and Italian units were garrisoning the hinterland of Franco, it would have been no use to deny the fact of intervention. Timid *démentis* would only have produced peremptory demonstration of the real situation. Why, then, if the fact was undeniable, not make as much propaganda out of it as possible? This propaganda had little chance of being contradicted. The Franco camp must swallow the attribution of Spanish successes to the Italians, their tongues in their cheeks; they could not venture publicly to quarrel with Mussolini. Nobody would say no to the Italian contentions. Everybody would attribute Franco's successes to Mussolini. And Mussolini, firmly believing in Franco's success, saw the world take Franco's successes as his before they had been achieved. But, as Lenin liked to say, 'you should not glory in victory before you have come out of the battle'.

There were, I repeat, Italian infantry units at the Guadalajara front, but few of them either of the army or of the militia. It seems that by far the major part of the Italians at Guadalajara were volunteers who had enlisted for Abyssinia and who, at the moment of embarkation, did not know that they were going to Spain. But these were not volunteers for the Abyssinian war; they had, I am told, been enlisted for the Abyssinian labour army, which had been formed recently. They were units similar to those known in Germany as 'voluntary labour service'. In one word, though all or most of these men had passed through the regular military service, they were not regular military units in any sense, but were formed into such only with a view to their utilization in Spain. Most of them had been landed in Cadiz during the last days of the Malaga campaign, but had not participated in the conquest of Malaga. By far the larger part were from Southern Italy. The majority were of peasant origin, as from all this one would expect. By no means an élite formation, then. (By the way: all the material I am giving here is derived from documents taken with prisoners. It was one of the most striking features of the battle of Guadalajara that, for the first time, the habit of killing prisoners was completely overcome in the republican camp. The political advantages of this correct behaviour became apparent immediately.)

Indications of the strength of the Italian contingent naturally diverge widely. Official sources from Valencia, in a natural attempt to give the republican success the widest possible importance, speak of five or six Italian 'divisions'. It would be unwise to take such assertions *á la lettre*. The impression of one careful observer carries conviction to me. According to him, two divisions were actually in battle, while a third one stood in reserve and was involved in the final catastrophe. These so-called divisions are very small, something like 3,000 men each. Both wings were protected, each by one Spanish division. Nine thousand Italians, then, and 6,000 Spaniards altogether on the fascist side. At the beginning of the fight the whole attacked sector was defended by one republican brigade of 2,000–3,000 men. Scouting, as usual, was very bad. The attack came as a surprise, with infinitely superior infantry forces and a good backing by artillery and tanks. The Government lines, naturally, broke at once.

After their initial success, the Italians lost all control over themselves. Drunk with the glory of their easy victories in Ethiopia, they saw final success already in their hands. They had decided to be in Madrid within four days, and told their troops so. They dropped every precaution, and advanced with entirely insufficient protection for the flanks. To wait for that would have forced them to slow down the advance, for, after all, their effectives were weak, not in comparison with the first republican contingents on the spot but with the geographical extension of the battlefield: a front of twenty miles, growing every hour as they advanced into enemy country. Moreover, they grouped reinforcements in masses on the main roads, and drew their staffs very near the advancing front line. According to all rules of reasonable warfare, it was madness. But if Franco was never able to make much of his successes, they would teach the Spaniards how to follow up an initial success with the destruction of the enemy. They had not even met this enemy.

Five republican brigades were thrown within twelve hours to the menaced spot. The Madrid command knew only too well that it was a matter of existence or destruction for the anti-fascist cause. One more success of the Italians, and republican Madrid was lost. Among the five brigades were two international ones, mainly composed of Germans and Italians, the best brigades of the whole Spanish army, wearing the names, respectively, of Thaelmann and Garibaldi. These two brigades are much superior to the military level even of the average foreign volunteers. They are composed of refugees, who, most of them, after having volunteered in Spain, could not even return to their first refugee abode and have no choice left but to live or to die in Spain. One German refugee machine-gun company, which had been thrown into battle immediately, with insufficient backing and with the sole aim of delaying the Italian advance until further reinforcements could arrive, was wiped out almost completely without wavering of its lines, in the successful fulfilment of its task. One out of the three Spanish brigades was composed of Basques, whose military abilities are much superior to those of the average Spaniard; the two others were élite brigades of the Fifth (communist) Regiment. As usual, the foreign volunteers bore the brunt of the battle. The Germans have to wash away the ignominy of their defenceless retreat before the forces of Hitler. The Italians found unimaginable bliss in fighting fascist troops, after ten years of exile, arms in hand, and beating them. The fact, politically so regrettable, that, in spite of innumerable declarations, political party units still exist, showed all its military value. The two brigades of the Fifth Regiment, almost exclusively communist, or anyway, exclusively under communist officers, showed the value of a morale based not only on military discipline but on common political conviction. With their success the communists refuted their own slogans concerning the dissolution of the political brigades.

The Italians, on their march, were first delayed, then

stopped in front, then attacked on the left flank, and considerably disturbed by this flank attack. But the event was finally decided by Russian aviation; 120 planes, bombers and scouts, attacked, not so much even the lines but the rear, bombing the troop concentrations on the road, the staffs, the artillery (all of them, as described, quite unprepared for such an event). The superiority of Russian over Italian scout planes has been well established during all these months of war, though not to such an extent as its superiority over the Germans. But until Guadalajara the superiority of the Italian bombers, both in speed and in exactness of bombing had been generally admitted. Probably Guadalajara does not give sufficient material for a reversal of this judgement. But the air battle of Guadalajara, the largest yet fought in Spain, has proved, it seems, that scouting, not bombing, is the decisive factor. A very considerable number of bombers will strike their objective, if they are well protected by scouts. In this case the effect was disastrous upon the enemy. After two hours of bombardment, the front broke, broke helplessly, without an attempt at further resistance. Only now did it become apparent how little value there was in the Abyssinian experience. In Abyssinia the Italians had no experience of being bombed. Before these bombs they ran, ran exactly as the first red militia units had run in Spain in August and September before similar experiences. Then, and only then, the flank attack showed all its implications. The Italian units, in their flight, were attacked individually by Government units, which had them completely at their mercy, because there was no organized resistance. All informants agree that the bombing was decisive, and after it there was no recovery: that the Government units recovered the ground lost the first day practically without resistance, and only stopped at their old lines on account of the scarcity of manpower.

There is no doubt that Guadalajara has changed the outlook of the war, that following that event new problems arise. It is worth while to discuss all the implications. It would, of course, be far from correct to suppose that the Italians will always run as they did in Guadalajara. Many elements of this defeat are incidental only. The Italians behaved as if there were no serious adversary. One experience of this kind will certainly suffice to teach them the contrary and make them act accordingly. Their troops were bad; their conduct is no reliable indication of the conduct of regular army units or fascist militia. Still, the fact remains that Italian units believed to be quite sufficient by their commands—after the Abyssinian experience—for the task, have been broken and chased over the country by forces smaller in number (a republican brigade counts 2,000 men on an average). More important, there have been real desertions, in numbers not entirely negligible, at an early stage of developments. Something like 1,000 prisoners have been captured up to now (if sources of information concerning this point are reliable), and most of them seem eager to explain that they have surrendered of their own accord. Given the reputation of both sides for shooting their prisoners, such declarations may perhaps be judged to be not quite genuine. But the fact remains and seems to be well established that whole groups went over at the first occasion offered, as soon as the Government lines stood firm. They had been furious at being sent to death in Spain instead of to work in Abyssinia, they explained; they had suffered heavily from cold on the Spanish highlands, and finally had decided to cross the lines—singing the *Bandiera Rossa* according to one source of information—in groups. Some of these deserters had been members of socialist organizations before the advent of fascism, but most of them had not. If one considers these facts one is induced to think that perhaps the surprise of Guadalajara is less indicative of the military value of the Italian army as reorganized by fascism than of the state of mind of the masses, in the Italian south at least. The propaganda value of the conquest of Abyssinia seems not to have been so great, after all, as was assumed by many observers.

We will not deal here with the implications of these facts for future developments in Italy. Neither will we discuss the possible international consequences. Mussolini can hardly accept defeat without reacting with more than aggressive words. The one aspect to be discussed here is the inevitable reaction to Guadalajara in the Franco camp.

In the preceding pages the intrinsic weakness of the Government camp in any and every respect has been discussed in detail. Up to now, Franco has lived by the mistakes, even by the stupidities of his enemies. He has been successful before Toledo, has reached the outskirts of Madrid, because neither the republicans nor the socialists were able to organize an army. As soon as he came up against something like organized resistance at Madrid, on 8 November, he had to stop. He overran Malaga, where nothing was prepared for defence. But every single time he met serious resistance, his advance was stopped. Franco has little push of his own; the movement behind him has obviously only a limited offensive power. He has won many successes because even a few battalions, indifferently commanded, but organized in the manner of regular troops, were sufficient to secure such successes. Would it be enough, in order to stop him, to organize a few brigades on a similar level on the republican side? If this is so, then the task is already achieved. Then, as so many times predicted, time will work for the republicans. They have, if nothing else, an almost unlimited reserve of man-power. Franco has not. First he had not dared to mobilize his rear. He has decided to try now; the two Spanish divisions on Franco's side at Guadalajara were largely composed of new recruits. They have accounted for even more deserters than the Italians, and these not non-political peasants but workers and agricultural labourers who hated the Franco régime. By staying still, however, Franco seriously menaces his own existence. His forces, lacking reinforcements, must decline. Those of his adversaries must increase. He needs more material help from abroad than he has yet received. It seems that at this moment pessimism is rampant in the fascist camp, exactly as it was in the Left camp in February.

But one must be careful not to jump to conclusions. Defence is infinitely easier than offence. The Government camp, if it has acquired defensive capacity, still lacks offensive power.

And the policy followed in these last few months has made it very difficult for them to launch a successful offensive. Politics will finally determine the course of the war, as they do in every revolution. What is the trend of politics in the republican camp?

The last few weeks, as far as one can make out from abroad, have been characterized by a break in the advance of the Communist Party. Two outstanding events symbolize a certain reshuffling of the political balance: the disappearance of General Kleber and the recall of the Russian ambassador, Mr. Rosenberg.

The disappearance of Kleber, the real commander-in-chief of the Madrid front, not a Russian, but a foreigner who has been in Russian service for many years, dates back to the end of January. From one day to the next, he not only had to leave his command, but actually disappeared, hiding himself for many weeks, afraid of the vengeance of his former subordinates. It is not true, as has been widely reported in the foreign Press, that he was caught by the rebels in Malaga. I saw him myself (though I had no occasion to speak to him) while he was said to be captured by the insurgents, but was actually hiding in the republican camp. The fact of his hiding is itself significant enough. The Madrid front was the one where the republicans had been able to repel serious attacks of the enemy. They had done so under the command of General Kleber, and there is no doubt that most of the military successes of the republicans on the Madrid front between November and January must be placed to his credit, so far, at least, as staff work is concerned. Military organization was mostly brought into line by other communists, from the Fifth Regiment, such as 'Carlos Contreras' (by no means a Spaniard, either) and Lister. What followed is characteristic not so much of the Spanish civil war in particular as of Spanish politics in general.

Kleber's successes roused an enormous amount of jealousy against him. A knot of intrigues, which I am far from being able to disentangle, ensued in the Junta de Defensa of Madrid. It appears that Kleber, an officer with an officer's

as if the Spaniards were simply being saved by foreigners. It was intolerable that these foreigners should take precedence over the Spaniards in matters of command. The power of decision had to be restored to a purely Spanish body, and the glory of the success ought to go to the Spaniards. Personal jealousy together with nationalism were stronger than hatred of the anarchists, desire to finish social revolution, and even the simple and primary desire to win the war.

The matter was only partly settled in a formal way. In a military sense the international brigades could do whatever they liked; if they chose they could march upon Valencia, take it, and institute what command and what government they liked. But for such action things are not ripe by any means. Such might be the course of a victorious general after he has ended the war, but not in the midst of an indecisive campaign. A *coup d'état* of the communists, not with but against socialists and republicans, would mean the end, the final success of Franco. They did not attempt it. They preferred to drop Kleber, to leave him to the vendetta of his personal enemies, which he escaped not without difficulty. It was a big blow to them. The anarchists had attained their immediate object.

If I am rightly informed, the story goes that in Spain after the fall of Malaga, under the impression of defeat, things changed profoundly and a general rally of forces took place. There is such a rally, but it has little to do with the fall of Malaga, whose political effects, as described above, were surprisingly small. In reality, the change started from the cr'
in the Madrid command, as a consequence of whi'
entirely Spanish *junta de defensa* was formed in Mad'
communists lacked strength to push through the
of the Government, and so abandoned this i'
days after, but a few days before the fall of
sequence, the problem of the general po°'
arose. Negotiations about Russian hel'
on the old lines failed, and becaus'
withdrew. The period when the '
and big political concessions for h'

communists remain a very influential party; they are, for the moment, not the paramount party.

The results of this reversal of positions make themselves felt in many ways. The socialists feel stronger again; they have little force of their own, but still command the machinery of the UGT. They have acted, in the last crisis, as a force with a policy of their own, and have regained a certain self-confidence. The communists, for their part, have had to bridle their animus against the POUM. The anarchists supposed the massacre of the POUM was intended to pave the way for the final attack against themselves. They dislike the POUM and have dealt it many blows in the first months. But since Russian and communist influence became preponderant, they have begun to protect the POUM, in order to protect themselves. The communists, now, in stopping their more ruthless attacks on the POUM, say themselves that they are doing so for the sake of a better understanding with the anarchists. On the basis of all that, a sort of armistice between communists and anarchists has been reached. It is not that they do not hate one another, or are not trying to prepare, both of them, for a final settling of their accounts. But for the moment both have renounced, partly at least, attempts to upset the balance by violent actions. Both have recognized that the war with Franco must precede civil war in the anti-fascist camp. In this one sense one can say that the catastrophe of Malaga has had its effect. Without it, the crisis in the Madrid command and the Government crisis might have had different consequences. The law which dominated all modern revolutions remains valid: defeat drives revolutions to the Left, success to the Right. This time, Malaga has prevented the communists from pursuing their attempts towards a *coup d'état* against the Left elements of the Spanish anti-fascist camp.

The effects, apparent in the success at Guadalajara, seem far to be beneficial to the Valencia camp. The administra-, which was completely paralysed by intrigues and by the aration of civil war in the anti-fascist camp, is working The coal crisis and the gasoline crisis have been miti-

THE BATTLE OF GUADALAJARA

gated by adequate administrative measures. Trains are running regularly again (in mid-February every journalist who travelled by railway from Port Bou to Valencia told of misadventures; to-day, the trains from Barcelona to Valencia take eight hours again, not more), and the military operations at Guadalajara were not hampered by gasoline shortage. Even the food situation seems to have improved, especially in Barcelona, with the smoothing out of political differences. The Catalan Government is buying food abroad.

The military command has undergone hectic changes. After the fall of Kleber there was at first no adequate provision for the Madrid command. This was one of the reasons of the Jarama disaster on the southern wing of the Madrid front. But then came reorganization. After the fall of Malaga, General Asensio was removed from his post of chief of the general staff at the Ministry of War in Valencia. In Madrid the communists were induced to put their foreign technical advisers at the disposal of an exclusively Spanish command. *En fin de compte*, they were thus persuaded to contribute to the fight their specific technical abilities, without securing complete political domination in return. Measures for the unification of the Catalan and the Spanish military command were taken. As Jarama corresponds to the transitional stage of chaos after Kleber's fall, so Guadalajara corresponds to the reorganized command. At the moment of the break-through of the Italian divisions, the Junta de Defensa was delegated the power to take all measures to meet the emergency, including the transference of troops from other sectors. Perhaps for the first time there was then a really unified command, because, at that moment, nobody had any fear of its success. Accordingly, it was successful.

V

CONCLUSIONS

The Franco rising is usually described as a fascist revolt; this habit partly derives from the fact that Franco himself identifies himself with international fascism. And, in a scientific sense, the term might pass, provided every dictatorship is called 'fascist' and fascism is simply used in the sense of 'a non-democratic régime'. But it is inexpedient to do this, because it bars understanding of the individual concrete dictatorships of our time, which differ widely between themselves in many respects. Fascism, classically represented in the present German and Italian régimes, means something quite definite. It means, first of all, a dictator who is recognized as the 'leader'; it means, secondly, a one-party system; it means, thirdly, the 'totalitarian state', in the sense that the régime dictates not only in matters of politics in the proper sense, but in every aspect of public and private life; it means, in the fourth place, that no force independent of the central party is tolerated in any field whatsoever; it means, moreover, that the party, by means both of conviction and violence, tries to get the unified consent of the nation and succeeds, to a large degree, in this attempt. It means, finally, that the totalitarian power is used in order to achieve a higher degree of co-ordination and efficiency in every branch of public life; fascism is the most powerful political agent of 'modernization' that we know of.

Hardly any of these features have their counterpart in the Franco régime. Franco himself, the leader, owes his role not to any real ascendancy over enemies and competitors, slowly evolved and solidly conquered, but to the chance that the other claimants to supreme command, Calvo Sotelo, Sanjurjo, Goded, José Primo de Rivera, are dead. This in the beginning is a difference of no slight importance. Its implications are emphasized by the fact that Franco has not, any more than formerly had Primo de Rivera, a 'totalitarian' party to back his aims. The two parties paramount in the Franco camp, the Falange and the Carlists (the former much more important than the latter) are both very far from being parties of Franco. The Carlists, who aim at the restoration of an absolute legitimate monarchy, are naturally at odds with both the Falange and with Franco, who are not monarchists. Besides there also exists, though with only feeble strength, Renovacion Española, the party of Alphonso XIII in exile. One sector of the Franco movement, then, is not fascist but monarchist. And this divergence of views on an important problem, a divergence shattering the Franco camp not much less than the anarchist-communist controversy is shattering the republican camp, excludes, at present, the very idea of a one-party system. Worse, still, there is notoriously deep disagreement between Franco and Falange, the fascist party proper. The Press of Falange always carefully avoids calling Franco the 'chief', the 'leader', or anything like it; they simply call him 'the generalissimo', the high commander, signifying that they only accept his temporary dictatorship as a war measure. They claim political leadership for themselves; try, not without success, to establish a party out of elements of all classes, take great care to group labour elements under their banner, and indirectly make it a reproach to Franco that he is not the representative of a popular movement of national resurrection—as they themselves try to be—but simply the leader of the military clique, which, after all is only the truth. There can be no real fascism, then, in the Franco camp, because the Fascist Party is against the general-leader, who, himself, has no political party at his orders. All this is not changed, in the least, by the superficial unification of Carlists and Falangists recently brought about by Franco.

CONCLUSIONS

Those two groups have been fighting one another all the time, with no less fury than anarchists and communists have fought one another in the other camp. None of them have renounced their political principles, and all the leading staffs remain in the unified party as they did in the two parties before their unification, each with its own following. It is a poor imitation, by a military dictator, of that fascist one-party system which has been achieved in other countries. There are few differences larger than that between an exclusively military, non-political dictatorship and a fascist dictatorship based on a wide political movement. Franco's régime is the former, not the latter. Already Spain has witnessed Primo's failure because he could not, as he wished, create a wide political movement to back his military dictatorship. In consequence, the Franco régime has little popular support, which is its chief weakness, and at the same time makes it something entirely different from genuine fascism. For months and months Franco did not dare to mobilize his rear. Finally, under the pressure of acute shortage of man-power he did so, with the result that the conscripts deserted *en masse*, at the first opportunity, in the battle of Guadalajara. Outside Navarra (which is Carlist), part of Galicia (which is more or less Alphonsist), and Majorca (which is the private domain of the tobacco king, Juan March), Franco has no popular backing. Finally, the Franco régime is anything but modernizing. A régime backed mainly by the Spanish Church and army could not be. In spite of all efforts to prove the contrary the Franco régime is really nothing but a repetition, with more violent methods, of the Robles régime, which, in its turn was a repetition of the Cánovas régime, of the restoration settlement, which so miserably failed at the end of the nineteenth century. The Spanish Right realize that the old gang will not do, that something new must be introduced, and try to *imitate* fascism, as the modern form of reaction. But the first thing genuine fascism would do would be to subdue both army and Church to the totalitarian party—as it has done in Germany and Italy—and to wipe out all the modes of life near to the heart of the old pre-capitalist traditionalist Spanish upper class. In

280

one word, in order to become genuinely fascist, the Franco régime would first have to destroy itself. As it is, it is simply a reactionary military dictatorship such as Spain has seen in dozens, with the difference that it is backed by foreign powers. The whole course of the civil war has demonstrated that, without this backing, limited as it is, Franco would no longer exist. This basic weakness of the revolt is in itself an indication that it is a phenomenon profoundly different from the supposedly parallel movements of its German and Italian allies, each of which arose on a basis of deep-rooted and very strong mass sentiments.

Every Spanish party, government, movement, has been caught between the pressure of circumstances which drive the country towards Europeanization and the country's deeply ingrained resistance. But of all classes of Spain, the old upper classes are least capable of Europeanizing themselves and the country. Franco has failed to be anything but the exponent of these old upper classes, incapable of modernizing, and equally incapable of merging with the masses of the people. The experience of 1707 and 1808 has repeated itself in 1936; the Spanish people stood out against its upper classes, and the upper classes proved to be powerless without the people. This, so far, is the main political result of nine months of civil war.

If it were only that, things would soon be settled, Franco would be defeated, the masses, after some upheaval, would probably sink back into their apathy, and nothing would be changed; but there were the foreigners. The Spanish revolution would probably have failed to achieve either democracy or socialism or anything else, and would certainly have failed to reorganize the country, had not the foreigner interfered and forced thoroughgoing measures upon the people. The history of the Spanish civil war, as far as the Left camp is concerned, is the history of the spontaneous resistance of the masses against two things: on the one hand against the revolt of clergy and army, and on the other hand against the necessity to beat down this revolt with modern means of warfare and organization. The masses wanted to fight and did fight heroically, but they wanted it to be a fight in the old guerilla

CONCLUSIONS

manner of 1707 and 1808, a rising from village to village, from town to town, against the threat of tyranny. That it could not be.

In order to understand it fully, one must remember that revolutions, in general, are moved, not so much by ideals as by necessities. This applies to the French, to the Russian, and to many other revolutions, to a much higher degree than is generally realized. The Bolsheviks, for instance, achieved their aims not so much because a few thousand intellectuals and workers had been convinced by the Bolshevist political programme, and had diffused this programme to a certain extent among certain limited strata of the small Russian urban proletariat; the Bolshevists won because the breakdown of the nation in war brought to the forefront the question of immediate peace, and the Bolshevists alone were prepared to carry this out. Similarly, in Spain the domination of the proletariat did not come about because a limited stratum of anarchists, and a still much more limited stratum of Trotskyists, dreamt of it (the communists had already ceased to dream of it), but because when the whole army rose in rebellion only the workers were able to defend the large majority of the people against army, Church, and large landowners. Every single step of the revolution, then, has not been brought about by the success of some sort of propaganda, by the spreading of some sort of abstract convictions, but by urgent necessities of the moment. In general, it is defeats which drive a revolution to the Left—not, as is generally believed, successes. It is defeats which ask for extreme measures of defence, and which bring into power the most advanced sections of the movement, because they alone are prepared and able to apply extreme measures. Thus the Independents overcame the Presbyterians, in the English revolution, as a result of the victories of the king over the parliament. Thus the Jacobins overwhelmed the Girondins, in Paris, as the result of the sweeping victories of the Austrians and Prussians in March 1793. Thus the Bolsheviks came in when Russia drifted towards a state of complete disintegration. Thus the revolutionary committees got power into their hands in Spain on the day when the republic crumbled under the stroke Franco had dealt it. The more advanced methods were supposed to bring about a greater measure of fighting power than the milder measures previously applied. And, with bitterness in their hearts, the more moderate sections, republicans, Catalanists, Right-wing socialists, co-operated in organizing that revolutionary power which was a menace to their very existence, because otherwise Franco would get in and destroy them immediately. This reluctant but real consent of the moderate elements, in the moments of disaster and of the greatest success of counter-revolution, to extreme revolutionary measures, is a common feature of every revolutionary crisis. Without it an advanced minority could never rule. In consequence, once the danger is over the more moderate elements invariably try, and generally succeed, to get rid of the more advanced section, whose help they needed in order to ward off the attempts of open counter-revolution.

This was at the root of the political change from parlia-mentary democracy to the 'double régime' of 19 July. After this day there were on the one hand the old legal govern-ments of Madrid and Barcelona, with no socialists and anar-chists participating in them, and with very little real power; and on the other hand the committees. At first the success of this system was splendid. In almost all the larger towns of Spain the insurrection was beaten. But then, surprisingly, came deadlock. The fact has a double explanation. On the one hand, after one or two weeks the insurgents got foreign arms of modern construction, and the popular forces of the militia conspicuously failed to make a stand against air-raids and artillery bombardments; on the other hand, this same militia, which had fought heroically in the old guerilla manner in its own street and town, its own village, failed to adapt itself to fighting in close units of modern type in the open field. The same men who had been heroes in the streets of Madrid became cowards on the battlefields of Talavera and Santa Eulalia. In other words, it was impossible to make the step from the traditional national guerilla warfare to modern warfare. The one effect of the formation of modern units was that the militia-men lost the opportunity to employ their guerilla instincts, without acquiring the abilities of the modern soldier.

For a couple of months, then, the Spanish revolution proceeded under a delusion. It was obvious that at least one of the two levers of the 'double régime' was defective: the legal Government. The Catalanists were not so bad, but the Madrid republicans, in these decisive first weeks, were really giants of inactivity. Remove them, then, overcome the double régime, create a government of the revolutionary parties, at one in spirit and action with the revolutionary masses: such was the intention. So Giral was replaced by Caballero, and later the anarchists were drawn close to the Government. The effect, to everybody's surprise, was nil. The new Government, though the radicalism of its political convictions was not in doubt, failed in every respect. It failed to reorganize; Toledo was as miserable a defeat as Talavera. And it failed to embark on a revolutionary social policy.

In fact, no such thing as a stronger revolutionary trend was needed in the towns. In the main industrial centres, with the partial exception of Bilbao, a widespread expropriation of industrial property had taken place, partly as a result of socialist ideals, but more frequently because the owners of the factories had fled or been killed. The workers had many more factories on their hands than they themselves or the administration could reasonably manage. Moreover, the attempt at thorough socialization was likely to lead to conflict between Spain and the great democratic powers. But it was different with the villages. Here the revolution, in fact, had been very slow. In some provinces, as La Mancha, the expropriation of large estates by the peasants and labourers had been spontaneous, but in the greater part of the country the agrarian revolution had at first simply been driven into the villages by the militia. If the Government wanted a broad popular rising, a real people's war, which was the one certain way to beat Franco, it must not play with 'socialist' industry in town, but make every effort to bring about a broad peasant movement and submerge Franco in the waves of revolting villages. In order to do so it must give the peasants tangible things, land in the first place. A good deal of the preceding diary shows how this task was not achieved. Caballero and his staff had never thought about both the technical and the political problems of a revolution. They had become, in old age, revolutionaries by disappointment, after a long and thoroughly reformist past. The communists, by orders from Moscow, had dropped every idea, not only of a proletarian, but even of a village revolution after the example of the French Revolution. The Trotskyists were repeating senseless formulae such as 'constituent assembly', taken out of the books about the Russian revolutions of 1905 and 1917. The anarchists played about with the creation of the kingdom of heaven in the form of the abolition of money and complete collectivization in the individual villages. In one word, all sections had been ready to ward off an armed attack, arms in hand. This was what made such a tremendous impression upon the Left in Europe, which, in other countries, had ignominiously failed to achieve this relatively simple task. But no party was able to organize resistance against even the small amount of foreign intervention with which they were faced, and none had any constructive idea whatsoever in politics. The creative political power in which both the French and the Russian revolution had been so rich was conspicuously absent in Spain. As on the Right every section of the Franco movement refused or failed to create something really new, so on the Left did every section of the labour movement, from the communists to the anarchists.

And thus the Caballero Government being a complete failure politically and administratively, the insurgents, helped less by their own valour than by Italian planes and German guns, arrived at the gates of Madrid on 7 November. It seemed that the supreme moment for the Spanish republic had come. At this moment Russian foreign policy veered round. It had not been pleased, at first, by the Spanish troubles, and for months refused almost every sort of help, to the bitter disappointment of the Spaniards. Now, finally, Moscow realized that, though it had kept out of the muddle, a defeat of the Left in Madrid would be as bad for Moscow as the defeat of Addis Ababa had been for the League of Nations. Moscow offered its help, and it was eagerly accepted.

The fact of foreign intervention is itself not peculiar to the Spanish civil war. The French revolution had to fight against infinitely stronger enemies—or at least these enemies put an infinitely stronger force into the fight against France—than is the case with Spain. After all, the amount of help given to Franco by the fascist States was limited; but it was too much for Spain. It had been too much, first, on account of the inexperience of the popular militia and the revolutionary administration. But the months between July and November showed that there was little if any adaptation to modern warfare and to modern military necessities in general in the Government camp. The anarchists, as the most genuine representatives of Spanish resistance to Europeanization in the labour camp, were least adaptable. But it is incorrect to say that this incapacity to adapt was mainly due to anarchist principles. The anarchists, in fact, stuck close to the ideals of a guerilla militia, a workers' rule in the factories, and an administration by more or less independent local committees. But the other parties, republicans and socialists, who proclaimed ideals borrowed from Europe, were in fact just as unadaptable as the anarchists. One section of the movement threw the responsibility of the failure on the other, but in reality they were all equally guilty of the general failure.

But by November it was clear that all that would not do, and that the republic would founder within the next few weeks unless the foreigners came to help. They came, Russian specialists and Comintern volunteers, and brought efficient help. They saved Madrid; they succeeded, for the time being at least, in turning the scales. But at the same time they introduced a deep change into the trend of the movement.

And now a significant phenomenon ensued. Every previous revolution, in Britain, in France, in Russia, had proceeded from the rule of moderate groups to the rule of more advanced groups, and, in this process, continually gained in efficiency. The Spanish revolution, too, had first followed this course. It had proceeded from moderate forms to more violent forms, from the rule of the republicans to the rule of the revolutionary committees and to the Caballero cabinet. But this swing to the Left had failed to produce results. Now, with the entry of the communists upon the Spanish stage, a much less advanced faction took the wheel. And, surprisingly, with this change the Spanish revolution won in efficiency. Obviously, two factors have co-operated to bring about this result. One was the obvious failure of the radical Left, in all its sections. The Left-wing socialists, the anarchists, and the Trotskyists proved, under the test of events, not to be either Jacobins or Bolsheviks. They proved unable to create an iron revolutionary dictatorship of the French and the Russian type. Just as Franco only imitated the superficial forms of fascism, so the advanced groups of the Left had only imitated the revolutionary tradition of other countries, without being able really to follow the model they had set themselves. One faction in each camp refused even formally to accept the foreign model, the Carlists in the Franco, the anarchists in the republican camp. The other factions proved unable to adapt their official models to the conditions of the spot. The Spanish labour movement, and the Spanish Left in general, had been able to *fight*, but was not able to organize an *efficient* fight. It was as little efficient, as little up to the needs of a modern war, as Franco on the other side. Spain, in all its sections and inimical parties, proved to be basically different from Europe, and to be partly unwilling and partly unable to copy European examples.

This was one aspect of the defeat of the Left not by Franco but by German and Italian planes, tanks, and artillery; though there was so little of all that help that a somewhat better organized movement must have easily overcome them. Neither was it, naturally, the Spanish communists who overcame the difficulty. It was the Russian specialists, the foreign technical advisers, and the international brigades. So far, the escape of the Government from destruction was due to the communists, not because they were communists, but because they were foreigners, better trained and more efficient. But there is perhaps another aspect of the fact, in which communism as such is of greater importance. After all, other revolutions had had to fight against inferior adversaries. Cromwell's Ironsides were a more efficient troop than Prince Rupert's cavalry, the 'columns' of the French Revolution superior to the Prussian 'line'. It needed a certain amount of time to evolve this intrinsic superiority, but the forces were never so unequally matched, never were they balanced so much in favour of the counter-revolution as in the Spanish case. Had the Spanish revolution met Franco only, it would probably have evolved a superiority over him of the same type as that evolved by the revolutionaries in France and Britain. But here the revolution met, not its own reactionary adversaries, but the strongest military powers of the world, though represented by third-rate and very small forces. Could a reactionary country like Spain adapt itself quickly enough to such an ordeal? It certainly could not. True, it could have done much more, infinitely more than it did, and that would have made an enormous difference. It would not have relieved the Government from the necessity of accepting foreign help, but it would have reduced the urgency of the need, would have put the Government in a position to negotiate, instead of being at the mercy of the foreigner. Still, the coming of the foreigner was inevitable. And it needed to be a foreigner with a ready-made organization, able to meet the Germans and Italians. This ready-made organization only the bureaucratic Russian State and its Communist International could provide. In a word, in order to fight, not counter-revolution in its own country, but international fascism, the Spanish revolution must appeal to a well-organized, ready-made force; to a force not itself in a state of revolution; to a non-revolutionary force.

In this tremendous contrast with previous revolutions one fact is reflected. Before these latter years, counter-revolution usually depended upon the support of reactionary powers, which were technically and intellectually inferior to the forces of revolution. This has changed with the advent of fascism. Now, every revolution is likely to meet the attack of the most modern, most efficient, most ruthless machinery yet in existence. It means that the age of revolutions free to evolve according to their own laws is over.

As it was, and as it had to be, because the failure of the Spanish Left coincided with fascist intervention, republican Spain was at the mercy of the force which brought help. The communists could dictate, and did dictate in the way described in previous chapters. For it was a force with a revolutionary past, not with a revolutionary present, which had come to help the Spaniards. The communists put an end to revolutionary social activity, and enforced their view that this ought not to be a revolution but simply the defence of a legal government.

This policy has several aspects, and they ought to be presented in clear distinction if the very complex evolution which followed is to be understood. First of all, one ought never to forget that communist policy in Spain was mainly dictated not by the necessities of the Spanish fight but by the interests of the intervening foreign power, Russia, which took account of Spanish situations and necessities only so far as was needed in order to win the war. It would be a gross exaggeration to say that the course of the Spanish revolution has been completely arrested by Russian intervention but it has been deformed and deviated, exactly as the course of Spanish counter-revolution has been, not arrested, but deformed, by the intervention of Italy and Germany in the Franco camp. The natural elements of Spanish affairs are reflected only indirectly in the present policy of the Spanish communists (whose actual leaders, during the decisive period, were not Spaniards but foreigners—Antonov-Ovseenko, Rosenberg, Kleber, 'Carlos,' André Marty, etc.). Spanish needs are broken, transformed by passing through the prism of Russian interests. This fact is in itself no reproach. It would be unreasonable to demand that an ally should care first not for his own interests but for the interests of the power he is allied with. The peculiarities of the situation only arise through the fact that Russia has in every country a party at its orders which claims to be a party of the national proletariat but in reality is completely at the orders of the Moscow Government. Moscow, it is true, proclaims a metaphysical preordained identity of the interests of every proletariat with the interests of the Moscow Government, but this is a proposition that can no longer be taken seriously.

The trend of Spanish events then, was diverted by the interference of a Power whose help had been sought on account of its higher technical standards in both military and administrative affairs. As a compensation for help this Power claimed and obtained—besides pay in cash for the arms it provided and for the other commodities it sold—a decisive influence upon the policy of the Spanish Government. The inability of the Spaniards in both camps to fight efficiently, an inability partly inherent in their general character, partly due to their deep-rooted reluctance to apply modern methods, had led, in both camps, to a deviation of events in the direction indicated by more modern foreign forces. The old tragedy of Spain, which is put under pressure from abroad but does not want to become modern, took this particular form under the circumstances of the civil war.

What were the results, in the Government camp? Taking the changes introduced by the communists separately, opinions will probably differ widely as to their value. To me it seems that quite a number of these measures were reasonable and inevitable. The Russian officers and the non-Russian foreign communist volunteers brought military success; not very splendid success, indeed, but enough to save the republic. The communists, moreover, claimed, and partly obtained the transformation of the old militia into something similar to a modern army, and again, I think, were right. The communists, moreover, demanded the creation of a centralized administrative power as against the chaotic rule of local committees; certainly it was a necessity of the war. They objected to the collectivization of the peasants' lots—it was belated wisdom, bought at a high price during the disaster of agrarian collectivization in Russia—but after all it was wisdom. They put a check to wholesale socialization of industry, which was dangerous from more than one point of view. In all these respects, the communists were the executors of the inevitable necessity of the moment: the necessity of concentration of all forces upon the essential aims of the moment. In all these measures they did exactly what other revolutions had done before them. Every single one of the great revolutions has started with a relaxation of central authority and, in the fight for its existence, has ended in an enormous increase of centralized authority. The Long Parliament broke the centralized administration of the Stuarts, but, after a few years of civil war, had to tolerate the military dictatorship of the Cromwellian generals. The French Revolution first introduced a far-reaching autonomy of local and departmental administrations, to be reduced, during the years of civil and international war, under the iron centralizaiton of the régime of Robespierre. The Russian Revolution started with the chaotic rule of the Soviets and ended in the iron dictatorship of the centralized Communist Party. Centralization and discipline are elements of modern life, most needed in moments of acute crisis. It is the basic weakness of the anarchists not to understand this; the weakness which they would have had to overcome if they were to take the lead. But had they been able to overcome it they would not have been Spanish anarchists, the specific representatives of the reluctance of the masses to adapt themselves to centralism and discipline. The change from the rule of the committees to the predominance of the Communist Party, in this sense, corresponded exactly to the change of the French Revolution from the Gironde to the Jacobins, of the Russian Revolution from the Soviet to the party dictatorship. In this sense the trend of communist policy was dictated by the necessities of the hour, and the particular feature of the event was only that there had been no national force in Spain capable of putting the inevitable change into effect and that the foreigner had to provide not only officers and arms but a new policy too.

But these changes do not exhaust the influence of communist policy in Spain. The communists did not merely object to sweeping socialization; they objected to almost every form of socialization. They did not only object to collectivization of the peasants' lots; they successfully opposed any definite policy for the distribution of large landed estates. They not only opposed, rightly, the childish ideas of local abolition of money; they opposed State control of markets, even of markets so easy to control as the orange market. They not only tried to organize a working police, but showed a definite preference for the police forces of the old régime, so hated by the masses. They not only broke the power of the committees; they were distrustful of every sort of spontaneous, 'uncontrollable' mass movement. They acted, in a word, not with the aim of transforming chaotic enthusiasm into disciplined enthusiasm, but with the aim of substituting disciplined military and administrative action for the action of the masses and getting rid of the latter entirely. Before Russia interfered, the communists said: 'This is not a proletarian, it is a bourgeois revolution.' The description reeked of a bookish scholasticism possibly valuable in sociological analysis *a posteriori*, but worthless in the practice of politics. But as soon as the Russians had interfered, the slogan became: 'This is no revolution at all, it is simply the defence of the legal Government.' This involved an express renunciation of all support of the forces of revolution.

This policy had the inevitable consequence implicit in it. The policy of the Communist Party goes directly against the interests and claims of the masses. The peasant does not get a clear promise as to more land but he does get requisitions. What is he likely to feel? The worker gets neither socialization nor increased wages. But he does get increased prices. What is he likely to feel? The housewives do not get more cash in hand, but markets are uncontrolled and there is no card-rationing system either. And prices are rising and food getting scarce. What are they likely to feel? It is true that Franco and in general the forces of the old régime are so hated that none of these folk withdraw their allegiance from the Government. But they withdraw their active support. There is no resistance to conscription; but there is very little volunteering. There are not very many peasant revolts; but there is an obvious slackening of the interest of the village in the movement. There are some bread riots, not very many; but there is an uneasy feeling in the homes and the women in the queues say: 'What are we suffering for? What has it all to do with us?' Or something to the same effect.

And this upsetting of the balance on the one side has its counterpart on the other side. What is lost in popular backing must be compensated by the creation of other pro-Government forces. The old civil service, the old police, certain elements of the old army, large groups of shopkeepers, merchants, well-to-do peasants, intellectuals, begin to take a more active interest in the Government than before, while the poor peasant and the industrial worker are drawing away from it. They are backed by an administration with totalitarian tendencies. Had they to bear the brunt of the battle they would fail, even more miserably than the committees and the militia of July. For while these forces of July had all the defects, but at the same time all the qualities, of the Spanish people, enthusiasm and capacity for self-sacrifice together with the traditional inability to wage a modern war, these newly rising groups are no more able, but less enthusiastic and self-sacrificing. They live, politically, under the protection of the foreigner.

A famous historical parallel may illustrate the meaning of all that. The first half of the programme of the communists in Spain was put into effect, in the French Revolution, by the Jacobins, by Robespierre. They introduced the iron régime of revolutionary centralization. They beat down enthusiastic nonsense such as the abolition of money, the expropriation of the well-to-do. But at the same time they broke with the hesitant and double-faced policy of their predecessors and gave the peasant the land of the aristocrat. The peasant soldier, in reward, gave them victory on the battlefields of Belgium. Then the revolution was safe. The strongest elements of the country were satisfied. The peasant had got what he wanted. The revolutionary dictatorship was no longer necessary. The classes which had been partly persecuted and partly just molested by this dictatorship, united and broke it. That happened in the month of Thermidor, in 1794. Then came the

CONCLUSIONS

régime of those who had made Thermidor, the régime of the Thermidorians. They abolished what had been intended to be only temporary in the revolutionary régime: they abolished the iron dictatorship, the emergency courts with their frightful powers, the censorship of the Press, the interference with the political opinions of the individual. At the same time they abolished the emergency measures in favour of the classes which had supported the revolution, abolished the control of markets, the measures of expropriation (with the exception of the chief expropriation, that of the land of the aristocracy and Church). They reverted to liberal principles, both in politics and economic life. And very naturally, they got the support of those classes which had not supported the Jacobins, classes which had not participated in the revolutionary fight, but were prepared to share its fruits. And to a certain extent they succeeded, because the danger for the new order was over.

To-day the communists in Spain combine both the revolutionary centralization of Robespierre and the Thermidorian policy of his successors. They make a dictatorship, but it is a dictatorship not in favour of the revolutionary classes. Such a policy could not last for a fortnight if republican Spain had to live on the enthusiastic support of the people; it can last, and will doubtless continue to last, because the Spanish people have failed to make their own revolution efficient. The Trotskyists, who complain so bitterly about this result, must blame themselves for it. In fact, they are even more to blame than any other group. They have, in their mechanical repetition of formulae from books about Marxism and the Russian revolution, been unable to create a mass movement at all. Anarchists and socialists at least succeeded in doing that. But probably in this case, as in so many others, it is superficial to blame individual groups and leaders at all. Had the Trotskyists in Spain not been dogmatic Marxists of foreign inspiration, they would have been nearer to Spanish realities. But then they would have been a genuinely Spanish movement, which is to say they would have been exactly like those socialists and anarchists who have so conspicuously not succeeded. From whatever aspect the problems of the Spanish revolution are treated, from whatever starting-point discussed, the final result is always that things might have been otherwise provided that—Spain were not Spain. Had the Spaniards been able to create a revolutionary movement strong enough to beat a counter-revolution armed with European arms, then Russian help would have been superfluous, then things would have taken another turn, then socialists and anarchists would have gradually merged into one single revolutionary party, backed by the spontaneous enthusiasm of both workers and peasants; they would have won the war, and created a new order of things, less dictatorial, more humane and more progressive than the present Russian régime. But that is all Utopian. In reality the driving force behind the rising of the masses against Franco was not a specific desire to create some sort of modern order of things on the European pattern, either liberal, democratic-republican, or socialist. As in 1707 and 1808, they rose simply to ward off an attack.

The difference was that in 1707 and 1808 this attack came from without, plus a certain amount of co-operation of the upper classes from within; whereas in 1936 it came from within, plus very strong co-operation from without. But in each case it was felt as an attempt at 'tyranny'; the fight against it as a fight for 'liberty'; and the claim at the bottom of the resistance every time was the claim to be left to live one's own life.

That this is the deepest impulse of the movement is not expressed in words—newspapers are written by Europeanized editors, and the popular movement is inarticulate as to its deepest impulses—but it is shown by acts. It was shown in 1808, when the peasants won their guerilla war but the officers were incapable of helping Wellington. It was shown in July 1936 when the masses won in the streets of Barcelona and Madrid, but refused to learn the first thing about modern war in the open field. It was shown after November 1936, when the appearance of the international brigades did not create any real movement of emulation, of competition in efficiency with the foreigner. The Spaniard is not a modern European. The foreigner is more efficient; he brings new methods, which are badly needed. So the foreigner is tolerated, and heartily disliked. But the Spaniard has not the reaction which would be instinctive with a Yankee, a Britisher, a German, and which Stalin is trying now to teach the Russian: the reaction to do as well or better than the foreigner so as to be able to get rid of him. Nothing of the kind.

In the international brigades there are some volunteers who have fought in the World War, but the majority have not; on the other hand, the Spanish militia has now months of war behind it, and the volunteers have had only four to five months' fighting in the peculiar Spanish conditions. Yet the superiority of the international brigades is undisputed—with the exception of certain Basque and Asturian units—for no conceivable reason except that the Spaniards are not eager to achieve equality. The same applies to war industry. The arrival of foreign technical specialists on the one hand, the ample supply of foreign war material on the other, is far from having created an eager drive towards improvement of the Spanish war industry. That is progressing very slowly, with severe setbacks. The Spaniards seem to feel, to a certain extent, that as there is foreign war material, things may just as well be left at that. Compare the enormous strides French armaments made during the two years of revolutionary dictatorship, with the help of all the best physicists and chemists of the period! The Spaniard does not want to Europeanize; on the contrary, now that his instincts of independent action have been thwarted and discipline has been imposed upon him, he is withdrawing from the jobs which are at the moment most important. These foreigners, after all, are unavoidable; then let them at least do the job and don't bother us! Such a sentiment is not directly expressed (the Spaniard would be too proud to admit that the foreigner does anything better than he himself), but dislike of the foreigners who have come to help is very openly expressed, as can be seen in the above diary. This is not nationalism in the European sense. Our heated nationalism is something specifi-

CONCLUSIONS

cally modern, twentieth century, and its core is the desire to
be more powerful, economically and politically, than our
neighbours. This desire is inconceivable to the Spaniard. His
nationalism is not the desire to beat others, or to pretend to
beat them, but simply the desire to be left alone. This desire,
in the Kleber-Rosenberg crisis, found pathetic expression.
The republic was jeopardized by this crisis, but never mind!
Even the political leaders were suddenly drawn into the
orbit of the popular feeling. First get rid of the foreign
command.

Certain conclusions can be drawn. They do not concern
the final issue of the fight between Franco and the republic.
This fight has become so largely a non-Spanish affair, dependent on foreign forces, which cannot be calculated from
an analysis of the trend of Spanish events, that prediction is
impossible. On the battle-field of central Spain, to-day, the
Comintern and the Fascintern are meeting in their first
military battle; the course of history has involved the Spaniards, but the Spaniards are only auxiliaries. But it is almost
certain, as the result of these first months, that Spain will not
become either genuinely fascist or genuinely communist (not
in the sense of Leninist communism of 1917, which is out
of the question, but of the communism of 1937). Neither, of
course, will it become a 'parliamentary democratic republic',
as the communists claim to be making it. Should the communists achieve their aims, destroy the Right, destroy the
Trotskyists, merge with the republicans and with the socialists, only the anarchists would remain in the field. The anarchists, however, are anti-parliamentarian by principle. It
would be a democratic republic with only one party. Russia,
as everybody knows, is a democratic republic with only one
party, since the new constitution; it is a strange sort of democracy. But the result of the Kleber crisis is to have made such
a result very unlikely. To sum it up: whatever the final result
of the armed fight may be, Spain will not emerge out of it as
a genuinely Europeanized country, be it in the fascist, the
liberal-democratic or the communist sense. It will remain
what it was, a country whose evolution has been arrested at

297

the end of the seventeenth century, which has since displayed an enormous amount of resistance to foreign intrusion, but no capacity for rejuvenation. There may be, in the end, a régime claiming to be liberal-democratic or claiming to be fascist; in reality, it will be something profoundly different from what these names designate in Europe.

Neither have any of the specifically Spanish factions, such as the Carlists and the anarchists, a chance to win. Carlism is more or less a local Navarrese affair. The anarchists are a half-religious Utopian movement; which has failed to achieve its task, and was bound to fail to do so from the beginning. It had extraordinary fighting powers, but, by definition, no power to organize. It has had to renounce all its panaceas; the fight against discipline, against politics, against the existence of a State and a government; has had to give ministers to the cabinet, and introduce discipline and the command of officers into its own units. Anarchism is deeply disturbed and even demoralized to-day. It is not the same thing for a movement to be in contact with 'lumpenproletarian' elements in the days of revolt, and yet keep in touch with them when it comes to participate in the Government. Here, too, is a source of disintegration. One must conclude that the anarchists have no chance to win either.

What will be the final issue? It is impossible to say. Perhaps it is not too rash to hint at one aspect of the situation. Before the revolutionary movement of 1930-1, actual power was in the hands of generals. If Spain is unwilling or unable to move away from its present form of existence, if the revolution is to fail, then it would be only natural that the régime at the end of the crisis would be the same as that before the start: a rule of the army. It need not be the Franco army. A republican army is in creation. And if one thing can be said about the present political situation in Spain it is that a successful republican general would have a good chance. The political leaders have already had reason to fear the prestige of Kleber, but Kleber was a foreigner, and so could hardly have won, and certainly did not want to win, the political allegiance of the country. And no Spanish general on the republican side has yet had the slightest success as a result of his own plans. It remains to be seen whether a successful general will emerge in the Left camp. If not, the army as such will probably have a very strong say, provided that the republicans win. If Franco wins, there will be a military dictatorship, whatever the official description it gives itself for purposes of propaganda. The likeliest conclusion, then, is that, in the end, the Comintern and the Fascintern will have fought out an important round in Spain, but that, for the Spaniards, things will remain essentially as they were, with the difference that foreign intrusion will be much stronger than before, and will work, not as a model, but as a disintegrating force upon Spanish civilization.

This civilization is not under discussion in this book, which is devoted only to the problems of the Spanish civil war. Still, at the end of the investigation, it is worth while to say one word about this Spanish conception of life, which is so unpermeable to European influence. The European, who instinctively only appreciates 'progress', change, is horrified by the stagnation of Spanish life, by what he must call Spanish inefficiency. This inefficiency, being almost the key to the present trend of events, had to be given ample consideration in these pages. But if the reader is inclining to conclude from all this that Spain is 'a rotten country', he is misled. The fact is that almost every foreign observer, whether watching the Right or the Left camp, has felt an almost magical attraction. Many a foreign specialist and technical adviser has dropped his job, in fury and despair, deciding 'to leave these wretched Spaniards to themselves', and still could not get away from them; people with a political faith usually ascribe it to the supreme importance of the Spanish fight for the future of mankind. Important as the Spanish civil war doubtless is, I still believe that its importance is sometimes exaggerated; but this is not the essential point. The deep attraction of Spain consists, in my opinion, not so much in its importance, but in its national character. There, life is not yet efficient; that means that it is not yet mechanized; that beauty is still more important for the Spaniard than practical use; sentiment more important than action; honour very often more important than success; love and friendship more important than one's job. In one word, it is the lure of a civilization near to ourselves, closely connected with the historical past of Europe, but which has not participated in our later developments towards mechanism, the adoration of quantity, and of the utilitarian aspect of things. In this lure exerted by Spain upon so very many foreigners—and the author of this book is emphatically among those who have been deeply attracted— is implied the concession, unconscious very often, it is true, that after all something seems to be wrong with our own European civilization and that the 'backward', stagnant, and inefficient Spaniard can well compete, in the field of human values, with the efficient, practical, and progressive European. The one seems predestined to last, unmoving, throughout the cataclysms of the surrounding world, and to outlive national usurpers and foreign conquerors; the other, progressive, may progress towards his own destruction.

GLOSSARY

Names of Spanish Institutions

Falange española, the 'Spanish phalanx', a fascist organization imitating the Italian fascists. Until his execution Sr. José Primo de Rivera, the son of the dictator, was its leader. General Franco is not a member.

Accion popular, the 'popular action', the party of the Catholic clergy, as far as they are not 'Carlists', and of their adherents; leader Gil Robles; now dissolved, at the demand of General Franco.

Partido tradicionalista, the 'Carlists', partisans of the junior line of the royal house of Bourbon, and of an absolute monarchy of the seventeenth-century type. Their stronghold is Navarra; their slogan 'The King Christ, and the Holy Virgin'.

Renovacion española, the party of ex-king Alphonso, has lost all practical importance since the civil war.

CEDA, Confederacion Electoral de Derechas Autonomas (electoral confederation of the autonomous groups of the Right) the united front organization of all the parties of the Right which, under the leadership of Sr. Gil Robles won the 1933 and lost the 1936 elections.

Partido radical, originally an anti-Catalanist, republican group in Barcelona under the leadership of Sr. Lerroux, suspected by many Spaniards of acting under the orders of the police; later spread over most parts of Spain, took office after the 1933 elections and entered into a coalition with the Catholic Accion Popular in 1934, which was the signal for the Asturias rising.

GLOSSARY

Union republicana, a small split to the left from the Lerroux party, under the leadership of Sr. Martinez Barrios, now president of the Cortes; the group to-day is the extreme right wing of the 'popular front'.

Lliga Catalana, the party of the Catalan industrialists, under the leadership of Sr. Francisco Cambó, regionalist, but anxious for the unity of Spain, and strongly monarchist; to-day the party sides with Franco.

Esquerra Catalana, the Catalan Left, originally founded by Colonel Maciá, now led by Sr. Companys, the president of the Catalan Generalitat; republican, strongly autonomist, and anti-socialist.

Izquierda Republicana, the 'Republican Left', the party which ruled from 1931 to 1933 and again from February till July 1936, under the leadership of Sr. Azaña, the president of the republic; republican, centralist, anti-socialist.

UGT, Union General de Trabajadores (general workers' union), the socialist trade-union centre, corresponding to the British T.U.C., collectively affiliated to the Socialist Party, whose main strength derives from the UGT. The communists too belong to the UGT. President: Largo Caballero.

CNT, Confederacion Nacional de Trabajadores (national confederacy of workers), the anarcho-syndicalist trade-union centre; leading personalities of the CNT must at the same time be members of the

FAI, Federacion Anarquista Iberica (peninsular anarchist confederacy), the political organization of the anarchists.

POUM, Partido Obrero de Unificacion Marxista (workers' party of marxist unity), a revolutionary socialist group, mainly in Catalonia; Left wing under Trotskyist influence; leaders Joaquin Maurin (executed in the Franco camp) and Andres Nin.

Cortes, the national parliament, consisting of one house of elected members only.

Generalitat de Catalunya, the regional government of Catalonia, instituted by acts of 1932 and 1936, with a president, a premier, a ministry of its own, responsible to an elected regional representative body and with special attributes defined by the law.

Ayuntamiento, the Spanish word for 'municipality'.

Alcalde, the Spanish word for mayor; he is named by the Government, not elected.

Seguridad, cuerpo de seguridad, the secret police.

Guardia civil, the gendarmerie, a special police corps, dating from the 'forties of the nineteenth century, run largely on military lines; the name has lately been changed into '*Guardia nacional republicana*'.

Asaltos, the shock-brigades, a second semi-military police corps formed in the first year of the republic.

Mozos de escuadra, the special police corps of the Catalan Generalitat.

Junta, a traditional form of revolutionary committee, first formed during the national war against Napoleon in 1808, and repeatedly since.

Reforma agraria, a department of the ministry of agriculture, entrusted with the parcelling of large estates under the law of agrarian reform, enacted in 1932 and restored in 1936.

SELECTED ANN ARBOR PAPERBACKS

works of enduring merit

For a complete list of Ann Arbor Paperback titles write:

THE UNIVERSITY OF MICHIGAN PRESS / ANN ARBOR